The Plume

A Civil War Love Story

Peter Hubin

Published by: Up North Storytellers

THE PLUME

A CIVIL WAR LOVE STORY

PETER HUBIN

Published by: Up North Storytellers
N4880 Wind Rd.
Spooner, WI 54801

Library of Congress No. 20155937631

ISBN NO. 978 1 4951 5162 0

Printed in the United States of America
By: Documation
       1556 International Drive
       Eau Claire, WI 54701

THE PLUME is historical fiction. The book is about soldiers in the 6th Wisconsin, Iron Brigade that fought at Gettysburg. A nurse from Wisconsin helped injured soldiers from that battle. President Lincoln asked for help to solve serious problems. This is a Civil War story about love and devotion.

PREFACE

1863 America was mired in a great Civil War. The young country was being led by President Abraham Lincoln as he sought to unify the country and end slavery. Walter, a young soldier from Antigo, Wisconsin and his brother, Royce were entering the fifth major battle of their two year enlistment. The battle was Gettysburg and Walter was very seriously injured on the third day and was unconscious for the next three days.

The first thing he saw when he regained consciousness was a very beautiful, smiling face telling him he would be alright. It was Florence, a student nurse from Wisconsin that was attending a special training session at Hagerstown, Maryland. When the battle at Gettysburg broke out, Florence and her fellow nurses rushed to nearby Gettysburg to care for the injured.

Walter's Commander exchanged plumes in Walters hat and when he was transferred to a hospital in Harrisburg, Pennsylvania he gave the precious plume to Florence as a symbol of their love. Walter was sure Florence would visit him or at least write a letter. Upon discharge from the hospital two months later, a crestfallen Walter began searching for Florence, but where?

By the end of September, Walter found out that Florence had been severely injured and was at a town near Gettysburg. He immediately went to her and helped her to recover. On November 19th, President Lincoln was coming to Gettysburg to dedicate the memorial and battlefield cemetery. Florence was now healed and Walter took her to Gettysburg to hear President Lincoln. He hoped they could meet this great man and they did! The President was impressed by the 6th Wisconsin Regiment soldier and the nurse that saved his life. Later he sent them an invitation to come to the White House as he had a task for them.

This began a relationship between Walter, Florence and President Lincoln that would last for nearly two years.

1

Walter and Florence were deeply in love and eventually married. Walters injury at Gettysburg continued to haunt him with 'battlefield memories'. The old injury had caused his heart and lungs to become more and more restricted.

Walter was instrumental in getting help for families of soldiers fighting in the war. Walter, Florence and Royce played a large part in getting improvements in the way the Union soldiers were treated.

Walter and Royce were part of a wonderful loving family. Walter was elected to the State Senate of Wisconsin and during his term the Civil War ended. Walter wanted children and a beautiful girl, Alivia was born to Walter and Florence. The beautiful plume was a symbol of their undying love for each other.

This story is fiction but is based on historical facts.

THE IRON BRIGADE

The Iron Brigade was on the move. It was June 30, 1863 and the huge 'Army of the Potomac' was in the process of leaving Maryland and entering Pennsylvania. The Iron Brigade was made up of the Wisconsin 2nd, 6th, and 7th, the 19th Indiana and the 24th Michigan. These regiments had shown extraordinary fighting ability at the second Bull Run, Antietam, Fredericksburg and Chancellorsville.

The Iron Brigade was one of the most admired among the many thousands of troops during the Civil War. They were very well trained, showed great discipline and team work and were very tough.

The Army of the Potomac was spoiling for a fight with the Army of Northern Virginia led by General Robert E. Lee. He had led his troops in to Pennsylvania looking to restock his hungry soldiers. Scouts for both huge armies kept their leaders informed. Both armies were spread out as Calvary troops rapidly ranged far and wide from the main body that was on foot.

Anticipation ran high that a confrontation was near. The Iron Brigade was made up of over 1800 men and the five regiments marched together. The 6th Wisconsin was led by Lt. Col. Rufus Dawes. He had overseen the training of most of the 420 volunteers that marched with him that day. He was an extraordinary leader and most of the young men admired him and responded by being outstanding soldiers. Marching rapidly along this huge throng was Walter Rounds and his brother, Royce. Walter was twenty years old. He was average size and looked very fit. Royce was almost a copy except he was twenty-two years old. Both boys lived just north of Antigo, Wisconsin and worked with their dad in a lumber enterprise. Royce planned to attend the University of Wisconsin and study forestry after the war.

3

All of the Wisconsin regiments received their training at a camp on the west side of Madison. A man by the name of Randall was Governor and was a very strong supporter of President Lincoln and his fight to end slavery. This training camp was named in his honor and was very well run. Wisconsin soldiers were very well trained and were regarded as among the very best soldiers.

Civil War uniforms showed tremendous variety. Many brigades had regiments made up of ethnic groups and their dress reflected their heritage. The 6th Wisconsin were distinctive in their dress also. They all wore black hats as did all other Iron Brigade regiments. The regiments wore dark blue tunics and light blue pants. They were made of wool and were very durable. The pants had a black piping down each leg and there was a 4-button fly. A black belt completed the dress and had a buckle that had U. S. on it. Lt. Col. Rufus Dawes had a feather plume in his hat as did many of his troops. The men were proud of their attire, but the wool fabric was warm, and the next day was July 1st and the troops were hot.

Word came down the line that the Confederates had been contacted near a small town called Gettysburg. This huge Union army had troops traveling over several different roads to accommodate this massive army of over 200,000 troops. Also in these huge columns of troops were supply wagons, artillery pieces and hospital personnel. Hundreds of horses were needed to pull and move things but not the soldiers, they were on foot. Each had a back pack with a bed roll. Each carried meager food supplies and water. The back pack also may have contained a small shovel. The soldier carried his own rifle, ammunition and a bayonet hung on his belt.

Both armies were spread over several miles and was difficult to know just where the adversary was located. Orders were given for brigades to take up positions in certain locations. Others continued on to reach their assigned positions.

Sporadic shots could be heard as fighting began in some areas but not in others.

Walter and Royce, along with the other 6th Wisconsin Regiment soldiers, were very apprehensive as they made preparations to spend the night. What will tomorrow bring?

GETTYSBURG, THE BATTLE

Walter, Royce and the entire 6th Wisconsin took up positions just as it got dark. Shooting ceased and troops settled in for the night. About all they knew was the rebels were west of their position and they were south of Gettysburg. Strategy was that several brigades of troops would be kept in reserve, near their anticipated place of deployment.

Artillery cannons were moved into position along this ridge that the Union troops were forming on. This line apparently was three to four miles long and faced the west, but was very irregular as troops sought to take advantage of trees, boulders, hills or anything that offered protection. Breastworks were put up to offer additional protection from the hail of bullets and cannon fire they knew would come.

In recent battles with General Lee's army of Northern Virginia, the Union soldiers had been forced to retreat. The Confederates had many well seasoned fighters and were feeling confident fighting the Yanks. The 6th Wisconsin dug in and waited in the oppressive heat.

The morning of July 1, 1863 dawned hot and bright. Very early on, the rebels charged all along the Union lines and fighting was furious. In front of the Wisconsin 6th, was a force of Mississippi soldiers. Both sides took heavy losses. Lt. Col. Dawes ordered his troops to 'fix bayonets' and after a few minutes ordered his troops to charge the rebels. Walter, Royce and the remainder of the 6th charged down the hill and routed the rebels. His troops trapped this huge force of Confederates in a railroad cut and killed or wounded many but captured close to 200 Confederates. This successful attack cost the 6th Wisconsin about a third of its troops so they were positioned on the right flank on July 2nd. Walter received a slight wound on his right arm but Royce was not injured. Once again they dug in and built breastworks.

By the second day, Union cannons were put in place to fire on approaching rebels. The Confederates were able to position their cannons and were aimed at the middle of the long Union line. The rebels charged the 6th Wisconsin and once again Lt. Col. Dawes ordered a counter charge. The 6th Wisconsin was joined by the 84th and 137th New York. The sight of these Union fighters rising up and charging their position caused the rebels to immediately retreat. The Union could reclaim breastworks that had been lost earlier in the day. Walter and Royce were not injured.

Both of these huge armies had been scattered over many miles and took about two days to get all the cannons positioned and all the supplies in their proper places. By now both sides had many thousands of troops killed or wounded. The weather was unbearably hot and most troops on both sides wore winter uniforms. Keeping the troops and the horses supplied with water was a serious problem. Fighting had been fierce but most knew the worst was yet to come.

The wounded were treated by doctors and nurses in make shift facilities. Some in Gettysburg but others in temporary tents along this long battle line. The word went out that any nurses or doctors should come to this Gettysburg area to help with the extremely high number of wounded. A group of nurses from Madison, Wisconsin had been at Hagerstown, Maryland for special training. There were twenty-seven nurses in that group, plus over fifty from other areas. They all took whatever supplies they could obtain and got on a special train that would be able to go from Hagerstown to near Gettysburg. Word spread of this huge battle and there would be many thousands that would be injured and would need care. In this group of nurses from Madison was a nineteen-year-old with the name of Florence. She and the others wondered what they would find on the battlefield. They had heard horror stories of limbs being amputated with no way to kill the pain. Serious wounds from cannonball, rifle fire or bayonets were anticipated, but the thought of what they would find was very scary.

July 3rd was a continuation of the hot dry weather. Most troops thought this would be the hardest day of battle as both sides had artillery in place and it was well known what cannons can do to troops. The rebels finally had the troops that had been on the road. There were about fifteen thousand fresh troops and they were lined up out of range of Union artillery.

At 12:30 p.m. a signal was given and rebel cannons opened up on Union positions. The Union answered with a few rounds, but they were saving their rounds for the Confederates that they knew would come across a vast open area in front of them. The roar of these cannons, which numbered about two-hundred was deafening. The smoke from the powder hung in the area like a fog and it was so thick that the combatants could not see each other at times.

Suddenly the rebel cannons were still. The fifteen-thousand fresh rebels moved out of the trees and formed up on an open field about a mile from the Union lines. The 6th Wisconsin had been positioned as reserve regiment and fully expected to be called into action. Walter and Royce were in the same squad and had some time to reflect on the past two days. They recalled the names of fellow 6th Wisconsin soldiers that they knew were wounded or killed. Both men had fought in other campaigns where many of their regiment died or were wounded, some very critically and may have died later. To begin with, both men developed strong friendships with squad members. As time went on, they both developed a more hardened attitude toward other troops. They worked hard to develop strong teamwork but began to realize they were all like chess pieces that could be moved around to fight the enemy. If a solder dropped out due to death or injury, another would eventually take their place.

There was a steady flow of new recruits to replace those soldiers killed or wounded in battles. Many troops were lost to sickness and poor health due to weather, poor food and diseases that swept through the camps. Health care was lacking and morale was a problem.

Walter and Royce were among the very best soldiers of the 6th Wisconsin. They were proud to be part of the Iron Brigade and admired Rufus Dawes as a leader they could trust and follow. Replacement soldiers would not always respond with the same vigor as some of the veteran soldiers. These veterans quickly informed these replacements as what was expected as a soldier in the Iron Brigade.

Walter and Royce felt that both of them had been very fortunate to not have been killed or wounded seriously. They had fought in four major battles and were now in the fifth. Both wondered if today would be the end of their story.

There was an eerie stillness after the cannon fire ceased. Word was passed back to the 6th Wisconsin that the rebels were advancing in the open field. The force was at least a mile wide and was headed toward the center of the Union line. That would mean the Confederates were heading right toward the 6th Wisconsin position as they waited in reserve.

The Union cannons began to open up at the advancing troops. Most shot canisters which are full of metal that acts like shot out of a shotgun and does deadly damage to soldiers. The rebels continue advancing disregarding the Union cannons. Finally, this huge body is within rifle range of Union troops and they open up with deadly results. Many have fallen but many more continue up the hill toward the Union lines.

The Union fire is deadly and the Confederates fire back. Some are now within one-hundred feet from withering fire from the Yanks. Many rebels continue and some reach the Union lines and attempt to climb over the breastworks. The call goes out to the reserve regiments and with a lusty shout.

Walter and Royce and the rest of the 6th Wisconsin charge into the fray with bayonets fixed. It was a terrible scene as grey coated rebels came over the breastworks and fought hand to hand with the Union troops. Shots were fired when targets presented themselves. Walter and Royce were within fifty-feet of the melee when Walter tumbled and fell. He rolled over and tried to get up but he could not! Then he saw the blood, his blood. He had been shot! He put his hand on his upper right chest and felt warm blood.

He woke up and saw he was in a tent. There were many other soldiers on cots like he was. He listened for shooting and there was none. He was very weak and felt terrible. He could see ladies tending to soldiers and wondered what had happened. He could just barely remember that he was shot … his memory was very hazy.

FLORENCE

In a few minutes, a nurse came to Walters cot and greeted him. She knelt down beside Walter and smiled at him with the sweetest smile he had ever seen. This lady was a nurse and she said her name was Florence and she had been taking care of him for three days. She told him a doctor had removed the bullet from his chest but he had lost a large amount of blood and he was very weak. She told him she could tell he belonged to the Iron Brigade and that he must be brave and strong. She said she would help him to recover. She left to attend another wounded soldier. Walter thought an angel must have visited him. This Florence was a very kind, sweet and caring person. Walter felt his heart quicken! Maybe he had seen her has he drifted in and out of sleep and now he thinks she is an angel. He hoped she is real and that he is alive. He wondered where Royce was. He drifted off to sleep.

Walter slept the remainder of the day. He was awakened by Florence bringing him an evening meal. Walter could see that it was early evening and other wounded troops were getting evening meals also. Florence helped Walter so he could sit on the edge of his cot. She put the tray on his knees and knelt beside him and fed him. Walter found that once he began to eat he realized he was very hungry.

As Walter slowly ate, Florence put her spare hand on his right shoulder near his injury but far enough away to not injure the wound. She wanted to stabilize Walter as he was very weak.

Walter asked Florence if she knew anything about his brother Royce Rounds.

"Your brother Royce came looking for you shortly after the doctor removed the bullet from your chest," Florence told him. "When he saw you, he cried. He could see you were in a bad way. In a few minutes he reached into his pocket and brought out a locket. He opened it and showed me a picture of your mother and father. He said the locket had been given to him as he was the oldest. If anything happened to you he was to give it to you until you are well. I put it under your pillow."

And with that she reached under the pillow and found the locket. Walter grasped the locket and held it. His lips trembled and his eyes watered. He opened the locket and looked at his parents.

"How was Royce?" he asked Florence.

"He had a bandage around his left arm above his elbow, but other than looking very tired he seemed fit. He asked me to hold on to the locket if you didn't make it. He would find me and ask for it back. He thanked me for the care I have given you and then he was gone. The 6th Wisconsin would be following the Confederates."

"What about the battle?" Walter asked, still quite groggy.

"The Union soldiers drove the Confederates off. For now there is no shooting," said Florence.

As Walter ate, Florence said, "Your commanding officer Lt. Col. Rufus Dawes visited this tent shortly after you arrived. Many of the men here were from the 6th Wisconsin and they appreciated a visit from him. He visited each and spoke to them. He stopped and visited the two Confederate soldiers also. They knew of the Iron Brigade and Lt. Col. Dawes. He was a very impressive man. The men were very pleased that he had stopped to see how they were doing. He thanked them for their service but now they must rest and get well.

"Then he came to your cot. He could see that you were asleep and did not want to awake you. He asked me about your progress and then he took off his black hat with a beautiful plume on it. He asked where your hat was and I told him under the cot. He reached under and pulled out your hat. He said he knew your plume had been hit by a bullet on the first day of fighting here.

"With that he removed the damaged plume from your hat. He then took the beautiful plume from his hat and put it on yours. He then put your plume on his hat. He put your hat back under your cot and stood up. There were tears in his eyes. In a moment he addressed all in that tent. He said that Walter Rounds is one of the bravest and very best soldiers he had ever seen. He truly expresses the spirit of the Iron Brigade. He said he will now wear Walter's plume as a symbol of the excellence shown by Walter as a member of the Iron Brigade.

"With that, he asked me to tell you about his visit and that he will now proudly wear your plume. He then stood at the end of your cot and snapped a salute to you. As he left the tent, the men that could, cheered. Before he left he pulled into a very upright position and then saluted the troops. Then he was gone . . . on to continue fighting the terrible war."

Florence continued feeding Walter until he could eat no more. He was tired and Florence helped him lie down.

"Do you know where my black hat is?" Walter asked. Florence reached under the cot and brought out the battered black hat with the beautiful plume on it.

Walter looked at the hat in amazement! The plume was beautiful! Florence handed him the hat and he stroked the plume. The soft, large feather had been a symbol of great pride as a token of honor and prowess for the members of the Iron Brigade.

SOLDIER IN THE NIGHT

Walter was tired. Florence tended to his medication and made him comfortable. He fell into a fitful sleep. Toward morning he awoke to sounds of soft crying coming from the soldier to his right.

Walter listened for awhile and then whispered, "Do you want to talk?" The soft crying stopped and for several minutes it was quiet.

"One of my brothers was killed as he fought beside me. A bullet hit him in the heart. I wonder what happened to his body? Did he get buried in a decent grave that is marked so that my parents, brothers, sisters and relatives can pay respects? Will the army notify my parents? They live near Boscobel, Wisconsin.

"Jody had a sweetheart and they planned to get married when he returned from service. Hilda wrote a poem to Jody and he carried it always and read it aloud often. I have it memorized.

> *"The winds of war are blowing*
> *Your heart tells me you are going*
> *With blue coat soldiers falling*
> *I know you hear the calling.*
>
> *"The tides of time are swelling*
> *The union is in danger of felling*
> *Our love is very strong and true*
> *My love, I will always wait for you."*

Walter was quiet as was the soldier. "I am tired of this terrible war," said the soldier after a long silence. "Too many deaths and injuries. We are but cannon fodder. What about Hilda and others like her? What about Mom and Dad? What

14

if we fail in our attempt to keep the Union whole? Are we sand on the beach of life? The waves pound on us and then retreat but we remain strong. A storm makes violet waves that destroy the beach. The storm fades and the beach is rebuilt. Is the sand beach the Union? Is the storm the assault on our democracy of the Union by the Confederates? Will there always be storms to test our resolve? You and I are minute players in this huge war. We are drawn into it because it is what we must do to preserve the Union. If we fall or are injured, men will say we did our part and we are heroes. Our families and our sweethearts may have resented our going to fight but deep down they will understand...I hope. For you and I we can hope we recover from our wounds and by that time this bloody war will be over and we can go home."

Walter was quiet as was the soldier. Finally the soldier offered, "We are animals and if we watch the wild populations we see periods of violet fighting sometimes to the death. Territory defense, mating privileges and fights for food are some reasons for fighting. Some animals get together in packs, flocks and herds to attack others, defend their territory or protect their life.

"Man is more highly organized so we get huge armies of men, arm them with terrible weapons that can kill at a distance and train them. We drill our soldiers to follow orders without questions. Punishment is meted out for violators of these orders. *Ours is not to wonder why. Ours is to do or die.*

"Some men can not stand this . . *follow orders or else.* Some men break under this training. Some don't break but have serious internal fighting going on in their mind. Many of us will be haunted by events during our enlistment. These may go on for the rest of our lives. Most of us don't want to kill anyone, but *kill or be killed.* Seeing many dead bodies, some are your fellow soldiers, some are Confederates and some are torn to bits by cannon fire. Those are terrible sights to see. We try to forget them but nightmares are constant re-minders. War is hell!"

The soldier thanks Walter for listening. Walter tells him. "I hope it helps you to heal and when you return to Boscobel you can leave all the ghosts behind."

"I had a sweetheart also," the soldier said. "Her name is Le-ona. I have a poem she wrote and gave me when I left home."

"With rifle in one hand,
My locket in the other.
You must defend this land,
Good bye to father and mother.

The march toward war is calling.
Many Union troops are falling
My love and these hills will call to you
Return sweetheart, our love is strong
and true."

Walter is silent as is the soldier. "You must return to Bo-scobel and put Leona's fears to rest as well as the fears your family has. Your letters home are a powerful link. We must win this war to keep the Union strong. I hope this battle is a turning point in a long struggle . . good night." said Walter.

GOODBYE, FLORENCE

Walter is concerned with his injury. Is it healing properly? He knows that many injured soldiers linger and then die. Florence comes in at dawn and changes the dressing on his wound. Walter asks about the wound.

"It seems to be progressing properly. After breakfast you will be moved on a special train and taken to a hospital in Harrisburg," said Florence.

"Are you coming with me?" asked Walter, hopefully.

"I must stay for a time, but then I will return to Hagerstown to continue my training," said Florence sadly.

Walter is crushed. Florence has been a bright light in Walters uncertainty since he has been wounded.

"Why can't you come with me? You are my savior and a very special friend. I don't want to be away from you . . even for a short time," said Walter sadly.

Florence finished dressing the wound and holds Walters hand. She looks into his eyes and smiles, the same beautiful smile that Walter saw when he awoke after three days. Walter reached for her other hand.

"Please don't leave me," Walter pleaded.

"I want to stay with you," Florence said. "I already asked if I could go with you and the answer was no. The matter is out of my control."

Breakfast arrived and Florence fed Walter. Shortly, hospital workers from the train began to arrive in the tent and began helping some soldiers toward the train. Walter felt great anxiety and asked Florence to get the black hat from under the cot. She presented the hat to Walter and he took the beautiful plume off the hat. He asked for Florence's hand and put the plume in her hand.

"This plume was presented from my commander, Lt. Col. Dawes. It is my second most prized possession. The first is my life and you saved it. Please take this plume as a heartfelt thank you."

"I would be happy and proud to accept the beautiful plume . . but only if I can return it to you some day."

Walter stood up and pulled Florence to him and gave her a kiss. Florence was embarrassed but returned Walter' kiss. She was flustered but returned to getting Walter's possessions ready to travel. The Iron Brigade uniform, the black hat, boots and medications were put in a rucksack. Walter wobbled to the cot next to him and shook hands with the soldier.

"Maybe I will stop at Boscobel someday and look you and Leona up. Good luck, soldier."

The orderlies approached Walters cot . . "You are next, Walter."

Walter requested that Florence assist him to the tent opening. Florence put her arm around Walter's waist and helped him toward the tent opening. He said good-bye to his tent mates as he passed their cots. When he reached the tent opening, he slowing turned around, pulled himself to full height and snapped a salute to the remaining soldiers. The salute was answered by all, including the two Confederate soldiers.

SAD PARTING

Florence watched Walter slowly make his way toward a horse-drawn wagon that would take him to the train to Harrisburg. Tears flowed and she cried. She ran and followed Walter before he was to board the wagon. She called his name as she approached and Walter slowly turned toward her. Finally she reached Walter and they embraced and kissed. They held each other as Florence held the plume out of harms way. After several minutes the orderlies insisted that Walter must continue so he does not miss the train. Florence walked a few steps holding Walters hand.

"What is your last name?" Walter suddenly asked.

"Porter, from Sparta, Wisconsin," replied Florence.

Walter boarded the wagon and it headed to the train. Florence sadly turned and slowly returned to the tent where she was met by her classmate friends, Rebecca and Beatrice. They came to meet her and she embraced both of them for several long seconds. Finally they turned toward the tent and walked arm in arm to resume caring for the few injured soldiers left in the tent.

The next day the remaining soldiers were transferred to another hospital in Harrisburg. Some were granted furloughs to return home for thirty days or more. These troops would begin by boarding a train to Hagerstown, Maryland. From there they would take trains toward their home towns. The two Confederates were taken to a prisoner camp by guards.

The two Confederate soldiers were both younger, seventeen and sixteen years old. Both were very appreciative of the care and treatment they received at the hands of the enemy.

"We certainly have a different view of the Union soldiers and the way we were picked up and brought to this tent and given care just like the Union boys. We have had enough of war. Since we have gotten to know some of these yanks, it would be very hard to shoot any of them. Anyway, thanks for saving our lives. We will never forget it or you ladies."

The same day, Florence and her twenty-six classmates boarded a train to Hagerstown to resume their special studies. Workers came to take down the tent, pack it and place it in wagons to be taken to the next battle. The little town of Gettysburg was beginning to return to the way it was on June 30, 1863. Many residents of Gettysburg fear that their little town will be drastically changed.

Florence has heard much about the bloody battle which killed or wounded more soldiers than in any battle to date. Both the Federals and the Confederates are Americans and many, many soldiers had relatives fighting against them. In some cases they faced each other through their rifle sights . . so tragic.

On the last charge by the Confederates against the battle line of the Union troops one amazing story is . . As the Confederates made their way across an open field for about one-half mile many were cut down by Union cannon fire. These troops reached rifle fire distance and many more were shot down. Still they continued upward toward the massed yanks behind breastworks and stonewalls on top of the ridge. As some Confederate soldiers got to within a few feet of the Union troops the Union boys raised their guns. They were so impressed by the courage of those fighters that they said they would not shoot and they could surrender or retreat. The story said that in some cases the opposing troops shook hands and some surrendered and some retreated.

RECOVERY AND REDEPLOYMENT

Walter arrived at the hospital in Harrisburg and immediately was placed under the care of Dr. Mast. The doctor examined the wound in Walter's chest and immediately was concerned that there may be infection in it. He swabbed the wound with liquid phenol. Walter felt immediate pain but it subsided in a few minutes. The doctor repacked and bandaged the wound. Dr. Mast knew Walter was a member of the Iron Brigade.

"Your wonderful fighting ability is well known." The doctor wanted to know about Walter's family. He told about his father, mother and brother Royce. He showed the locket with a picture of his mother and father.

"My family lives near Antigo, Wisconsin. My dad is in the lumber business. Royce and I hope to join him in that business after the war. I do have a younger brother, Ernest, and a younger sister Bertha. They are still in school."

Dr. Mast continued to treat the wound in Walter's chest. Finally, the infection was under control. However the doctor sensed that Walter was struggling with 'battlefield fatigue' which can seriously affect the mental outlook of a soldier that has been in battle. Dr. Mast visited with Walter and found out about Florence and felt that was a positive sign.

Dr. Mast arranged for Walter to be part of a group of injured soldiers. This group met each day for at least one hour. A Dr. O'Brien led the discussion and interacted with the men. Two men were familiar to Walter as they were from the 6th Wisconsin. One man was from an Ohio regiment and the other from the 1st Minnesota.

To begin with, Walter doubted the value of these meetings. At first he was very quiet. The other men were very reluctant to say very much either. Day by day, Walter warmed to the group and he felt more comfortable speaking out. Most of the group were deeply troubled by the awful loss of life. Having comrades fighting beside them and getting killed a few feet away.

"One minute alive and well with hopes and dreams . . the next minute he lies dead."

The 1st Minnesota man saw Confederates blown to pieces by cannon fire on the last day of fighting at Gettysburg. He really struggled with that memory.

"I was one of the very few from the 1st Minnesota that was not killed or wounded at Gettysburg," he said. "We had two-hundred-sixty-two men on July 1st but only forty-six were left standing after the big battle on July 3rd. Nearly all the men I knew were killed or wounded. This includes a brother that was killed on the first day. The Confederates breached our breastworks and fought hand in hand. We had fixed bayonets and I killed a man with a thrust to his chest. I can still see that young mans eyes as he looked at me as he died." There was a long pause. "I don't think I could go into battle again."

For the next few days, the discussion among the group was almost nonexistent. Dr. O'Brien talked about battlefield fatigue. He explained the way to healing is to talk about events on the battlefield or elsewhere.

One day one of the other 6th Wisconsin soldiers said, "I am afraid to go home. I don't want to act like we have had to for the last two years. I won't know how to get along with my family, neighbors and friends. I am afraid. We have all gotten so used to people dying that I think I will have an unhealthy attitude toward the value of the human life."

Walter talked about Florence and how she had helped him deal with the terrible things he had seen. He is hoping to get a letter from her soon. He is concerned about Royce and wonders where the 6th Wisconsin is located. He wishes there was a way to write him a letter.

"The hospital will supply the paper, envelopes and stamps," said Dr. O'Brien. "The letter will be sent to *The Department of War, Washington, D. C. Please forward to Royce Rounds, 6th Wisconsin regiment.* It may take some time but Royce will get the letter eventually."

After almost two months at Harrisburg hospital, Dr. Mast declared Walter ready to leave the hospital. Paper work was filed with the war department. Shortly a representative of the Union army visited Walter with his new orders. Thirty day leave and then report to Camp Randall at Madison, Wisconsin. Walter would help train replacement soldiers.

SEARCH FOR FLORENCE

Walter really longed for Florence. She had grabbed his heart and he thought about her often. He kept looking for a letter or some word from her. Dr. O'Brien telegraphed a hospital in Hagerstown to inquire about Florence or the training program she is on. He got a response but his source could not find Florence or the training program she was on.

In about an hour the doctor received a telegraph message that said, "When many of the injured soldiers from Gettysburg were moved here we were overwhelmed. The program you inquired about was cancelled and the nurses were sent back to Wisconsin."

Walter was heartbroken. Why didn't Florence send a letter? Maybe she didn't know the address. He hoped she was not sick or hurt. Maybe something happened to her family.

SPARTA

Walter decided he needed to go to Sparta and find Florence's parents and maybe Florence. He needed to find her, so he went to the train station and began his journey to Sparta and Florence.

His route took him through Pittsburgh, Chicago, Madison and finally Sparta. Train travel did not agree with Walter, but it was bringing him closer to Florence . . he hoped. He did enjoy viewing the scenery from the low mountains in Pennsylvania to the tall buildings in Chicago and Pittsburgh to the flat rich fields in Wisconsin to the Coolies near Sparta.

When he got off the train at Sparta he inquired where the Porter family lived. He had no luck for some time. He wandered around town and came to a building called Village Hall. He went in and inquired if anyone in this building could tell him where the Porter family lives. A lady got up from a desk and directed him to the land records department.

Walter inquired to an elderly man and he opened a large book and presently found the address for the Porter family. This man gave Walter directions to find the house. Walter thanked the man and headed out to find the Porter house. It only took a few minutes. A knock on the door was not answered. Walter had noticed a 'for sale' sign in the window. Now what? Maybe the neighbors could tell him something. The house to the south looked promising. There were some kids toys on the porch. Walter went to the door and knocked. Shortly the door opened and a lady asked if she could help. Walter explained about Florence and then asked about the Porter family.

"They moved in about two years ago. The father died about one year ago. There is a daughter and I only saw her once. I have not seen her for three or four months. The mother lived alone but about a month or so ago, she left with valises. She left on the train going east," said this helpful neighbor.

The lady was very friendly and wanted to help Walter. "When they moved here Mr. Porter was quite ill. They had land in northern Wisconsin and had a home on a lake. Mrs. Porter said it was a beautiful home but it was quite remote. Her husband got ill and was told that Dr. Penner in this town may be able to help him."

Walter thanked her and went to the house north of the Porter house.

There was no answer at this house but someone definitely lived there and apparently was not home. Walter went back to the Porter house and looked at the for sale sign. It had an address if anyone wanted to inquire. Walter went back to the Village Hall and asked for directions listed on the for sale sign.

Walter found the address and saw it belonged to an office of a land agent. He entered and an elderly man rose from his desk and came to the counter. Walter explained who he was and why he wanted to know where Mrs. Porter was so he could find her daughter Florence. The man went to the file cabinet and produced a file and began leafing through it.

Finally the man produced a small piece of paper.

Please sell the house as is, including the furniture and appliances. $2,650. Will contact you with address.

Thank you.
Mrs. Porter.

"This was under my door one morning about the 5th of August. I have not heard anything from Mrs. Porter. Apparently she left quite suddenly and no one seems to know where she went. When I put the for sale sign in the window the neighbor to the north was in her yard. I asked about Mrs. Porter and the neighbor did not know but wondered if she had moved back to the house on the lake in northern Wisconsin."

Walter went back and went up to the neighbor north of Mrs. Porter's house. A pleasant lady came to the door. Walter explained who he was and what his interest in Mrs. Porter was.

"Olivia left very suddenly about August 5th," the lady said. "She was very friendly and we visited occasionally but didn't say anything before she left. She did say she had a daughter, Florence, I think, that was studying to be a nurse. I wonder if she moved back to her home on the lake."

"Do you know where the home is located or any town near by?" asked Walter.

"No, only that it was up north and on a nice lake. She loved the house and it sounded very nice. It was much larger than this home. It was on the north side of the lake and a little above the lake," the lady replied.

Walter was trying to get a picture of Mrs. Porter. He pictured a pleasant, friendly person, possibly accustomed to a life of moderate luxury.

"Did Olivia ever say why they left the lake?"

"Apparently Mr. Porter owned a large acreage around the lake and their home. It sounded like several thousands of acres. It sounded like Mr. Porter invested heavily in a gold mine in Montana. I got the feeling that he borrowed money and put the land up for collateral. The mine was a dud and to cover his loan, the bank or whoever, took all the land," said the friendly neighbor to the north.

"Why did the Porter's move to Sparta?" Walter asked.

"Mr. Porter spent time here visiting his mothers brother, his uncle, when he was younger," said the neighbor.

"Do you know who that was?"

"Olivia told me a name once, but I forgot it. She said he and others formed a company to build a railroad line. He moved to Madison and apparently had no ties to Sparta anymore."

Walter enjoyed talking to this lady and asked her name, if that was permissible.

27

"Of course it is permissible. It is Antoinette Zimchezk."

Walter blushed for being straightforward more than he usually is around women. He guessed this lady to be a few years younger than his mother.

"You are really smitten by Mrs. Porter's daughter aren't you?" Antoinette said with a smile.

Now Walter really blushed. He looked down and kicked at the ground for awhile.

"Florence is the most beautiful, caring person that I have ever met - she saved my life," Walter said after a long pause. "The first thing I saw after three days was her beautiful, smiling face leaning over me. She told me I was going to be alright and she would take care of me. At first I thought I was seeing an angel. Florence assured me she was no angel.

"Florence tended me for another week in this large tent full of injured soldiers. Many were from my regiment, the 6th Wisconsin. There were two Confederate soldiers being cared for in that tent also. My brother Royce fought by my side and he received an injury to his arm but after one and one-half days, the 6th Wisconsin gathered what was left of the four-hundred-twenty men that were able to fight. Sadly over two-hundred were either wounded like me or killed. These weary men under Lt. Col. Rufus Dawes grouped up with the rest of the Iron Brigade and continued pursuing the rebels. I have heard nothing directly but I know the fighting is still bitter and going from battle to battle. I wrote Royce a letter and hope he gets it."

Walter was about to thank Mrs. Zimchezk for all the information when here comes a girl, about ten years old, and a boy of about fourteen years old walking into the yard. These were Mrs. Zimchezk's children returning from school. The children were very polite and friendly.

"This young man, Walter, was a soldier in the 6th Wisconsin regiment," their mother told them. "He fought in many battles but was badly wounded at Gettysburg. He is still recovering.

We have been talking because Mrs. Porter's daughter was a nurse caring for the wounded at Gettysburg. Walter needs to find Florence. . .he has special feelings for Florence. He has not heard from her since he was transferred to a hospital in Harrisburg, Pennsylvania. Florence was assigned elsewhere. He knew that Florence was from Sparta so he came here to find her. You know Olivia and she went away and we don't know where she went. We are wondering if she went to Florence, wherever she is."

It was a beautiful, late September day and it was early evening. Walter had enjoyed talking to Antoinette. The children were in awe of a real Civil War soldier in their front yard. They asked questions and were polite. Jenny was the girl and wanted to tell them about Florence.

"Maybe she is Florence Nightingale," she said with an impish smile.

"Florence is a real beauty," Walter replied. "She has a friendly smile and great compassion for her patients. She is about nineteen or twenty years old with long, light brown hair and brown eyes. She has a medium build and is fairly tall, about as tall as your mother."

"She sounds like she looks like Olivia," Jenny said excitedly. "She must be a very nice person and I can tell you really like her. . .very much so."

About this time a tall man walked into the yard. "Hello, Father," Jenny said as she went to him and gave him a hug. Caleb, the son went to his father and put his hand on his shoulder and greeted him. Antoinette gave Abner a hug and a kiss. Abner approached Walter and offered his hand. He and Walter greeted each other with a firm handshake. Walter could feel great strength in the very firm handshake.

"Abner is a cooper," Antoinette told Walter, "and makes barrels for a living."

Abner was taller than Walter but with the same medium build. Walter thought this man looked very strong.

Antoinette told Abner about Walter and why he was there. Abner asked if Walter had secured lodging for the night.

"I have not," replied Walter. "I passed an inn earlier and thought I would inquire there."

Abner asked, "Is there room for Walter at the supper table? And is a bed available for this brave soldier?"

"Of course, there is," Antoinette replied. Abner told Walter, "This family would be honored if you would share our meal and spend the night with us."

Walter gently kicked the ground and started to mumble when Abner went to him and put his arm around Walters shoulders and said, "We will not take no for an answer."

Twilight was upon this little group of people who were under a beautiful maple tree. It was adorned with its fall color of deep red leaves. The temperature was pleasant, and the sky was blue with a band of faint red on the horizon. Walter thought this must be heaven on earth, far from the terrible events of the war. He briefly wondered if Royce was some place as friendly and beautiful at this moment. His thoughts were briefly about Florence and was concerned that so far he could not find out where she was.

Antoinette prepared supper and the rest of the group settled in the front room. Caleb was interested in what a mini-ball was.

"They are small cannon balls," replied Walter, "that are loaded into a cannon and fired into advancing troops. It is like giant birdshot from a shotgun except they are deadly at a range of one hundred to three hundred or more feet. Many men can be felled with one shot."

"We heard that our northern troops are called Blue Coats." Jenny said. "Did you wear a blue uniform?"

"I did," Walter replied as he got into his rucksack and produced his Iron Brigade uniform which was dark blue with light blue trousers. "All the Iron Brigade troops dressed like this and wore the flat black hats."

"In looking at the uniform," Jenny said, "I can see where you were shot in the chest. That was terrible."

"Walter, would you tell us what the Iron Brigade is?" Caleb asked.

"It was five regiments and about two-thousand men when it was at full strength. It was made up of the 2nd, 6th and 7th Wisconsin that trained at Camp Randall in Madison. The 19th Indiana and 24th Michigan make up the other two regiments sometimes call the *black hats.* This brigade was very well trained and were fierce fighters. We have suffered great losses but new replacements are trained to take their places. I have been in several battles and Gettysburg may be my last as I would not be able to hold a rifle to my shoulder and fire it. I have been assigned to Camp Randall to train Wisconsin troops."

"Many young men from Sparta have left for the war," said Abner. "Several have been wounded or killed so our little town has had plenty of agony about this terrible war."

"Father went to sign up for the war," said Jenny, "but he couldn't and was told that his job making barrels was very important to the war so that will be his contribution. That was fine with me as I didn't want him to be hurt or away from us. Mother goes down to the church and tears sheets into strips to be used as bandages."

Abner got up and lit two lanterns.

Antoinette called the group to the table. Hot dish and fresh bread was the fare and Walter thought it was wonderful. This was his first home-cooked meal in over two years.

"What did you eat when you were fighting?" asked Jenny.

"I have to tell you that I have walked many hundreds of miles. I had a back pack with a few clothes, a bed roll and a small tent. I carried a rifle and plenty of ammunition. I had a cup for water, coffee or tea and a small kettle I made pork and beans in at night, and buried the kettle in the hot coals of the camp fire. In the morning it would be nicely cooked by the time I dug in out of the coals. The cook wagon provided the pork and beans plus hard tack. For lunch we ate hardtack and supper was more hardtack and bologna. Once in awhile, ham, pork chops or roast were available. We had to do our own cooking, which I have to admit I was not good at but I got better.

"Some days we marched twenty to twenty-five miles and the food wagon had a hard time keeping up. We procured food as we traveled when we could, chickens, eggs, hogs, garden vegetables, apples, fruit, etc. Most times we paid, but not always. We were always hungry and hardtack got mighty old. It kept us alive, though. We rarely had fresh bread."

"What about your family? Where do they live?" asked Antoinette.

Walter dug into his pocket and produced the locket with the pictures of his mother and father and passed it to Jenny. "Edward and Alice are much like you folks. Mother is a wonderful homemaker and is a caring, loving lady, maybe a little older than you. Father runs a lumber business which is north of Antigo, Wisconsin. Royce and I work with my father producing maple flooring. Before I went into the army he obtained several thousand acres of timber land that had never been logged. Father is working toward making a large mill that employees many workers that can produce huge amounts of maple flooring along with other wood products. I know he is trying to get a railroad into the site of the mill."

After supper, Antoinette produced a fresh apple pie which was a real treat for Walter.

"How are you going to find Florence?" asked Jenny, "and can I help?"

"I need to find out where Mrs. Porter went," said Walter as he leaned back and scratched his head. "I think she is with

Florence who I hope is not injured or sick. I will check with the land agent tomorrow and give him an address where he can send me a letter in the event Mrs. Porter contacts him regarding the sale of the house. If the house get sold, Mrs. Porter will have to present a deed and when she does, perhaps she will have to list some address. Once I have that I will travel there and find Florence. Yes, Jenny you can help. If you notice that Mrs. Porter comes home . . tell your mother and father so they can go and ask her for an address of where Florence is located. I will write down the address of my parents home near Antigo, as well as my address at Camp Randall if it is more than thirty days from now."

"There is a train to Madison at 11:10 a.m. each day," Abner informed Walter. "From Madison you can take a train north to Antigo to visit your parents. I bet your parents will be happy to see you since you have not been home for over two years. Maybe Royce will have sent them a letter to keep them informed of his health and other things."

Walter asked for the address for the Zimchezk residence so he could contact them from time to time. Caleb volunteered his bed to Walter as he could sleep on the divan for the night.

"I sure would like you to visit my class," Jenny said. "My classmates would really like to meet a soldier from the Iron Brigade. We studied about that and the Civil War."

Walter was taken aback by Jenny's request. He said, "I would be uneasy going into a room full of young students."

"Please say that you will do it. I am sure that Miss Nichols would approve."

JENNY AND WALTER

"Miss Nichols lives only two blocks away," Jenny said. Maybe Mom and I can take you over to her house and ask permission to have you visit my class."

Walter was feeling like he should be willing to visit Jenny's class. Jenny was certainly thinking it would be a good idea and went up to Walter to plead with him.

"Go see Miss Nichols."

Off the three of them went. Miss Nichols was home and welcomed the group into their home. Jenny introduced Walter and explained that she would like Walter to meet her classmates tomorrow morning. Miss Nichols was very impressed with Walter and why he was visiting Jenny's home. Jenny had already asked Walter if he would wear his uniform and he said he would.

Miss Nichols gave her approval and said, "I will be looking forward to tomorrow morning." Jenny was very excited!

"I am looking forward to it too," said Walter, "even though it is very frightening."

The next morning, Walter came to the breakfast table dressed in his full Iron Brigade uniform including his hat. When he walked into the room the entire family looked in awe!!! Walter was impressive!!! His dark blue tunic and light blue trousers with the black piping down the legs, a black leather belt with a large brass buckle with U.S. on it was over his tunic. He had his dress leggings on above his boots and they were light colored.

The most impressive item of his dress was his large flattop black hat. The brim on the sides was slightly curled. An upside down brass horn with a brass number six inside the curl of the horn adorned the front. A blue cord with tassels toward the front finished the adornment of the hat.

Walter removed his hat and sat down for breakfast. Jenny was bubbling with excitement and Antoinette tried to calm her down. Breakfast was finished and it was time for Abner to go to work. Walter thanked Antoinette and Abner for the meals, the hospitality, the understanding and appreciation of his feelings for Florence.

Jenny, Caleb and Walter headed off to school. Word had spread about an Iron Brigade soldier that was going to be at school. Several people lined the sidewalk and street to see Walter and thank him for his service. Walter was proud of his uniform and his service and he appreciated the thanks sent his way by the people of Sparta.

All three completed the four blocks to school and found the school yard full of students and some adults. All were awaiting the arrival of the Iron Brigade soldier. Once in the school yard, Walter and the kids were swarmed by the students. Many wanted a closer look at the uniform. Some wanted to touch Walter and his uniform. Most were in awe that a Civil War soldier in full uniform was here.

The bell rang and Jenny took Walter by the hand and led him to her classroom. Miss Nichols welcomed Walter and all the students. After roll call was taken, Miss Nichols called on Jenny to introduce her visitor.

Jenny was excited and told her classmates, "Walter fought at Gettysburg and was severely wounded in his chest. A very pretty wonderful nurse cared for him and made him well. He was moved to a hospital and he lost track of Florence. He knew she was from Sparta so he came here looking for her or someone who could tell him where she was. Florence's mother lived next door to us and Walter went there hoping to find out about Florence. Olivia was not home so Walter came to our house to see if we could help. That is how Walter found me."

Miss Nichols asked if anyone had questions and nearly every hand went up. Walter was nervous. He answered the questions as best he could. Many had questions about his uniform. What was the Iron Brigade? How were you wounded? One boy wanted to know if he was hurt during Pickett's Charge? Walter said he had very little information about Gettysburg names and asked the boy, "Was that on July 3rd?"

"I thought it was," the boy said, "and it was when many thousands of Confederates advanced on Union troops."

"That was where I was wounded," said Walter. "The 6th Wisconsin had suffered huge loses during the first two days of Gettysburg. We were in a reserve position in about the middle of the three or four mile long line of Union troops behind breastworks and rock fences. The Confederates had concentrated their cannon fire in the middle of the line in hopes of being able to break through. Some Confederates did break through and we were called into action to support the first line troops who suffered very heavy loses from cannon fire. We had fixed bayonets and my brother and I were entering the fight when I got shot. I woke up in a hospital tent three days later. That is where I saw Florence, smiling and leaning over me, telling me that I would be alright."

"The class tried to learn more about the battle at Gettysburg," Miss Nichols told Walter. "There has been great interest in the battle because three Sparta boys fought there also. They fought for the 2nd Wisconsin and the 7th Wisconsin. As you have said they were members of the Iron Brigade. Unfortunately all three boys were killed at Gettysburg . . two on the last day. All three boys were in my classroom a few years ago and it makes me very sad."

The students had more questions.

"What do you eat while fighting?"

"Where do you sleep?"

"Where is your rifle?"

By now all the students moved in around Walter. "Do you have to go and fight again?"

"I am on leave," explained Walter, "and am going to visit my parents for a few days. I will have to report to Camp Randall at Madison to train more Wisconsin soldiers. No I don't think will fight again. My injury will not allow me to shoot a rifle again."

There was a knock on the classroom door. It was a reporter from the Sparta paper along with a photographer. Miss Nichols was consulted to see if a picture or two could be taken with the soldier and the students. Miss Nichols said that it was alright with her but she would ask the young soldier. Walter said it would be alright. Pictures were taken as were notes about questions the students asked.

"There has been great interest in you since you arrived in Sparta," the reporter said. "Maybe much more than you realize. Three of Sparta's young men fought at Gettysburg and were killed. We know the fighting was extremely brutal and deadly. You were severely injured, but survived. You are a hero, my friend, people of this town would like you to know that we really appreciate your service in the face of terrible fire power. We all hope you can find Florence and she is alright."

"I need to catch the train and I must leave." Many students came up and shook hands or gave him a hug. Jenny had tears streaming down her face as she said good-bye and asked Walter to bend down and she gave him a kiss and a hug. Walter thanked Miss Nichols and when he got to the door he turned and pulled up in a salute to the students. Finally the good-byes were said and Walter left the classroom . He made a quick swipe of his eyes with the back of his hand to dry tears. He did not know why he was so emotional. Maybe it was Jenny's farewell hug and kiss. Maybe he hoped these young students won't have to go to battle.

Outside in the school yard were dozens of men and women. As soon as Walter stepped out there was a rousing cheer and clapping. Walter was taken aback. Several came forward to shake his hand and thank him for his service. Finally he was able to put his rucksack over his shoulder and head to the land agents office.

The land agent was in his office and Walter asked if there was any news. No, was the answer. Walter gave him a paper with this parents address.

"I will be posting at Camp Randall in Madison for several months. Any news about Olivia Porter would be very important to me. I need to find Florence."

The agent assured Walter that if the house sells, Mrs. Porter would have to transfer the deed and there is a line for the name and address of the seller.

"Young man, I will keep a sharp eye out for anything that may help you find Florence. The whole town will be helping! Now, you better hightail it to the train station!" The agent reached out and said, "Walter, thanks for your service and good luck."

Walter arrived at the train station on time. He asked for a ticket to Madison and asked the cost.

"Walter," the ticket agent said, "for you there is no cost. Some people in Sparta have left funds to cover your ticket wherever you are going."

Walter was stunned! Why would people do that for me, he thought.

"Of the four people we know that fought at Gettysburg," said the agent, "you are the only one that survived that terrible battle. We know you came perilously close to not surviving. You offer hope to us in Sparta and besides you seem to be an alright guy. Is Lt. Col. Dawes as good of leader as has been reported?"

"Sir, Lt. Col. Rufus Dawes is a giant among men. He has intense eyes and a vision for the future. He is very sincere, knows all his men and is extremely well respected. He makes us want to work as a team, defend each other and present a

unified force as part of the Iron Brigade. He will be my friend
for life as I know I will be his friend for life. Sir, we love Lt.
Col. Dawes. Yes, he is an outstanding leader."

GOING HOME

Walter thanked the ticket agent as he heard the locomotive of the train, its bell clanging and blowing steam as it pulled into the Sparta station. Walter boarded and found a seat opposite of a middle age man that looked friendly . . at least he smiled at Walter as he sat down.

"Albert Cutler," said the man as he held out his hand.

"Walter Rounds, nice to meet you."

"You look like a veteran of many battles," Mr. Cutler stated. "Am I correct?"

"I have fought in many battles as a member of the 6th Wisconsin in the Iron Brigade," relayed Walter.

"I know that the 6th Wisconsin fought at Gettysburg along with the 7th Wisconsin that my youngest brother and his friend are enlisted in. I got a letter from my brother recently and he told of the heavy loses both sides endured. Both my brother and his friend were wounded but are recovering and are on leave now."

"Is your brother discharged from the military service now?"

"No," Albert said, "he has been reassigned to Camp Randall to train new recruits."

"That is my assignment also, after a few days of leave with my parents near Antigo."

Walter and Albert made small talk. All at once the train was in a tunnel and the train was in complete darkness. In a few minutes the train immerged from the tunnel and back into the light. Walter made a comment to Albert about all the steep hills and long valleys that the train is passing near.

"This is the coolie country of Wisconsin," Albert offered. "Apparently the last glacier did not get this far and this is very old country. We can see how the rivers cut the land as they run to a larger river and eventually into the Mississippi River. Apparently this happened over a period of many million years. Also we can see some places where the rock layers are exposed. Fossils found in these layers indicate that all these layers were at the bottom of the ocean or large lakes. Now the tops of the ridges are about one thousand feet above sea level. Either the ocean sunk or the land rose up."

Walter was interested in what Albert said. He was just not in the mood to pursue any discussion. He felt a sadness leaving the students when they seemed so very interested in being around him, touching his uniform and being so kind and polite. He hoped they didn't get the idea that war is a good thing.

Miss Nichols sure seemed like a very nice person. Her students seem to look on her as a good friend. She certainly seemed like a very good teacher. Walter once again thought about those bright and happy faces of the young students. Will there be terrible battles like Gettysburg in their life? Will the world be peaceful so they can lead happy lives? He felt his eyes water as he looked away.

Walter wondered why those students affected him like they did. His search for Florence brought him to Sparta and he felt a great sadness for not being able to find any information about her whereabouts. Walter wondered if he felt a great appreciation from the people of Sparta for what he did as a soldier. The town was in mourning for the three young men who died at Gettysburg. The entire town seemed to know he had come there to find Florence or find out where she is. Walter felt the powerful message from the people of Sparta that they want me to find Florence and they will do all they can to help me locate her. Walter can still picture her beautiful face, smiling at him as he awoke from his injury. It brought a lump to his throat. Where is Florence?

"Do you travel much?" Walter asked Albert.

"I travel some when I am needed," responded Albert.

"What line of work are you in?"

"My company makes sawmill equipment. If a mill operator has a problem or questions I will visit the mill and try to solve the problem and answer questions."

"What powers your sawmills?"

"We have developed three sizes of stationary steam engines to run the head rig or to run the jack shafts that power smaller saws, like edger's. Other jack shafts can power planers, blowers to move shavings and sawdust. Currently we are developing a very large band saw that will be the head rig in a large mill. We are still developing that mill but it won't be ready for a few years. It looks promising. We are working on developing a large band saw that has teeth on both sides of the blade so it will cut both forward and backward."

After a few minutes, Walter said, "My father has a lumber company and he plans to produce hard maple flooring and oak flooring. Before the war he acquired several thousand acres of land north of Antigo."

The train was slowing down as it approached the Madison depot. "Do you have a card I could give to my father?"

Albert produced a card and told Walter, "My company provides customers with ideas of arranging sawmill and processing equipment for the best efficiency for the site selected."

Walter said good-bye to Albert and got off the train in Madison. He inquired about a train to Antigo and the ticket agent replied, "Leaves at 1:15 p.m. Need to change at Wausau."

Walter found a room to use to change back into his civilian clothes. There was a lunch counter at the depot and Walter sat down and ordered soup and a ham sandwich. An elderly man took the stool next to Walter.

In a few minutes, the man asked, "Didn't I see you with your Iron Brigade uniform on just a few minutes ago?"

"Yes, you did," said Walter. Nothing more was said for a few minutes.

Then the man asked, "Do you know any Negro's?"

Walter wondered where the man was going with that question. He chose to ignore that question and continued eating lunch.

"They should all be slaves," the man continued. Now Walter knew this man was a bigot and wanted to goad him into a discussion that could only turn out bad.

Walter finished lunch and paid his bill and got up to leave.

"You don't say much, do you?" The man said.

"Mister," Walter paused and looked at the man. "They are human beings and they should not be slaves, just as you and I are not slaves." He picked up his rucksack and turned and left the lunch room. He could feel his anger rising but the farther he walked away from the man the more the anger subsided. He wondered if the man was from one of the Confederate states or was he a man who really thought slavery was alright.

Discussions about slavery were common place among the 6th Wisconsin troops. Most of the men were like Walter from rural Wisconsin and they had no contact with Negro's and knew very little about slavery. Most felt like Walter though, it was wrong.

Walter boarded the train to Wausau. It was a town on the Wisconsin River near some waterfalls. The car was not crowded so Walter selected a seat so he could sit by himself. He really wanted to sit alone and deal with his thoughts. He was headed home so he should be happy, but he seemed to be under a dark cloud and it made him feel strange.

Once again his thoughts were about Florence. Walter just knew Florence would have made contact with him while in the hospital in Harrisburg. Something must have happened. Did Confederates sabotage the train and it crashed? Did she get captured by the Confederates to tend to Confederate soldiers? Somehow, none of those theories seems plausible. Maybe Florence doesn't feel about me like I do about her. Walter knows he is young and not very experienced with dealing with young ladies he is attracted to, but he felt the attraction went both ways.

Dealing with those 'what if' thoughts was troubling and didn't do anything to make Walter feel any better about Florence. What he did know was that he wanted to go and search for her . . but where? If only someone would buy Mrs. Porter's house. Then what . . the land agent in Sparta has no address to contact her at. Apparently whoever makes an offer to buy her house will have to wait for Mrs. Porter to inquire if anyone has expressed an interest in purchasing the house. Surely, she would have to include an address where she could be reached. All at once, Walter thought, maybe he could buy the house!!! Mrs. Porter will have to list an address. Next thing, where will he get $2,650.

As the train proceeded north, Walter was deep in thought about how he would get funds to buy Mrs. Porter's house. He also was going to be short of time as he already used five days of his thirty day furlough. He doubted that his mother and father could afford to help him. Maybe Grandmother Rounds but Walter doubted it. She was elderly and since Grandpa Rounds passed she seems to be struggling financially.

The train rumbled north and Walter kept thinking. Maybe he should talk to the bank at Antigo. The more he thought about it the more he thought it might work. But what about collateral. He had only $760 in the bank and $1,435 in back pay. Even if the bank loaned him enough money to buy the house, how would he pay for it. If he could buy the house, then what? If I can locate Florence and we could marry we could live in the house. Then what? I would need a job to not only pay for the house but to live also. That requires paying for food, clothes and heat. Who will hire me? I may not be able to work because of my injury.

The train made a stop at Portage and Walter got up and walked to another car. He immediately recognized one of this 6th Wisconsin fellow soldiers. He greeted him and immediately Walter could see the soldier had lost his left arm near the shoulder. The two were happy to see each other and Walter remembered his name was Ted Liskau and he lived near Merrill prior to the war. Ted and Walter compared notes on their injuries. Ted was hit with a piece of a cannon wheel that got shattered by a Confederate cannon ball. His arm was nearly cut off and quick work by one of his squad members saved him from bleeding to death. The arm was amputated.

"I spent a week in a hospital tent near Gettysburg. I was transported to a hospital in Harrisburg and was there for over two months. I have been discharged and am heading home." said Ted.

Walter and Ted continued talking. Walter inquired whether there was a girl waiting at home.

"Yes, there is - her name is Matilda and we were planning to marry but I have been away a long time. I hope we are still friends and there is not some one else."

Walter told Ted what happened from his injury and how he met Florence. He told about his not hearing anything from Florence but he was hoping to find her. He also said he has to report to Camp Randall and train new recruits.

"What are your plans when you get home?" inquired Walter.

"My dad and my uncle have adjoining farms and I expect to continue working for them. Clearing land, logging off the best timber and planting crops to increase the size of the two farms. I hope to purchase my own land soon, but having only one arm there may be a change in my plans."

Walter told of his plans to continue helping his father develop a large lumber operation to produce hard maple flooring as well as red oak flooring.

The two Iron Brigade soldiers talked of some of the men they knew in the 6th Wisconsin. Walter found he really didn't like talking about the way they had lived, the battles they fought, the death and injuries and the hardships the men endured. Ted seemed to run out of enthusiasm for discussion for the past also.

The train pulled into the station at Wausau and Walter shook hands with Ted and shouldered his rucksack and told Ted good-bye.

"Good luck, best wishes for you and Matilda. Also on developing your own land."

Walter got his ticket for Antigo and found the train would pull out at 4:35 p.m. Walter had twenty-five minutes so he headed to the lunch counter and ordered a bowl of soup, a chicken sandwich and a glass of milk. This would be the first milk Walter had had in about two years and it was delicious.

Walter boarded the train to Antigo as light was beginning to fade. He admired the beautiful leaves on the maples, ash, aspen and oaks. This was a time of the year Walter and Royce would hunt for squirrels, partridge, rabbits and sharp tailed grouse. In November they hunted white tail deer.

Both men really loved the woods. The overhead branches and thick tree trunks made the woods a place of mystery and pleasure. Other animals provided excitement and in most cases were not hunted. Black bears were encountered at times as were timber wolves, bobcats, raccoons, fishers and badgers. Also seen were eagles, owls, hawks and great blue herons. The forests were huge and wild as very few people lived near Walter's home.

Settlement in northern Wisconsin was slow as railroads and roads were being built. The railroad ended at Antigo and roads were more like trails. Settlers were purchasing land, clearing it and developing farms in the Antigo area. The land was flat and fertile. Where Walters parents lived it was hilly and rocky, apparently remnants of the glaciers. While not desirable for farming, it was wonderful for trees. Walter's father and mother inherited several thousand acres of forest land that his father was planning to develop for their lumber enterprise. A fast moving river ran through this huge forest in a southeast direction. Someone had named it the Wolf River as there were plenty of timber wolves in the area. The river had a large population of trout but was dangerous to fish because of boulders and fast moving water.

Walter was looking forward to seeing his family and hopefully getting some news about Royce. His sister, Erna was the oldest, next Royce and Walter. Ernest was fifteen and Bertha was twelve. Ernest and Bertha were attending school in Antigo and had to live with a family in Antigo during the week. Father would come and pick them up and bring them home for the weekend. Today was Friday but it was too late to get a ride home with him. Walter thought he would spend the night in Antigo at the hotel and walk home in the morning. It is sixteen miles and it should be easy. He hopes his injury was healed enough to enable him to walk home.

ANTIGO

Walters train arrived at the Antigo depot and Walter departed. He was walking toward the hotel when he heard someone call his name. He turned around and saw one of this friends from school, Hal. They met and Hal welcomed Walter back to Antigo. He knew Walter and Royce fought for the 6th Wisconsin and he had heard how the regiment routed the boys from Mississippi and captured many at Gettysburg. Walter was glad to see an old friend. They hunted squirrels and partridge together when they were about fourteen years old.

Hal was just getting off work at the shoe and boot factory in Antigo. He was on his way to meet two of his friends at a tavern on Fifth Avenue.

"Come on, Walter . . it is too late to walk home anyway," urged Hal.

Hal introduced Walter to his friends sitting at the table. They worked together at the shoe and boot factory and were not familiar to Walter. All three young men had received exemptions from military service because of their work at the factory. Good boots were of great importance and Weiner Shoe and Boot Company had a great reputation. It also had a contract to produce one-hundred-thirty-thousand pairs of boots for the Union army. They needed all the workers they could get to meet their quotas. They had factories in three other cities in Wisconsin. Walter wore a pair of Weiner boots that he had since he volunteered two years ago.

Hal and his friends drank beer, but Walter drank coffee. Hal and his friends had many questions about serving in the military. Hal produced a newspaper clipping about an editorial that appeared in a Madison newspaper. Hal read the clipping as he and his friends felt they would be affected by the message it spoke of.

Hal read, "The political view of the war was shifting from each state providing volunteer troops selected by volunteering. But now President Lincoln has control of procuring troops for the Union army. He works with the states but the federals decision of who would be drafted or selected as a volunteer was final. The Union needs more troops as it needs to win this war. The Emancipation Proclamation was presented which changed the focus of the war from uniting the Union and, in addition, it was to free slaves."

All of this was well known to Hal and his friends. They felt certain that they would be drafted soon and their work making boots would not keep them from being deferred.

They all had read about the three days at Gettysburg. They asked many questions of Walter about the battle and his injury. They admired his bravery in the face of such a terrible onslaught. Several patrons at the tavern stopped and thanked Walter for his service.

A man approached the table and said, "Fighting this war to free Negro's is wrong. They will all end up on relief and we will all have to pay. They don't have a brain in their head and they are lazy." The man slurred his words and was unsteady.

Walter did not say anything for about a minute. Finally he said, "Would you want to be a slave? Maybe the four of us will knock you over your head, steal your wallet and put you in irons. We could take you to a factory in Milwaukee where no one would know you. You would have no proof of who you are and you would be required to work long hours for no pay, but a little something to eat. We would make a nice profit from turning you over to the factory."

The man stepped back and said, "You can't do that. It is illegal. I have my rights."

"Negro's are human beings and in America they have rights also and that is what this war is about," Walter told him.

The bartender and another patron approached the man and told him it was time to leave and escorted him out the door.

Walter felt betrayed. Right here in his home town. These men expressed very strong anti-negro language. How could that be? Apparently the war was bringing forth very strong anti-negro feelings.

THE CROWD

"It is getting late and I need to get a room at the hotel," Walter said. Goodbyes were said and Walter departed the tavern. He continued to the hotel and he could hear shouting coming from a crowd gathered on a street corner. There were twenty to thirty men and some women in the crowd. Walter stayed about one-half block away until he could find out what this gathering was about. He heard several voices objecting to the forthcoming draft or conscription that President Lincoln had ordered to obtain enough soldiers so the union could win this war.

"It is not fair - who will provide food for our families."

"There already is a serious shortage of able bodied men now."

"Our farms and town are being neglected with mostly old men, women, children and cripples to do the work needed."

"We already have sent many of our men to battle and at least six are dead and at least that number are injured."

"It was one thing to preserve the Union but another to free the slaves and confiscate southern property." That speaker drew loud applause and shouts of approval.

"Maybe Wisconsin should stand alone and make our own rules about who will serve."

"That won't work - we are part of the Union. And Union means we all stick together."

"Our boys write back and tell us there is not enough food, blankets, replacement shoes and clothes."

"Some regiments have not been paid for months."

The crowd has grown to fifty or sixty. The police chief and a deputy show up and study the crowd. Walter sees that there seems to be three or four men and one woman doing most of the talking. Walter is surprised at the remarks that he is hearing! There seems to be a great deal of unrest about issues

51

Walter was only somewhat aware of. He did know that the little town of Antigo had supplied their fair share of soldiers and that definitely worked a hardship on farms and businesses. His fathers lumber enterprise lost two hard workers when Walter and Royce volunteered to fight for the Union. However, he was doing it as part of Wisconsin service to the Union in its struggle with secessionists' from the southern states.

Someone walking past Walter recognized him and he said nothing until he joined the people gathered.

"There is an Antigo soldier, severely wounded at Gettysburg, standing a few feet away. I would like to invite him to come and talk to us. Maybe he can help us understand what lies ahead."

"Yes, yes, let's see if he can talk to us."

They asked Walter to come in and talk about his experiences. As Walter approached, the crowd broke into loud applause and cheers. One of the speakers asked Walter if he could comment on some of the things that were said. Walter was cautious. He realized this group could get out of control easily. He also thought the police chief and the one deputy would have a difficult time if things got ugly.

The crowd gathered around Walter and he stated, "I have been soldiering for the past two years. I just see what is in front of me and we don't get much in the line of news about things back home. Mothers and Fathers don't tell about hardships in the hometown. They want to do all they can to cheer us up. Recently I have been aware of objections to the upcoming draft and the Emancipation Proclamation. I just learned about those since my release from the hospital a week ago. Yes, from time to time there is a shortage of food, blankets, replacement clothes and maybe boots. I can tell you that I am wearing the same boots that I was issued when I joined up and they were made by Weiner Shoes and Boots, maybe by some of you right here in Antigo.

"There have been shortages of ammunition. Weather can be brutal and we live in tents. Another thing we are short of is soldiers. At Gettysburg the 6th Wisconsin, my regiment, lost half of our four-hundred-twenty men. At Antietam it was close to the same ratio. Men die from sickness, cold, poor food, but yet we must keep fighting the Confederates. Some of us are going to come home with terrible thoughts in our heads. Having a fellow soldier killed a few feet away, seeing remains or bodies blown apart by cannon fire and other terrible sights are hard to get out of our minds.

"Managing a huge war like this, with Americans fighting Americans can be very difficult. We are aware that there is political fighting that holds down progress. President Lincoln is a great leader. So is my commander, Lt. Col. Dawes of the 6th Wisconsin. Please support our troops."

When Walter finished there was loud applause. Many came and shook his hand or slapped him on the back. The crowd faded away from the light of the gas street light. No more shouts were heard. The police chief came over to Walter and thanked him for his service and for his eye opening talk.

Walter proceeded to the hotel and obtained a room for the night. The hotel had a dining room so Walter ordered a steak, baked potato and a glass of milk. The steak was excellent and Walter was full and content at the conclusion of the meal. He returned to his room and contemplated what the crowd had said. Apparently there is great concern for conditions at home as well as concern for upcoming events like conscription. Walter knew that many of the people that live in Antigo and nearby are new to Wisconsin. Hal and his friends had said that new immigrants who had voted would be eligible for the draft. Those that had not voted apparently will not be drafted. This was cause for a great deal of bitterness toward these people new to Wisconsin. Perhaps the rules for draft eligibility will change if more soldiers are needed. Hal said that about

53

one-third of Wisconsin's population are new immigrants and resentment is building because of the draft rules as set down by the federal government. Walter hopes that compromise can be reached and he knows the best solution is for this terrible war to end.

THE LETTER

Walter's thoughts turned to Florence. He took up pen and paper and wrote her a letter dated September 20, 1863, Antigo, Wisconsin.

Dear Florence, My heart is breaking. I have not heard anything since we said goodbye as I got into the wagon taking me to the train to Harrisburg. We said a tearful goodbye then you were gone. My last memory of you is you waving goodbye as the wagon departed for the train. That image is crystal clear in my memory. Each day in the hospital, I looked for a letter from you or better yet, I hoped you might visit me. I spent most of my time thinking about you and how strong our feelings are for each other.

As the days wore on I began to wonder why I had not heard from you. Had you gotten sick? Did you go back to Wisconsin? A doctor at Harrisburg telegraphed the hospital in Hagerstown and was told that the influx of the wounded soldiers forced them to abandon the nursing program and the nurses went back to Wisconsin. I wondered if you may have stayed to care for the wounded like you did for me. I hoped that you were doing that as your loving care will help many wounded soldiers have a full recovery.

As time went by, I gave up on that idea as I know you would have contacted me. You have the beautiful plume that I know you will return to me and now I am really worried. Your strong character dictates that you will return it, so I am beginning to think dark thoughts that something must have happened to you.

I was discharged from the Harrisburg hospital and went to Sparta. I located your mother Olivia's house but she was not home and the house was for sale. The for sale sign gave an address of a land agent in Sparta. So I went to inquire about the house. He told me he found a note under his door on the morning of August 5th and the note asked the agent to sell the

55

house for $2,650 as it included appliances and furniture. It was signed by Olivia Porter.

Your mother pulled up stakes and moved in a very short period of time. No one knew a thing about where she went. I am of the opinion that your mother received information about your situation which caused her to abandon Sparta and go to you. I am afraid you are very sick or that you have been badly hurt.

I need to find you, Florence, and if I can find an address wherever your mother is, I will come there to find you. If someone buys your mothers house, she will have to present the deed, signed by her and listing her address. I am trying to raise enough money so I can buy the house so I can get the address as to where she is. So far I have not been able to arrange to carry out the transaction. Of course, someone else may buy the house and when the land agent hears from your mother and he has a return address, I would then be able to find her and then you.

Florence, you are about all I think about all the time.

Your loving friend, Walter

HOMECOMING

Walter folded the letter carefully and put it in his rucksack, thinking about what lies ahead. He was due to report to Camp Randall by October 14, 1863. He needs to send a letter to the land agent in about a week. He needs to find enough money to buy Olivia's house in Sparta. If he can get enough money to buy the house, he would have to go to Sparta, give the money to the land agent and then wait to hear from Olivia.

If he does get an address of where Olivia is and he goes to find Florence he will run out of time. Maybe he should go to Camp Randall and try to get discharged from his military service. Walter signed up for thirty months and he has served nearly twenty-five months. His only chance is to claim his injury is causing great trouble. That would be stretching the truth but he knows others have done something similar to leave the military early.

Walter would prefer not to be untruthful. He is looking forward to seeing his mother, father, Erna, Ernest and Bertha. He hopes there is news about Royce and maybe he is home and has recovered from his injury. Walter was up before dawn, shaved and cleaned up. He shouldered his rucksack and headed toward home. The gas streetlights were still on as Walter headed north. It began to rain, more like a light drizzle but enough to be a nuisance. It may make some parts of the road slippery. Walter got to the edge of town as there was a little light in the eastern sky. He broke into a slow run like he had done on many long marches.

As Walter ran he envisioned how his parents home would look. Their home and lumber enterprise was on the southern edge of the huge forest his parents owned. The setting was beautiful. A large house with dormers and wrap around porch that was on the east, south and west side of the house This large house was tucked into the south side of the gently sloping hillside and had several large red oak trees on all sides of the house. The main entrance was from the south and it opened to a cloakroom and then into a large dining room. A large fireplace was at the west end of that room. In the north-west corner was a living room. The kitchen was on the east side and the bedrooms were upstairs. Father and Mother built the house in 1856. It had been a wonderful loving home growing up in his later childhood. He was anxious to get home and especially wanted to talk to his mother.

He doubted there would be any great changes to the house or the lumber enterprise. Maybe Fathers lumber enterprise may have changed but with the war going on getting additional labor would be very difficult. Walter was very curious about what plans his father had to expand the lumber operation. What would it be named? Rounds Lumber, Rounds Flooring, Northwood Flooring, Wolf River Flooring? Walter enjoyed thinking about a possible name. He thought his mother would be the one to come up with just the right name.

Walter guessed he would see great changes in his two younger siblings. Being two years older and at ages when rapid growth can occur he expects that both would have grown taller. Walter wondered if any of the teachers would have been drafted or taken other jobs to help the war effort keep going. Walter was hoping that farms and businesses around Antigo would be able to carry on in a productive manner. Walter wondered what his older sister Erna was doing. She was living at home when he went into the service and may still live there. He imagines his mother appreciated the help. Maybe she helps in the lumber mill also.

Walter finally got home. He found he had to stop more times that he expected. Maybe he is not healed up yet. It was Saturday morning and Ernest was the first to spot Walter as he walked toward the house. "Walter's here!" shouted Ernest to alert the rest of the family and they all came running. Hugs and hand shakes were in abundance.

Mother offered breakfast and Walter gratefully accepted. The dining room table was where the family gathered while his mother Alice fixed bacon and eggs for Walter. Coffee and donuts were offered and happily accepted by this happy crowd. Walter delivered an update on his health and how Florence had saved his life. He also told about his efforts to find Florence.

"Sounds like you are in love with Florence," said Bertha. Walter blushed and looked down.

After a wonderful breakfast, Walter inquired about what was happening to Royce.

His mother said, "We received a letter recently and Royce said he is alright. The injury to his upper arm is healing and he expected to be home the third week in September for a furlough."

Walter's father Edward said, "Since this is the third week in September he could be here any time. That would be great to have you two war hero's here at the same time."

"What is happening in your life?" Walter asked Erna. "Not much," was Erna's reply. "I have been helping father with the wood and have done quite a bit of the cooking to help mother. Father has been teaching me to run the sawmill and I like it."

"Wow, Erna the sawyer. Are you pretty good?" Walter teased.

"At least as good as you would be if you could learn to be a sawyer. It might be too difficult for you," was Erna's teasing reply. This brought laughter from the family. "Erna is indeed a very good sawyer," said Edward, "and this lets me do other jobs like rip the boards to the correct width, put boards in the drier or put boards through the planer."

Walter told of meeting Albert Cutler on the train and produced the card with Albert's information on it.

"They are developing a very large band saw with teeth on both sides of the blade. It would be the head rig of a very large sawmill."

"What the heck is a head rig?" asked Bertha.

Ernest offered, "It is the main saw that cuts the logs into boards."

"Good answer," said Edward.

Edward was looking at the card and saw that the Cutler company advised on sawmill location and placement of various pieces of machinery.

"They have three different sizes of steam engines to run sawmill equipment," Walter said. "I think Mr. Cutler would come here and give you an opinion about these things if you contacted him."

"Want to go squirrel hunting?" Ernest asked Walter.

"Yes, just as soon as I find out what is going on in Bertha's world. I bet she has a boyfriend!"

Bertha squirmed in her chair, twisted her napkin and fixed her eyes on her hands in front of her. "Well, he is a boy and we are friends but it is not anything very serious."

Walter laughed, "I doubt a cute girl like you would have any trouble having a boyfriend."

THE HUNTERS

Ernest left the table and returned with two small caliber rifles and a game bag.

"Let's go get us some bushy tails." Ernest was fifteen and built like Walter and Royce, medium build, strong features with light brown hair and eyes. He looked alert and able to take care of himself.

Ernest and Walter walked northeast and after walking for ten minutes, Ernest signaled halt. They were on the edge of a small valley that had many red oak trees, many of which were very large. There was still a lot of leaves on the trees so squirrels would be difficult to see. Ernest selected a large basswood tree and they went and sat with their back to the tree.

Ernest quietly said, "Father told me about this valley and this tree. If we sit quietly and watch those four large red oaks, the squirrels will think we have gone and begin to move. Wait for a good clean shot in the head and shoot." They sat about ten minutes when Walter saw a gray bushy tail of a squirrel begin to move like a flag was being waved.

Walter squirmed around and got his rifle in position for a shot. In a few seconds the entire squirrel came into view and Walter had a clear shot at about a hundred feet. He shot and the squirrel dropped and after a few kicks it lay still. The small recoil did not hurt Walters injury.

"Don't move - others will come out. Oops, there is one now." A few seconds later another squirrel dropped and was still.

The boys shot two more each and were about to go and pick them up when on the other side of the valley, Walter saw a brownish-orange fox squirrel jump up on the trunk of a large oak tree. Walter took aim as he had a clear head shot. The shot was about two-hundred-twenty feet away and required Walter to aim above the head to allow for the amount the bullet will drop. Walter fired and the squirrel did not move. Another shot was heard and the squirrel dropped and did not move. Walter said "Great shot, brother." Unbeknownst to Walter, Ernest had taken a bead on the squirrel also just in case Walter missed.

"Hey brother, who is the best shot? Huh, huh." He reached out and playfully punched Walter in the shoulder and then gave Walter a hug. "It is great to have you back. We have all been worried about you and Royce, but Mother was very frightened that something would happen to you guys. The accounts of Gettysburg were the worst. Mother was sure both of you were wounded or killed. When she got a letter from Royce that you were critically hurt and he was wounded, Mother cried for two days. When she got your letter and one from Royce that you were coming home, Mother just kept singing and she smiled all the time she was not singing."

As the two headed for home with their squirrels, Walter relayed, "The last two years were rough. Many times I thought about what I wanted to do if I survived the war. It was to be with my family and be able to go out in these beautiful woods and go hunting. Going home was a comforting thought in many terrible places I have been." Walter thought about Ernest and hoped he would not be drafted. Maybe the war will be finished soon.

HOW CAN WE HELP

Walter and Ernest returned home and saw their mother and father sitting on some lean back chairs under the big oaks southwest of the house. The temperature was very pleasant and the sun was peeking through the clouds. The boys went to their parents to report their good luck hunting. They made small talk and Ernest could see his parents wanted to talk to Walter.

"I will clean these squirrels and maybe Mother will fix them for supper," said Ernest.

"That would be possible if they are not shot up too much," said his mother.

"All head shots, Mother. We are crack shots and one of us is a better crack shot than the other!"

Edward and Alice invited Walter to take a seat in one of the lean back chairs.

"We know how you went to Sparta looking for Florence and we know of your plan to learn of her mothers address. Why do you think something happened to Florence?" asked his mother.

"The last day we were together she said she would be going back to Hagerstown after one day of closing up the hospital tent. She was going to resume the special nursing program at the hospital there. When I had not heard from Florence after three weeks my doctor at Harrisburg telegraphed the Hagerstown hospital and inquired about Florence. He was informed that *because of the great number of wounded soldiers from Gettysburg, the special nursing program was suspended and the nurses went back to Wisconsin.*"

"What city in Wisconsin did the nurses come from?" asked Edward.

"Florence only mentioned the University and no more. We really didn't visit much as I was very weak."

63

"I can only think of the University at Madison," Edward said.

His mother said, "You could send a letter the University of Wisconsin and explain the circumstances and hopefully they could give you some information. Send it General Delivery, Medical School."

Walter relayed, "Antoinette mentioned that Mr. Porter came to Sparta because the doctor there could help him with whatever was ailing him. Mr. Porter also used to visit Sparta and spend time with his mothers brother, his uncle, when he was young.

"I could write to Antoinette urging her to see if she could remember Mr. Porter's uncles name. Maybe he has kept in touch with Florence. Apparently he moved to Madison to form a company to build railroad tracks."

"The company building the railroad track to the mill is from Madison," said Edward. "Maybe the uncle of Mr. Porter is one of them. They will be coming is about two weeks. We could inquire if this man is one of the owners. Living is Sparta at one time would be an opener for discussion."

Walter said, "Another interesting thing is that the Porter family of Sparta used to own a large tract of land in northern Wisconsin. They built a very nice home on a lake on that property. Apparently Mr. Porter put the land up for collateral to borrow money on a gold mine in Montana. The mine was a failure. Whoever had loaned the money took the land to cover the money lost when the mine failed. Mrs. Porter and Florence lived there but had to move to Sparta. Apparently Olivia Porter really enjoyed the home on the lake. I wonder where in northern Wisconsin that land with the lake was located?"

"Should I postpone the idea I had of buying the Porter house in Sparta?" Walter asked his parents.

His mother said, "Maybe we should see if we get any leads on the letters you will send out on Monday."

That was good news to Walter as it was looking like it would be difficult to raise the $2,650 to buy the house. What if Olivia Porter did check on the sale of the house . . it could drag on and on. Returning to service at Camp Randall is looming also.

About then Bertha joined the group and joined the discussion. She wants to know what Florence looks like and what kind of person she is.

"Florence is very pretty. She has medium length light brown hair and brown eyes. She carries herself with dignity and has wonderful posture. She has a medium build, a little taller than Mother and is as kind of person that I have ever met. She is a true healer and tended to all my medical needs at the hospital tent. She is a very sweet person and you would like her."

Just then two men on horseback rode up to the group. It was a neighbor about five miles closer to Antigo but on the road to the mill. His name was Stanley Diercks and his fifteen year old son James. They dismounted and tied their horses to the hitching rail.

"Walter, we thought that was you double timing past our place this morning. How are you?" As both men extended their hands in greeting to Walter.

"We heard you were seriously injured at Gettysburg and wanted to see how you are doing."

"I am feeling better and my wound is still healing so I have to be careful what I do."

Stanley said, "We know that Gettysburg was terrible and we know that you were at Antietam and that was also a terrible battle. Are conditions for you soldiers as terrible as we are hearing?"

"When the 6th Wisconsin was organized we were supposed to have a thousand men in that regiment. We left Camp Randall with less than that number. We were part of the Iron Brigade which was the 2nd, 6th and 7th Wisconsin, 19th Indiana and later, the 24th Michigan.

"We fought at the second Bull Run, Fredericksburg, Antietam, Chancellorsville and Gettysburg. I don't know where they are fighting now. Each battle had men killed or wounded and our numbers declined. We suffered great losses of men due to typhoid, diarrhea and dysentery. These loses were even larger than the casualties in battle. Food was undependable depending on where we were and if we were fighting or getting ready to fight. We started out being assigned in teams of six to provide food for themselves. We had to do our own cooking and most of us did not know how. Teams lost soldiers and were not replaced so eventually it got down to two or three working together to provide warm meals. Hardtack was the main food we ate, sometimes rancid or infested with weevils. It did keep us alive. Fresh meat was rare. Salt pork and salt beef didn't spoil but it was so salty it was nearly impossible to eat. After about a year, the army provided men to act as cooks and provided wagons to carry the food.

"We each carried half of a small tent that we combined with another soldier. Brother Royce shared a tent with me. We had a blanket, and in the winter we had two to keep us off the ground and keep us warm. The cold weather caused inflammation of the lungs that took thousands of soldiers. Summer was better, but muddy roads, heat and rain made life miserable.

"There are several hundred thousand troops fighting in many places. One main goal is to keep the Confederates from obtaining food and munitions. Each battle reduces their numbers just like the Union loses soldiers. We can recruit or draft more soldiers but because the south is a much smaller territory to draw from, eventually the north should prevail. One serious problem is the quality of men that are supposed to be soldiers. Many of the new recruits are weak and not up to the rigors of marching and fighting. Some have handicaps, some were just unwilling to take orders and to fight. My regiment had an outstanding leader in Lt. Col. Rufus Dawes. He made us help the weaker soldiers to become better. We drilled often as we all needed to know what to do in a battle. We had to be a team and be able to depend on each other in battle."

Erna and Ernest had joined the group and listened to Walter tell of the conditions he had endured for the past two years. Walter observed the looks of astonishment as he spoke. Apparently the news in the papers didn't go into detail of the topics Walter brought up.

Stanley told Walter, "It sounds like you and Royce were very fortunate to still be alive. It sounds like this huge Union army has serious problems to overcome."

"Early in the war," continued Walter, "some battles were fought with both sides facing each other and firing away. These soldiers were like cannon fodder if cannons were present. The forward troops had no chance to avoid death or injury. Our 6th Wisconsin was never ordered to fight in this manner. We all had muskets with rifled barrels. We had to open a cartridge with powder, pour it in the end of the barrel, put the bullet in and ram it down with the ramrod. The gun hammer was cocked and a percussion cap was attached. The gun was ready to fire. A soldier would get off about two shots per minute and that caused the barrel to heat up. When gun powder was poured in it stuck to the inside of the barrel and caused the bullet to stick. The ramrod needed to be pounded with a rock in order to get the bullet where it needed to be. After several shots my musket was useless and someone behind me would trade muskets with me. Our regiment mostly tried to seek protection from trees, hummocks, rocks, breastworks or wherever we could. Lt. Col. Dawes would not let us fight unless we could have some protection. We did charge from our positions and had good success routing the rebels and we captured many especially at Gettysburg."

By now it was late afternoon and Stanley and James remarked that they needed to leave. They raise large plots of potatoes and have many bags to sort and prepare to haul to Antigo and load on railroad cars. Goodbyes were said and Stanley shook Walters hand and thanked him for his service. Alice told the family that fried squirrel was on the menu for tonight.

Edward and Ernest had chores to do and Erna and Bertha would help with supper. Walter asked for paper and envelopes and retired to write letters.

Hospital Administrator
University Hospital
C/o General Delivery
Madison, Wisconsin

Dear Administrator:

My name is Walter Rounds, 6th Wisconsin Regiment, Iron Brigade, I Corps, Army of the Potomac.

I was wounded on the third day at Gettysburg. I was unconscious for three days and when I awoke, a very caring nurse was by my side. She looked after me for the next week with loving care and she saved my life.

I was transferred to a hospital in Harrisburg, Pennsylvania and spent two months there before being discharged and given a thirty day furlough. This very kind nurse was named Florence Porter and she was from Sparta, Wisconsin.

She was attending a special nursing training session at Hagerstown when fighting at Gettysburg started. These twenty-seven nurses rushed to the region near the battle to attend injured soldiers.

I have not been contacted by Florence in any way since then. I found out that because of high numbers of wounded at Hagerstown the special nurses training was cancelled and the nurses returned to Wisconsin.

My question is: Were these twenty-seven nurses in training at the University hospital in Madison? I really need to find Florence. She saved my life! Any information on her whereabouts would be helpful so I could go to her. I am fearful that she may be sick or hurt.

If you could give me an address or other information so I could go to Florence it would be very much appreciated. Thank you.

Please send any news to Walter Rounds, c/o General Delivery, Antigo, Wisconsin.

Sincerely,
Walter Rounds
6ᵗʰ Wisconsin Regiment

P. S. Lt. Col. Dawes is the Commander of the 6ᵗʰ Wisconsin Regiment. He could verify my injury and the care Florence Porter gave me.

Walter also wrote to Antoinette Zimchezk in Sparta and asked her if she could try to find out what Olivia Porter's husbands first name was.

Also Walter asked if Antoinette or anyone could find out the name of Mr. Porter's uncle on his mothers side. Maybe he could be in contact with one of Florence's relatives. Walter asked if there had been any activity involving Olivia's house and stop to see the land agent also. He asked about Jenny, Abner and Caleb.

Alice announced that supper was ready. The family gathered around the big dining room table. The fried squirrel and other dishes were served and eating began. Walter looked at his loving family. He was thankful that he could sit down and eat with everyone like he did before he went in to the service. His mind flashed to the many thousands of families that will never sit down to eat with fallen soldiers. His heart was sad. He quickly remembered how thankful he was.

ROYCE RETURNS

Sunday morning breakfast was prepared by Erna. There was pancakes, fried eggs and toast. Happy conversation was heard around the table as this wonderful family all joined in. Bertha had heard comments by people against the war and she was troubled by them. Ernest said several kids at school talked against the war and trying to free the slaves. Who are slaves and why are they slaves?

Edward quietly answered, "They are human beings like us but with black skin. Many were abducted from their homes in Africa and brought to slave markets in Charleston, Savannah and other seaports where they were sold to land owners. They were taken to plantations or other places and put to work. Most received no pay, or very little pay. They worked long hours tending crops especially cotton. Owners could be very brutal and beatings occurred. Families were separated, deaths occurred and these people had no rights.

"The Mason-Dixon line was surveyed and large granite markers were positioned to mark the division of the north from the south. The north was basically against slavery and Wisconsin is strongly in that camp. The south favored slavery but parts of states leaned toward anti-slavery. Maryland and northern Alabama are two that come to mind.

All at once, Erna screamed, "**Royce is here!**" Everyone went to the windows and saw that indeed Royce was coming up toward the house. The family ran out and met Royce as he came up on the front porch. He put down his rucksack and greeted everyone with big hugs. Everyone had huge smiles of happiness that Royce was home.

Royce told Walter, "I have something for you." He dug in his rucksack and produced an official looking envelope and gave it to Walter. Walter opened the envelope and slid the letter out and read it. His face broke into a huge smile as he embraced Royce.

"**I am discharged from the Army!**" It was signed by Lt. Col. Rufus Dawes.

"I am discharged also," Royce told the family. "Lt. Col Dawes summoned me to his tent and told me that both you and I were among the very best soldiers in the 6th Wisconsin Regiment. He said he was very sorry to see us leave, but both of us had served above and beyond what was asked of both of us. He gave me the discharge papers, saluted and gave me a big hug. He said someday he would hug Walter also."

Walter and Royce hugged and Walter felt like a heavy weight had been lifted from him. To not have to return to military service was to make both men feel like they were free - free to make plans for the future.

Walter dug in his pocket and produced a locket and said to Royce, "I have something to return to you."

Royce accepted the locket with their mother and fathers picture in it.

"Whatever happened to the nurse in the tent at Gettysburg? She certainly was your guardian angel."

Walter updated Royce on efforts to find Florence, including telling about letters he and their mother had written to be mailed tomorrow.

Royce told Walter, "When I visited you after you were wounded, you had not woke up yet. Florence told about the Doctor removing the bullet. She said it would take time but she was encouraged by your progress even though you had not been awake yet."

"Not long after you visited, Lt. Col. Dawes also visited the tent according to Florence. He visited each cot including two Confederates. When he got to me he reached under my cot for my hat. He told Florence that he knew a bullet had hit the plume on my hat during the first day at Gettysburg. He took my damaged plume out and replaced it with his own large, beautiful plume. He put my damaged plume on his hat and said he will wear it in honor of Walter Rounds. He then snapped a salute to me and left to continue fighting.

"When I was going to be transferred to a hospital in Harrisburg, I gave the beautiful plume from my hat to Florence and told her I would find her and the plume once I had recovered. Florence told me she would take good care of it and return it to me when we met again. I know she is taking good care of the plume and wants to return it to me. Something has happened to Florence and I need to go to her. I know Florence has feelings for me and wants to find me also."

Alice made bacon, eggs and toast for Royce, who like Walter, was thankful for his mother's cooking.

"Another thing I really enjoy," Royce said, "is sitting on a chair to eat, or just to rest."

Walter concurred and added, "It was rare that we sat on anything except the ground."

Royce added, "Sleeping in a bed is way better than sleeping on the ground in a small tent." Royce caught up with what was happening in Erna, Ernest and Bertha's life. He also noticed that Ernest and Bertha had grown taller.

Royce dug in his rucksack and produced a carefully wrapped object. Royce said, "My regiment and many others were on the march near the Virginia/North Carolina border. I saw a group of Negro's sitting along the road we were on. As I approached, a young boy ran to me, took my hand and said, 'Please, Mister, go to my grandmother with me.' I followed him to the group beside the road and this elderly Negro lady gets up and handed me this.

"Give this to your mother," she told me. "Thank you for fighting for us."

"I thanked her and hurried to catch up to my troops. The little boy and two others ran beside me. He said 'thank you Mister - good luck.' The boy stopped and we marched on. I could not look at it until we took a rest. So Mother, here it is.

I am sure the Negro grandmother would be proud that I delivered it to you."

Alice opened the carefully wrapped article and showed great surprise at what she uncovered. Bertha had crowded around to look over her mother's shoulder and looked very pleased with what they saw. It was a necklace made out of a piece of dark brown wood. It was a disc about an inch and one-half in diameter and a one-third inch thick. On the front the word HOPE was carefully carved into it. Alice ran her fingers over the beautiful smooth surface. Bertha reached and felt it also. Both of them were pleased by the beauty of the necklace.

Alice turned it over and saw carefully carved into it were the words, '*Mother to Mother*'. Alice looked at Royce, "Of all the hundreds of Union soldiers marching by, why were you singled out to receive this beautiful necklace?"

Royce said, "I waved at the group and said hello. Maybe that is the reason."

Alice clutched the brown wooden necklace and her eyes took on a faraway look and she was silent for several minutes. The other members of the family all silently wondered about Alice's reaction. Finally she returned from her faraway trance and the entire family was at ease.

"Alice, you scared us," Edward finally asked. "Is everything alright?"

Alice gave a little chuckle and said, "I guess it was scary. I was just trying to picture this Negro grandmother with her family and grandchildren around her and tried to imagine what their life had been like. Were they slaves? What will they do when this war is over?"

Being Sunday morning, Edward told the group they would hold church service there today. Bertha passed out some hymnals, Erna went to the piano and Edward opened the bible which was on the lectern in the living room. Edward asked Bertha which hymn she wanted. "*Rock of Ages* on page 129."

This family could sing! They really belted out that song. Edward asked Alice to read a scripture of her choosing. It spoke of a good Samaritan. Ernest's turn was next and he chose, "*This is My Fathers World,* page 281." Erna was chosen to give the sermon. With a small delay, she spoke about being dependable, to do what is required or expected of everyone.

Walters turn to select a hymn, *The Old Rugged Cross,* page 76. Alice was asked to pretend there were small children in the sanctuary. What would you tell them as they gathered around you. Alice pretended to wait for the little ones to get comfortable around her. She pretended to hold a puppy. She told about the puppy needing to be cared for, fed and kept out of harms way. The puppy is counting on me to take care of it until it gets bigger. Can you think of anything else that needs to be looked after and loved? Lots of baby animals and finally a little girl said, little kids, and everyone smiles and Alice is finished pretending.

Royce, what is your hymn? *Climbing Jacob's Ladder,* page 237. Erna what is your hymn? Erna answers, "It is not a hymn but it could be, *When Johnny Comes Marching Home.*"

Walter makes a request to Edward. "Let Royce and me sing a song we often sang in our camps. It is called *Tenting Tonight on the Old Campground.*" Both men got up and stood close together.

We're tenting tonight on the old campground
Give us a song to cheer
Our weary hearts, a song of home,
And friends we love so dear.

Many are the hearts that are weary tonight.
Wishing the war to cease . . many are the
hearts that are looking for the right. To see
the dawn of peace.

Dying tonight - - - - - dying tonight
Dying on the old - - - - camp - - - - ground

By the end of the song, both men had their arms around the other. Tears were in their eyes. The entire family is in tears as these two brave men gave them a look into the past horror of war. The sadness of death and injuries. The terrible conditions and the ever present thought of going home.

A WALK IN THE WOODS

Finally, Edward offers a prayer and the service is finished. Ernest asked Royce, "What would you like to do?"

Without hesitating, Royce said, "Take a long walk in our woods. Anyone else want to go?"

Everyone except Alice and Edward wanted to go. Ernest offered, "I will take a .50 caliber rifle just in case we are attacked by some wild critter."

Alice packed some ham sandwiches and they were off to the woods. Royce leads the way and heads north-northwest toward the west boundary of their property which was ten miles from north to south and ten miles from west to east. It was about sixty-four thousand acres. Most of this land was purchased by Alice's family and given as a wedding gift when Edward and Alice got married in 1839. Apparently Grandfather Miller was a land developer in Philadelphia and was very wealthy. He and Grandma Miller were killed in a train wreck and left the remainder of this large tract of land to Alice and Edward.

Royce was very happy. He loved this beautiful forest. The land was rolling and covered with large maple trees as was most of the territory they covered in the first two hours of walking. The maples became more sparse and were replaced by beautiful stands of red oak. Finally they reached the northwest boundary of this huge forest. They proceeded north for a few hundred feet and took a break to eat the sandwiches.

Everyone was enjoying the forest, no one was complaining.

ATTACK

They had gone about one-half mile when Royce came to some strange marks on the forest floor. The group gathered around trying to figure out what the marks meant. The tracks were in a gentle swale that ran north and south. Walter looked around the nearby area to see if anything seemed unusual.

The group studied the marks. They didn't look like anything anyone had seen before. The area the marks covered was about six feet in diameter. It had been scratched but in no particular pattern. Ernest looked at the surrounding trees looking for evidence of a large bear marking his territory. He saw no evidence.

Finally, Erna asked. "Does anyone notice a faint smell in the air?" No one else had noticed.

Finally, Ernest noticed a low hanging branch over the marked area was broken and some bark knocked off.

Walter said, "It could be a scrape by a buck deer, but this is a giant scrape."

"Could it be an elk?" Bertha asked. "I heard a kid at school talk about his dad seeing an elk northeast of Antigo."

The group continued east when all at once there was a high pitched bugling sound that stopped everyone in their tracks. The bugling started again and by now it appeared to be just over a small hill to the north of the group.

"I will go up and look over the hill to see if I can see anything," said Royce as he moved quietly up the small hill as the remainder of the group watched. In a few minutes, Royce returned and reported, "There is a bull elk and several cows just over the hill. They did not see me but I think we had better get out of here."

The group turns south toward home when all at once another bull starts bugling south of them. Once again the sound stopped everyone cold.

"This bull may be looking for a fight with the one over the hill and we are right smack in between these dangerous critters," Royce said. "Let's head west and get out of here."

The bull to the north bugled and appeared on the top of the small hill. There was instant panic in the group. The bull from the hill was headed right for them.

"Find a tree to climb - over here," Walter said as he took Bertha's hand and ran to a white oak with low branches. He boosted Bertha and she continued climbing. Erna was next. Ernest found a tree with low branches and he climbed it carrying the .50 caliber rifle. Royce climbed up the tree with the girls. Walter jumped and tried to grab the branch with his left hand as his right hand and shoulder were of no use to do anything over his head. He fell and he saw the bull coming right for him! He scrambled to his feet and went to the opposite side of the tree just as the bull tried to hit him with his huge antlers. The bull stopped and looked for Walter on the other side of the large oak tree. The bull took a few steps so he could get at Walter with his antlers. Walter was able to keep circling around the tree and the bull kept swinging his large antlers at him.

The girls, Royce and Ernest watched in horror as they realized Walter was in serious danger. They continued to shout encouragement at Walter who was beginning to tire. He realized that he had not fully recovered from his injury.

The bull was beginning to realize that Walter kept the tree between them. He paused and looked around after several tries to get Walter with his antlers. All at once, a very loud bugle came from the south. Just then another huge elk bull came running toward Walter and the first bull.

Walter was in a life threatening position. The first bull was on the north side of the tree so Walter was on the south side . . the side the new larger bull was coming from. Walters brothers and sisters now screamed at the top of their lungs. The new bull continued at a slow run right at Walter.

The bull was within thirty feet of Walter when the first bull went around the east side of the tree and prepared to fight with the big bull. The smaller bull held his ground and the big bull moved rapidly and within seconds he was about to engage the smaller bull.

SHOWDOWN

Walter was really frightened! With the smaller bull within arms reach for the past five or six minutes his adrenaline was very high. As the two bulls prepared to do battle, Walter looked for a safe place to run to. The closest trees were at least forty feet away and were a smaller diameter than the big oak he was by now. He knew that once these bulls starting fighting things could happen very fast. The small bull could be pushed back on the same side of the tree that Walter was on. That could be the end if he wanted to dispatch Walter before he continued fighting.

The big bull was just about to engage the smaller bull when it stopped and flung its huge antlers around a few feet from the smaller bull. Maybe he was trying to intimidate the smaller bull so they would not have to fight. Walter watched from behind the tree, peeking from around the south side. The family was terrified. They knew Walter was in a very dangerous spot.

The small bull put on a show of shaking his antlers. The two beautiful bulls faced off for about a minute. Finally, the small bull backed up one step. The two continued swinging their antlers. The small bull backed up another step. Now Walter is exposed more to the small bull. If that bull decides to get Walter, Walter will have to circle the tree right into the big bull. Walter had taken one step to his right to put more room between him and the smaller bull and now he was partially exposed to the big bull. After one or two minutes the big bull turns his head to the left and notices Walter partially hidden by the big oak tree. Royce has broken off a small dead branch and throws it at the big bull as it is closer to being under him. His aim is good and his small branch hits the big bull on this back. This causes the big bull to take two or three steps toward the little bull who backs up three or four steps. Now Walter circles to his right but then he is exposed to both bulls.

Walter thinks he should take a run for it to a tree about forty feet away. He thinks that even if he reaches the tree and one or both bulls come after him he will be caught or speared by one or both of the elk. The two bulls are standing looking at each other when a rifle shot is heard. The small bull drops, kicks a few times and is dead.

Walter can't believe his eyes. Ernest has shot the elk from his perch in a nearby tree. His .50 caliber bullet hit the bull in the brain and killed it. The big bull comes up to the downed elk and gives it a root with his antlers. He pushes the dead elk a couple of feet, raises his head. Walter is completely out of sight because he has the tree between himself and the bulls head. He can watch the elks body for any motion that the bull may do. After about seven or eight minutes the bull breaks into a trot going toward the north. Perhaps he detected the small herd of elk near where Royce had seen the small bull. In a few minutes the big bull was out of sight. The group in the trees were thinking about coming down to earth. All at once, a high pitched bugle was heard, a minute later a second bugle was heard fainter than the first.

Walter went to Ernest's tree and urged him to unload the .50 caliber and drop it and he would catch it. That done, Ernest shinnied down like he does that all the time. Royce and Walter helped Erna and Bertha down and the girls promptly hugged all the boys which were busy hand shaking and back slapping each other.

"Lets hightail it for home before the big bull comes back," Royce said emphatically.

Forty-five minutes later the exhausted group arrived at home. They had double timed all the way home. Edward and Alice were quickly told about the elk and the boys announced they would go back and salvage the meat. By now it was mid-afternoon and that project would take two to three hours or more.

Bertha told her mother all about the entire scary event.

"Those mean bulls looked really dangerous. I was sure Walter would get speared by those huge antlers. He was so brave."

RECOVERY

There was a logging road that ran within two-hundred yards from the dead elk. They could take a team of horses and a wagon to carry the meat back home. They would have to carry the quarters of the elk to get them on the wagon. Edward suggested using a stout pole and butcher hooks to carry one quarter at a time. Edward knew where these items were located and went to get them and he would go along to assist. Sharp knives were rounded up as well as several sheets to cover up the meat. A meat saw was taken as was a high powered rifle in case the big bull, or some other bull showed up. Several lanterns were also taken.

The team of horses and the wagon proceeded north on the logging trail. When they reached the spot closest to the elk, they tied the horses and took what they brought and went to find the elk. In about ten minutes Ernest led them to the elk. Ernest seems to have uncanny woodsman skills.

As the group approached the dead bull, they saw a pack of five timber wolves approaching from the east. The pack had not detected the group and cautiously approached the dead bull. One wolf was black, two were light reddish color and two were grey. The animals were impressive with their long legs, long tails and large muzzles. All appeared to be over one-hundred pounds.

The group quietly watched the wolves for three or four minutes. They decided to scare the wolves off and take care of the bull. Ernest fired a shot into the ground near the pack. The five wolves ran nearly in the direction of the group, apparently they could not tell where the shot came from. The group shouted and waved their arms. The wolves stopped briefly and then headed east away from the group at a high speed. The wolves had gotten to about forty yards from the group and all were impressed by the size and strength of these brutes. This was the first time any of the group had seen timber wolves up close.

The elk was gutted, skinned and quartered. Edward estimated that it weighed six-hundred-fifty to seven-hundred pounds when it was alive. A butcher hook was attached to two of the quarters, a stout rod was slid under the other end hook and the two men hoisted the rod onto their shoulders, with the quarter swinging between them. Two others hoisted another quarter and the group headed toward the wagon.

It was hard, heavy work but eventually the four quarters were loaded on the wagon and wrapped in sheets. One last trip was made to bring the head, heart and liver plus the elk hide to the wagon. It was getting difficult to see so lanterns were lit to see the logging trail to get back home.

On the way back home, Ernest, carrying a lantern, walked ahead of the team of horses. Two lanterns were lit and they were held in the front and rear of the wagon. Walter and Royce sat in the rear of the wagon. Royce had the rifle and both men watched for any sign of the wolf pack.

What a scary day! What started as an enjoyable walk in the woods sure turned deadly. Walter was thankful he was not hurt by the elk bulls but he was still thinking about the incident. He could not get over how close he was to the smaller bull, especially.

"How are we going to process this meat?" Royce asked his father.

He replied, "Since it is not cold we will have to smoke some, can some and make jerky. We will eat the liver and heart. The meat scraps, neck meat and flank meat will be made into sausage. Your mother is going to make a marinade to season the jerky before it is dried. We will be busy tonight."

No sign of the wolf pack and the procession reaches home. The meat is brought into the house and the task of preparing it begins. All seven family members pitch in and begin making strips of meat for jerky. These are put into the marinade that Alice prepared. This was familiar work as venison jerky was made several times in the past few years. Roasts were prepared to be smoked and a smokehouse fire was started. Alice selected the cuts she wanted to can. She had the jars washed and ready so as meat became available she filled the jars and when she had the correct number of jars she put it in the canner and put it on the stove. Canned meat was favorite of the family, so was sausage, jerky and smoked meats sliced thin and made into sandwiches.

Finally about 10:30 p.m. the meat had been cut up and started on its way to being preserved. The meat to be made into sausage was in three large crocks and will be taken to Peroutka's Meat Market in Antigo tomorrow. It will be mixed with pork and other ingredients to produce some very tasty sausages.

RETURN TO SCHOOL

Alice was up at 5:00 a.m. the next day which was Monday. Bertha and Ernest had to go back to school for the week. Breakfast must be prepared and eaten, the wagon loaded with the sausage meat, the elks head and antlers and hide. It was decided to get the head mounted and the hide tanned and possibly made into a jacket. The sixteen mile trip takes over an hour and school starts and 8:25 a.m. Walter and Royce will drive the team and wagon about three blocks from school to let Bertha and Ernest off to walk to school. They room with a nice family on Claremont Street who treat them like they were their own children.

"Have a good week in school. See you Friday afternoon," said Royce.

Next stop was a taxidermist to drop off the elk head and hide. The taxidermist was amazed at the size of the elks antlers.

"The bull that this guy was going to fight with had larger antlers than this one. Luckily they didn't fight and only shook their antlers at each other. We think that if we had not shot this one, there would have been a huge fight and this guy would have lost . . the other bull was larger by quite a bit," said Walter.

The taxidermist was interested in what happened so Royce told him what had taken place. The taxidermist concluded that Walter was indeed lucky not to have been hurt or killed.

Next stop was Peroutka's Meat Market. The meat was transferred into Peroutka's containers and ingredients to be added were agreed on. The meat market was a place that Walter and Royce really enjoyed visiting. The place smelled great with cured hams, bacon, sausages and faint smoked smell made a persons mouth water. The display cases had displays of beef, pork and lamb plus chicken, ducks, liver, heart, tongue and head cheese. The work area had pine shavings on the floor which added to the ambiance. Walter and Royce could not resist, they bought a small ring of bologna to eat on the way home, if they could wait that long.

"See you in three weeks, boys," said Mr. Peroutka.

Next stop was the post office to mail the letters that Walter and Alice wrote. Edward added a letter to Mr. Cutler in Milwaukee, stamps were purchased, attached and letters were put in the mail slot. Walter was very hopeful that the letters he was mailing would bring news about Florence. She is constantly in his thoughts. He is very concerned that Florence is ill or injured.

CONFRONTATION

Alice had given Royce a list of suplies to purchase so they drove the wagon to the general store on Fifth Avenue. As they approached the front door of the store they could see a group of four or five tough looking men assembled near the door.

"You boys going to fight for Lincoln?" asked a burly man dressed in buckskin. Walter and Royce continued toward the door.

"I asked you boys a question - are you going to fight for Lincoln?"

Royce and Walter stopped and faced the man. "Why do you ask?" said Royce

"We don't think we should be fighting to free the Negros. We don't have any around here, why should we free them anyway?" said the buckskin man. There was a lengthy pause.

"We have both spent two years fighting the Confederates. Mr. Lincoln believes all men are created equal and no one should be a slave to anyone against their wishes. Royce and I both feel the same way," said Walter.

"You boys fought at Gettysburg and Antietam?" asked the burly man.

"We were members of the 6th Wisconsin and the Iron Brigade," Royce told them. "We fought there and in Chancellorsville, Bull Run and Fredericksburg. We both were injured at Gettysburg. We have seen plenty of death and injury in two years. Mr. Lincoln's goal of unifying the Union and abolishing slavery is consistent with the democratic government where laws are made by representatives of the people selected by the majority of the people voting in each district. That privilege is worth fighting for. Excuse us, we have work to do."

The burly man reached for Royces hand and then Walters. "Thanks for your service boys, your explanation of our country cleared up my thoughts. I am sorry to have challenged you who have already served our country with distinction."

The other men shook Royce and Walter's hand and thanked them for their service. Once again Walter is surprised at the attitude of some of the people back home. Maybe there is a basic mistrust of government. They maybe read that the Union troops have struggled in their battles with the Confederates. Since the army is directed by the government it is easy to see how people don't trust the government. They read about shoddy shoes, clothes, blankets and other problems like food quality and distribution to the troops. Maybe that is where much of the distrust comes from. Walter knows that there are many immigrants in America and especially around Antigo.

Royce and Walter were waiting for the clerk to finish filling the order Alice sent along when a lady that Walter recognized approached them.

"I overheard part of your talk to those rough men. I was proud of your response and I agree. Thank you for your service." This lady, Mrs. Fermanich lived next door to the home that Walter and Royce stayed at so they could go to school in Antigo.

The supplies were loaded on the wagon. Edward needed a dozen files to sharpen the saw blades, including the blades for the big saw. The owner told the boys that he had just received a large order of cant hooks, axes, logging chains, caulked boots and work clothes.

"We don't know what father has in mind but he is getting a railroad track built to our property. We expect he has plans to expand the lumber enterprise," said Royce.

HEADING HOME

Royce headed the team toward home. Walter produced the ring of bologna from its wrapping, cut it into bite sizes and offered some to Royce. He took care of eating his share.

"I am disappointed in what some of the folks around here think about the war and why we are fighting it. Those men at the store sounded like Confederates," said Walter.

"Two of the men were familiar but the others were not. Us being gone for two years would have allowed time for lots of new settlers who move into this area," said Royce.

"Many may be moving from countries where the government was corupt and people distrusted motives of the government," added Walter.

"What about you, Royce? Is this war really worth all the deaths, injuries, destruction and expense?"

Royce was silent for some time. "You and I were soldiers and our job was to fight. The little information we received about things back home, Washington, D.C. and the government was sporadic and much of it was rumors passed on in the ranks. We both studied about the Union in school. We thought our constitution was the rule book for the United States to live by. The Mason-Dixon line was established to separate the so-called southern states from the northern states. The southern states chose to seceed from the Union and went to war to defend their choice. Northern states objected realizing that their founding fathers wanted one nation, where all men were created equal."

There was a long pause as the boys drive the team northward.

"You and I both knew that what the south was doing posed a serious threat to the United States of America. We did not understand slavery but both of us and our family were definitely against it. It was a basic human right to be free. I admire President Lincoln's courage and stand behind him and I think you do too, Walter."

"I agree with you," said Walter, "but it bothers me when I hear objections about the war and our efforts to free the Negros. You and I have very little contact with Negros but I know one thing, they are human beings and deserve to be free. Maybe if we had more contact with them we would feel different."

The boys and their team of horses were approaching Stanley Diercks potato farm, when they met two big freight wagons loaded with double layers of potato filled bags. These bags weigh one-hundred pounds or so each and each load required four horses to pull it to the railroad spur in Antigo. Each load had two men riding on the load to transfer the bags from the freight wagon to the boxcar. The first load was driven by Stanley and he stopped his teams by Royce's team

"Heard you got chased by a big bull elk, Walter. Did it hurt you?"

"No," Walter replied, "I kept the big oak tree between us but when another bigger elk showed up they had me trapped so Ernest shot the smaller bull and the big bull left to find the cows that started the big showdown. We ended up being right in the middle of it. When we get the sausage done at Peroutka's we will drop off some for you."

"Did you get a good yield this year?" Royce asked Stanley.

"It has been a good year, high yield and harvest conditions are good. I used lots of horses to dig the spuds. The price looks good too. Your dad said the rail line would get started soon. That would be good for both families. I've got to get these spuds in the boxcar. Good to see you boys. Good-bye."

Stanley snapped the reins and heavy wagons rolled toward Antigo. Royce shouted and started his team and as they passed Stanley's potato farm they could see several people in the fields filling bags with potatoes.

"That looks like hard work," said Walter.

As they drove on, Walter asked Royce, "What are your plans since you don't have to do any more soldiering?"

Royce was quiet but soon responded. "I want to go to the University of Wisconsin in Madison and study forestry. It sounds like Mother and Father plan to develop a large flooring mill. Their large holding in forest land should be managed carefully so good high quality trees will constantly be available to harvest, even in one-hundred years or more."

"That sounds like a great idea. We both have great love of the forest and especially our large holdings," added Walter.

"What are your plans?" Royce inquired.

"Find Florence! I hope to receive some encouraging news in the mail within in the next few days."

Home was in sight and what a sight it was. The broad roof with the large overhang and wrap around porch with dormers was an eye pleasing sight. All comfortably nestled among the beautiful large trees. The large stone fireplace and dark green vertical siding gave the house a welcome home appeal. Royce drove the team up near the house and the supplies were unloaded.

ERNA THE SAWYER

Erna and Edward were processing wood so both men went to watch. Erna was sawing some hard maple logs into boards. A large Case steam engine was the source of power. A large pulley on the steamer drove a wide belt that powered a jack shaft. It is a shaft that power is supplied to and it in turn can power other machines by engaging a belt on the jack shaft that drives the machine. Most of the power for the steamer went to power the sawmill when it was sawing. Erna would use a cant hook to roll the log onto the carriage of the sawmill. She would use the cant hook to position the log so it would produce the greatest amount of high quality wood. She next clamped the log into position to hold it steady once the sawing started.

Erna moved the carriage forward into the spinning saw blade. This saw had a second blade positioned above the first to handle very large logs. The first cut produced a slab which was taken away to burn in the steam engine. Next cut provides the board with bark on both sides that needs to be edged so it is set aside. Erna continued breaking the log down until it has been reduced to a cant which is a big square timber. She then proceeds to cut one-inch thick boards until the cant is all sawed.

Walter and Royce watched Erna and Edward deal with the lumber. It was lunch time so all four headed for the house to see what Alice had fixed for lunch. On the way to the house, Erna asked Walter to hold back. They stopped and let Royce and Edward continue on.

"If you need a few hundred dollars to buy the house in Sparta, I will lend it to you with no interest. Just pay it back when you can." Walter was astounded. He gave Erna a big hug.

"I really appreciate the offer. I will wait to see if I get any response from the letters we sent today."

During lunch, Edward said, "A large block of land that adjoins our property on the east is for sale. It was owned by a bank and they want to sell it. Apparently the land was put up for collateral and was taken by the bank to settle the debt. Alice and I made an offer and the bank has accepted it. There are about forty thousand acres in that parcel. I would like the two of you to take the afternoon and ride horses around the property and see what we are buying. Apparently there are a few lakes on this land."

Edward produced patents for each of the sixty or so sections. These showed they were sold by the United States of America to the Great Northern Land Company. "The agent for the bank was here this morning and we completed the deal."

THE NEW LAND

Walter and Royce were excited about the prospect of exploring this new land. They saddled up two horses and each put a Sharps rifle in the rifle boot on the saddle. They both thought about Ernest bringing the Sharps rifle for no apparent reason but it probably saved Walter's life.

They started toward the northeast on a well established logging road.

The two rode side by side and Walter asked, "How much money did Mother inherit from Grandfather and Grandmother Miller?"

"First they inherited the remainder of one-hundred sections of land when Grandfather and Grandmother were killed in the train wreck in Philadelphia. I know they received some money at that time but I don't have any idea how much," said Royce.

"Mother and Father are quite tight lipped about finances. I remember when we lived in Philadelphia, Grandfather was a very well respected land developer and owned several of the large buildings downtown. I know that Mother worked for him and handled his money and paid his bills. I know that Father attended college at the University of Pennsylvania into the 1840s around the time you and I were born."

"What did Father study at the University of Pennsylvania?" asked Walter.

"He studied Mechanical Engineering and after he graduated he worked for Grandfather Miller looking after the railroad steam engines and the wagon factory. He ended up running the wagon factory. Grandfather Miller had many different enterprises plus he owned many acres of valuable land just outside Philadelphia."

"I liked living in Philadelphia but I didn't like living in our row house," said Walter. "Grandfather and Grandmother certainly had a large elegant house and it was fun to visit there.

The carriage house and livery were the best. They sure had plenty of people working for them. Mother was their only child and is certainly not one to put on an artificial front. She seemed very much like Grandmother Miller."

"How did Mother and Father meet?" asked Walter.

"Grandpa Rounds had a large tree nursery and Father and his brother Douglas worked for him. One day Father made a large delivery to Grandfather and Grandmother Miller's estate and our mother showed the boys where the small trees were to be planted. They apparently were attracted to each other and began dating. They were married in 1834. Later Father was attending the University of Pennsylvania to be an engineer. Mother began working for Grandfather Miller doing book-work for his many enterprises. Erna was born, then me and then you. Mother had to take time off from work while we were small," explained Royce.

"Why did Grandfather Miller buy the large tract of land that Mother and Father inherited?" asked Walter.

"Apparently Grandfather knew this land in Wisconsin had recently been surveyed and the United States wanted to sell it as it needed money. Grandfather knew many people and must have heard about this huge tract of forest land and being wealthy he bought it sight unseen," was Royce's reply.

THE BLUE LINE

Walter and Royce finally came to trees that were painted blue on their bark. This marked the east edge of their original property and had been marked with blue paint by surveyors. They worked off quarter corner monuments to locate all the forty acre parcels in this sixty-four thousand acre parcel. This part of Wisconsin was surveyed in 1839.

The men rode their horses into the new land and found the going was easy. The huge trees blocked out light so there was very little undergrowth. They had to duck under limbs once in while. They had gone about a mile when Royce suggested that they ride south for awhile. They were both impressed by the huge maple, oak and cherry trees that they encountered on this rolling terrain.

They came to a small lake of about twenty-five acres and were impressed by its beauty. Larger trees surrounded its shores. A point reached into the lake on the south side. A fairly steep hill rose up from the north side of the lake. There were giant white pines growing on that hillside.

Royce commented, "I could build a home on that point. It is beautiful."

Walter wondered if there were fish in the lake. All at once, a large bass jumped near the southwest shore where the men had stopped to admire the lake.

"Guess that answers your question, Walter. Let's go around and ride out on the point so I can pick out a place for my house," taunted Royce.

"We may have to arm wrestle for it," countered Walter.

They went out on the point and dismounted. They walked to the edge of the lake and found a sandy beach that stretched on either side of the point which stood a few feet above the water.

"This is one of the most beautiful places I have ever seen," exclaimed Royce, obviously very pleased with their discovery. Both men looked around and took in the beauty of the scene in the mid-afternoon sunlight and shadows. They were impressed by the colorful forest of huge trees, dressed in their glorious fall colors.

Royce reached out and put his arm around Walter, "Think about all the poor souls that have died in this war that will never see a sight like this, unless there is one like it in Heaven."

Both men sat on a log, looking at the ground between their feet and were taken back to the terrible fighting they had witnessed and taken part of.

Finally Walter offered, "We are very, very lucky brother. Maybe we were spared for a reason, maybe to do some good for mankind."

A long pause and then, "We come from good stock. If we try to lead honest, decent lives where we treat everyone with dignity and respect we will be proud of the footprint we made while we were here," replied Royce.

Just then, a small flock of beautiful red birds with black wings flew past the men.

"What beautiful birds," remarked Walter.

The birds flew to the southeast and Walter took the reins of his horse and followed them as he wanted a better look at them.

The small flock flitted from branch to branch and both men could follow by walking rapidly. The birds finally began to move east away from the small lake. After about two-hundred yards the men could see another lake, larger than the first one. The men stopped to admire this lake. It was at least two-hundred acres and had a point reaching from the south side. It also was surrounded by huge maple, oak, basswood and cherry trees. A point reached out from the north side of this lake and blocked the mens view of that portion of the lake.

As the men looked out at the lake, they could not believe the natural beauty that they had seen and were now seeing. They had temporatily forgotten the red birds but here they came back to them. The men listened to their chirping but the flock slowly flew away following the edge of the lake.

"Let's follow them, they seem to be leading us somewhere," said Walter.

The flock followed the shoreline and the men led their horses as they tried to keep up with these mysterious birds which neither man had ever seen before. They continued to a point on the north shore and they could see that there was a much greater part of the lake which they had not seen.

The mysterious birds fluttered just in front of the men and they followed.

"It seems as though these birds want to show us something," offered Royce.

They approached a point that had protruded from the north side of the lake. The birds stopped flitting and now sat on a tree on the very tip of the point.

"Looks like they led us on a wild goose chase," Royce said.

"Let's go to their tree, maybe there is something there," countered Walter.

The men led their horses up to the tree that the red birds were in. Not a peep out of them. They did not fly as the men and horses approached the tree. Finally they were directly under the birds. Walter looked toward the east along the shoreline.

"**Would you look at that?!!!**" exclaimed Walter. Royce got up and stood beside Walter.

"That is a huge house, it is beautiful," whispered Royce.

About that time the flock of red birds flew toward the house.

"Let's go and see that house," said Walter excitedly. Off they went. The two hundred yards didn't take long to cover. They saw a large house with a wide veranda on the south and east side. It sat on a slight rise about a hundred feet from the lake. It had a large roof with a wide overhang and had two dormers facing the lake and two facing north. It was a large house made out of logs. It had large windows looking out at the lake as well as to the north up a hill. There were huge stone chimneys located on each end of the house reaching taller than the peak of the house. The men stopped and stared. What a wonderful house, Walter observed.

"It looks like no one has lived here for some time. I see a small tree growing up in front of the steps to the veranda," noted Royce.

The men tied the horses and approached the house. They went up the few steps to the veranda. They were impressed by the huge trees surrounding the house and as they climbed the steps a good sized red oak acorn clonked Walter on the head.

Royce tried the door and it opened. They stepped into a hallway with large closets on the east side. The hallway led to a large living room on the left and a large dining room on the right. All the furnishings were still in place. The floors were all oak and the walls were the other side of the logs that formed the house. Several large pictures hung from the walls where there was space. The living room furniture was made up of one divan, four padded arm chairs, and two rocking chairs made out of oak. A large bookcase stood to the right of the fireplace. A plant stand with empty flower pots stood on the left side of the fireplace. Oil lamps stood on three small tables near the padded chairs and divan. Three oriental rugs were on the floor near the chairs and another was on the floor near the fireplace.

The dining room was to the right of the living room and the main feature was a large round oak table. It appears to be able to seat at least twelve people. This room had similar beautiful pictures and oriental rugs.

The kitchen was north of the dining room. A large wood burning cook stove dominated the kitchen. A hand water pump was by the sink. Several oil lanterns were located on the cabinet tops and table. The cupboard was stacked with dishes, and pots and pans. The drawer contained silverware, very nice silverware.

A stairway led upstairs to four bedrooms, each with a dormer. All rooms had beds, dressers, closets, braided rugs, pictures and night stand with oil lanterns. One bedroom was like a magnet and Walter was pulled to it. He stood looking at the room. All the clothes were gone but the furniture appeared to all be here. He went to the night stand in the room and opened the small drawer which he found was empty.

Walter looked around the room. What about the closet, he said to himself. The closet was a walkin with a door which Walter opened and walked in. There were no clothes hanging on the rod below the shelf. The closet was empty but Walter reached up and felt the top of the shelf. His hand could barely reach the back of the shelf but he felt the entire four feet of the shelf on the east side of the closet. He did the same thing on the west side and on the final corner his hand detected a paper object. He exerted himself and was able to drag the paper to the edge of the shelf. He brought it down and looked at it. It was an envelope, addressed to Miss Florence Porter, Post Office Box, Antigo, Wisconsin. **Walter could not believe his eyes!!!** This must be the beautiful house on the lake that Antoinette told Walter about when he was in Sparta. Olivia Porter and Florence spent summers here and now it belongs to Edward and Alice Rounds.

THE LETTER

Royce had been exploring the other bedrooms and was now entering the bedroom Walter was in. Royce looked at Walter who was frozen with a 'this is incredible' look on his face.

"What is wrong?" an alarmed Royce asked. Walter still had a faraway, blank look on his face as he held the envelope in his hands. Finally, Walter seemed to come out of his trance.

"This is Florence's room. This house used to belong to her mother and father and was lost to that family when the bank that lent them money foreclosed. The money was to finance a gold mine in Montana. The gold mine failed," explained Walter.

"What is in the letter?" asked Royce excitedly.

"I am afraid to look and hope I am not just imagining this," Walter quietly said as he looked at Royce. Walter opened the already open envelope and took the letter out and it read, *Dear Florence, Imagine that! Another birthday rolled around. I hope you and your mother can visit me this summer. I would like to take you both to Washington, D. C. to see the Capital and White House. We could also visit Georgetown and do some shopping there. I will be looking for a note from you and hope you can visit. Have you decided on a career yet? Enjoy the lake. Hope you have a Happy 18th Birthday. Love, Aunt Azalea.*

Walter slowly turned to Royce. "I wonder when she was eighteen years old?" Both men were quiet and deep in thought.

"Look at the envelope and see if there is a post mark," Royce offered.

Walter looked at the envelope with a return address on the upper left hand corner and a postmark on the upper right side to the left of the stamp. The postmark was from Chambersburg, Pennsylvania and stamped May 15, 1860. Walter counted on his fingers.

"Florence is twenty-one years old," exclaimed Walter excitedly, "the same age as I will be next month."

Walter had already noticed that the envelope had been closed with sealing wax with the initials of AR indented into the warm wax. Walter looked at the return address which said, A. Rupp, 123 Greenwood Street, Chambersburg, Pennsylvania.

"Finally I have an address that I can write a letter to and ask if Florence's aunt can tell me any thing about my Florence."

Royce came up and put his arm around Walter. "You finally have a lead that may get you to Florence. You know what? If we don't head for home now, we will be lost in the dark. Put that envelope in your pocket and lets head for home," instructed Royce.

The men untied the horses and retraced their path around the west end of Florences' lake. They passed on the south-side of the small lake and headed straight west to intersect the property blue line and then find the logging road.

As they rode, Walter asked, "Would Florence's aunt be a sister to Olivia or Mr. Porter?"

Royce was quiet but then, "We don't know if Rupp is the married name or maybe she has not married. She could be a sister to Olivia and her maiden name may have been Rupp. It could be that Mr. Porter has a sister Azalea but then got married. Besides that, it really doesn't make much difference as long as she is Florences aunt," said Royce as he ducked under a low hanging branch.

The men reached the logging road and followed it home in the gathering darkness. The evening sky was clear and the sunset was interesting as the men viewed its lowering path through the trees. They noticed a beautiful rose color on the horizon from south to east and to the north. What a day.

Walter was in deep thought. He calculated the time it would take a letter to get to Pennsylvania and back to be at least a week. That is providing Florence's aunt will return a letter immediately.

THE REPORT

Walter and Royce walked into the house just in time for supper of fried elk loin. Royce waited for an opening to tell what they had discovered today. Edward showed surprise at the discovery of a small lake. He explained that he had never crossed the blue line and really didn't know what the property was like. He did not want to trespass.

Walter told about the flock of red birds luring them from the small lake to the larger lake.

"Scarlet tanagers," said Alice. "Quite unusual but I did see a flock of four last year, they are friendly to people."

"They led us to a big beautiful house on the north side of a larger lake. I found this letter," Walter said excitedly as he dug in his pocket and handed it to his mother, "and it was written to Florence. She used to live in that house! I still can hardly believe it."

Walter said, "I will write a letter to Azalea in Chambersburg and see if she has any news about Florence." He also added, "When we fought at Gettysburg, the city of Chambersburg was not very far away."

Erna got up and found an atlas that had a map of the states on it as they were in 1860. She found Pennsylvania and a little searching near Gettysburg she found Chambersburg, about fifty or sixty miles west of Gettysburg. Walter was silent and seemed lost in deep thought.

Erna was still looking at the Pennsylvania map. "Look here," she announced. "We know that the nurses program that Florence was on was cancelled because of the heavy casualties at Gettysburg. The nurses went back to Wisconsin. Maybe Florence was on her way to visit you at Harrisburg before she went back to Wisconsin. If she left Hagerstown, Maryland headed for Harrisburg, Pennsylvania she would go right through Chambersburg."

104

"I am going to Chambersburg," Walter announced excitedly. "I know that Florence is there, I am sure of it." Walter was silent.

Alice remarked, "Three or so years ago I was at the general store in Antigo and the clerk asked if I knew the lady and her daughter that live on a lake about fifteen miles north of Antigo. I told the clerk that I did not know them. The clerk did say they told her they go on the Lily Road. Maybe they are east of you."

"It looks like there was a trail going east of the house," Royce added, "so maybe there is a trail that goes around the east end of the lake and then south toward the Lily Road."

"What does the timber look like?" asked Edward.

"From what we saw," Walter told him, "there is a wonderful thick stand of maple, oak and basswood. On the north slope by both lakes there are huge white pines. The house was made out of smaller peeled pine logs and we could see some stumps where they were cut. We did not see any other evidence of where trees were cut. Remember we saw only a small part of the forty thousand acre parcel but we were very impressed."

"We were fortunate that the sale of the wagon factory in Philadelphia was completed," Edward wanted the family to know, "and the funds arrived just in time to complete the purchase of this new property. We plan to hire surveyors to find the corners of each forty acre parcel that touches the boundary. They will paint the blue line on the perimeter. That way we are identifying our boundaries so people would know they are trespassing if they cross the blue line. Likewise, we would know we would be trespassing if we crossed the blue line."

"Walter," Alice asked, "don't you think you should wait for responses from your letters?"

"Mother," Erna interjected, "we can see how much Walter loves Florence. Wild horses couldn't hold him back. He is heartsick with worry about Florence. Finding that letter today was like throwing a big log on that fire burning inside of Walter." Erna got up from the table and came to Walters chair and gave him a big hug.

"Little brother, my war hero, leave at first light and catch trains all the way to Florence. I will ride my horse to the train and lead yours back home."

"I will have breakfast ready by 4:30 a.m. so you and Erna can get an early start," said Alice. "And Walter, I want you to know that it will be a very happy day when you bring Florence to me. She must be a wonderful lady."

"You are going into war territory," Edward reminded him. "Better take your discharge papers in case you run into some local vigilanties that are looking for draft dodgers and deserters." Edward reached into his wallet and produced $200.00 and gave it to Walter.

"I feel just like Alice about your Florence. She must be a special lady and I am very much looking forward to meeting her."

THE TRIP

The next morning Alice had bacon, eggs and toast ready at 4:30 a.m. The entire family sat down and dug into the feast. Small talk accompanied the breakfast. Royce hoped he could explore the new land.

"Maybe Erna and I will go with you," added Edward. "We are anxious to see the big house."

"Don't expect to see it without me," said Alice.

Time to leave. Edward produced a surprise and gave it to Walter. It was a six-shot revolver and a box of shells.

"This just arrived before you got home. Take it in your rucksack. I hope not, but you may need it. Just aim and pull the trigger. Walter held the revolver in his hands and looked at it with a grin on his face.

"Wow, thanks Father."

Goodbyes were said, good luck was wished and then Erna and Walter spurred their horses toward Antigo and the train station.

Walter and Erna arrived at the train depot. The proper ticket was purchased for Madison and the train leaves at 8:10 a.m. Erna waited until Walter had purchased the ticket.

"I wish I had someone who was trying to find me and working on it as hard as you are." Walter chided her gently.

"Don't worry. There is a guy for you." Walter paused and looked at the floor.

"I want to tell you a secret just between the two of us. I gave Florence the plume from my hat that was given to me by my 6th Wisconsin commander, Lt. Col. Rufus Dawes. I know she has the plume and that was the best I could do at the time but we both think of it is as an engagement commitment." Erna gave Walter a hug and a kiss. They said their goodbyes and both had mist in their eyes.

MADISON BOUND

Walter boarded the train for Madison and took a seat opposite a stylishly dressed elderly lady that smiled and said hello. The lady was very easy to visit with and was going to Madison also. She was going to testify before the State Senate about the dreadful state of the many families in the Antigo area and surrounding area. So many families have the main breadwinner going off to war. Many of these families are destitute and many businesses are struggling because there is a shortage of workers and less money to support our businesses.

Walter was impressed by the enthusiasm of the nice lady.

"What is your name?" Walter asked.

"Ann Freiburger," she answered. "What is your name,?" she inquired.

"Walter Rounds, nice to meet you."

"You are Alice's son, the war hero. I heard about what you said to the crowd downtown a few nights ago. I must say, that you made an admirable impression on the people there. I have heard from three different people how impressed they were with your words and with you personally."

The two of them visited and Walter told Ann what he was trying to do. Walter could tell by her expression that she was very hopeful that he could find his Florence.

"I am scheduled to testify to the Senators at 1:15 p.m. today at the Capital and I am prepared. My presentation would be many times more powerful if you were with me and could add to my words. After all, a Wisconsin soldier seriously injured at Gettysburg while fighting as a member of the 6th Wisconsin Regiment in the famous Iron Brigade under the command of Lt. Col. Rufus Dawes would make a powerful statement that would be difficult for the Senators to refuse."

"What are you asking the Senators for?" asked Walter.

"An immediate $3.00 per week, plus $1.00 per each dependent living in the soldiers family and be paid for by state funds. So a wife home with three children would get $6.00 per week available at each counties courthouse or satellite location approved by the county board in each county. Payment would be by vouchers to purchase food, fuel, clothing, shoes and medicine. The merchants would present these vouchers to the county courthouse or approved satellite site. The county would be responsible for distributing vouchers and paying merchants for vouchers they honored. Each county would be reimbursed at the rate of 3% for funds distributed on a monthly basis. This program would be strictly voluntary and the soldiers family would not have to participate unless they wanted to. This program is for soldiers in active duty and ends thirty days after they are discharged. Only dependents of active duty soldiers are eligible." Walter was impressed with what Ann was going to present.

"Where will the funds come from?" inquired Walter.

"I will suggest a temporary tax on whiskey and tobacco," Ann responded.

"What do you want me to do?" asked Walter.

"Just stand by me and let me introduce you, maybe support my message with your own personal observations. What do you say? Are you going to help me fight for the families of soldiers."

"You drive a hard bargain. How do we get to the Capital?"

"We walk as it is only a short distance from the train depot to the Capital," added Ann.

SENATORS AT THE CAPITAL

Walter and Ann arrived in Madison with enough time to get lunch at the depot lunchroom. They arrived at the Capital by noon and looked for the Senate Chambers. There were many women and children beginning to arrive at the Capital.

As Walter and Ann approached the chamber, Ann said, "There is Senator Robert Haynes, the Senator from our district. He lives at Wausau. Come on, I will introduce you." Senator Haynes warmly greeted Ann and she introduced Walter.

"Ah, my friend Lt. Col. Rufus Dawes wrote me a letter and he told of two soldiers from Antigo that I should know about since they lived in my district. He said that you and your brother were among the very best soldiers that he had ever led. Rufus and I grew up together and he is very interested in what goes on in Madison."

Walter was surprised that Commander Dawes would mention Royce and his name to Senator Haynes.

Walter and Ann were escorted to their place in the Senate Chamber. Many women and children looked down from the balcony. Others began to fill in behind the seats and desks. Finally the Chamber was called to order and business was conducted on two other bills before them. Finally at 1:30 p.m. the President of the Senate called on Senator Haynes. He introduced Ann and told about her passionate appeal to him to aid the families of active duty soldiers and many, many were having a difficult time surviving with the main bread winner at war.

Ann was warmly welcomed and loud cheering and clapping came from the families. Ann introduced Walter and the Senators gave him a standing ovation. Several shouted 'thanks for your service'. Ann made her presentation and was politely received. There was enthusiastic approval from the families. Finally Ann asked Walter if he had any comments. Walter had sized up this group of Senators and felt they were not very sympathetic to the plight of the families.

"I know that President Lincoln will be activating the draft soon. This war has been very expensive and many men on both sides have died. The Union needs more troops if it is to win this war. That means more men will leave their families. Many will not have the means to support the families but these men will be fighting for a great cause. There is no doubt that there has been great disruption in many communities. I have seen it at Antigo. It has caused great unrest as these families feel there is no one aware of their plight. They need help and you are the hope for these families here today and throughout the state. I urge you to reach out to these families as they are part of each soldiers thoughts as they fight. Thank you," said Walter.

Walter sat down to loud cheering and clapping. The Senators began debating Ann's proposal. The main objection was funding this endeavor.

One Senator took the floor and told the other Senators, "A soldier worried about the welfare of his family but doing the bidding of his country needs us to do the right thing. If the rest of us need to contribute more to ease the suffering of the families, I am in favor of it."

Another Senator got up and said, "I think the allowance is too high and want it cut in half." A third Senator said, "That would be like cutting the ammunition that each soldier needs in half. And I will not support that."

That brought strong voices of approval from most of the Senators. The President of the Senate asked, "Are there any more additions to the bill in front of us. If not there will be a roll call vote." One by one, the Senators voted and it passed with only two dissenting votes. The families cheered loudly and the President thanked the families, Walter and especially Ann. She was honored with a standing ovation.

TRAIN TO CHICAGO

Walter thanked Ann for her good work and said goodbye, telling her that he will see her in Antigo someday. He made his way to the railroad station and asked about a ticket to Chicago. "Leaves at 5:20 p.m." replied the ticket agent. Walter paid for his ticket and settled on a bench to wait. Several groups of mothers and children filled the depot and sought tickets to return home. Several groups were headed north to Antigo. That train was leaving at 4:30 p.m. As that train was loading passengers, many went past Walter as he sat on the depot bench and just wanted to thank him for his words today and for his service in the military.

Walter went to the lunch counter and ordered a ham sandwich and a glass of milk. The 5:20 p.m. train to Chicago loaded passengers and Walter looked for a seat. There were some families on the train and very few seats were open. Walter approached an empty seat that was next to a young lady that was about Walter's age. He inquired if the seat was available and the young lady replied that it was. Walter stowed his rucksack and introduced himself.

The lady responded with, "Nice to meet you. My name is Beth McLaughlin." The lady was trim and neat with attractive brown hair. She was a pleasant person in Walters estimation.

"Do you live in Madison?" Walter asked.

"I am going to the University but I live in Janesville. I take the train in the morning and again in the evening," she said.

"What is your field of study?" asked Walter.

"I am studying nursing. Where do you live?" inquired Beth.

"A small town up north in Wisconsin - Antigo."

"You are certainly not heading home now. Where are you going?"

"Chicago tonight, then on to a town in Pennsylvania near Gettysburg." When Beth heard Gettysburg she straightened

112

up and turned in her seat to look at Walter. She had an expression that Walter could not recognize.

"Did you fight at Gettysburg?" Walter was confused now and looked at Beth with an inquiring look.

"Yes, I fought all three days with the 6th Wisconsin regiment. I was injured on the last day and was unconscious for three days. Why do you ask?"

Beth explained, "I was with twenty-six other student nurses that were enrolled in a nursing program in Madison. We had gone to Hagerstown, Maryland to take part in a special training course on treating heart patients. When the war broke out at Gettysburg, we all volunteered to go there and help out. A special train took us close to Gettysburg and we began working in field tents."

"You were there!" Walter exclaimed. "Then you know Florence Porter." Walter could hardly contain himself.

"Yes, I know Florence, she worked in a different part of the battlefield at Gettysburg. We all returned to Hagerstown on a train about July 13th. The hospital in Hagerstown was overflowing with injured soldiers from Gettysburg so the heart program was cancelled. We all went back to Madison, except Florence, Rebecca and Beatrice. Those three were going to Harrisburg to visit a soldier Florence had nursed backed to health. This soldier was from the 6th Wisconsin regiment and had been transferred to a hospital in Harrisburg."

"Florence, Rebecca and Beatrice were the best of friends but they have not returned to Madison."

"I was that soldier Florence nursed back to health," said Walter. "Actually she saved my life. I am on my way to find her. I found a letter Florence received from her Aunt Azalea who lived at Chambersburg, Pennsylvania. That town is between Hagerstown and Harrisburg. I was in a hospital in Harrisburg for two months and expected Florence to contact me, but I never heard from her nor received a letter. I have had the feeling that something has happened to Florence. It sounds like Rebecca and Beatrice have not returned to Madison either."

"We, the other nurses and I, wondered if they got jobs and stayed in that area. Since no one heard news like that we doubt that has happened. We wondered if the Confederates blew up their train or if there was a deadly storm like a tornado or a deadly fire or an earthquake."

Walter told Beth about Sparta and Florence's mother leaving town and putting her house up for sale.

"It sounds like her mother got some terrible news from Florence, or about her, for her to leave at the drop of the hat without telling her neighbors anything. Makes it sound like she went to be with Florence," Beth mused.

Walter was elated to have met Beth and had received information about Florence. Beth seems like a very nice person and Walter not only was pleased to have learned about Florence, but he enjoyed being in Beth's company. She was a nice looking lady about Walters age with light brown hair, which she wore in braids pulled into a bun. She had fine features, was of medium build and had a pleasant, friendly face. Walter found himself attracted to her. Walter felt his face flush and he leaned back in his seat and tried to calm himself. This was not right. Beth was not Florence but she was disrupting his feelings for Florence.

Walter had never had serious feelings for any girl before he met Florence. He liked girls, was a good dancer and attended dances when he could. Girls seemed to like him but he just never felt swept away like he did with Florence, and now with Beth.

Walter asked Beth for an address he could write to when he had news about Florence. Beth found paper and pencil and wrote her parents address in Janesville. Beth smiled at Walter as she handed him the paper. Their hands touched and Walter felt his face flush again.

"I come home every work day about this time. My parents have some health issues that are improving so I may not need to return each night. If you are in the area, feel free to stop and visit me. I am sure my mother and father would like to visit with you." Walter thanked Beth for the address and also for the invitation to visit her.

The train slowed down and the conductor called out 'Janesville'. Beth got up to leave so Walter got up and stepped into the aisle to let her pass so she could exit to the rear of the car. As Beth left her seat she put her right hand on Walters left arm. She looked into Walter's eyes, leaned forward and kissed him on the cheek. Walter reached out and hugged Beth. In an instant they parted and said goodbye. Walter watched her leave the car and as she walked toward the depot. Before she disappeared she turned and waved to Walter. Walter sat back on the seat and felt strange. He had a faraway look on his face as he gazed at the seat in front of him. He wondered what had just happened. Florence had stolen his heart, he thought, but this Beth seemed to be tugging at his heart also.

CROWDED TRAIN

Passengers got on at Janesville and the car was crowded. Two middle ages ladies came into the car and all the seats were occupied except the seat Beth had occupied. Walter saw the predicament and stood up and offered his seat to the two ladies. They gratefully accepted and thanked Walter. He grabbed a hand strap hanging from the ceiling and stood near the two ladies.

The train began moving.

"You look like you just saw a ghost," said the lady closest to Walter.

"Well, I didn't," said Walter. "I did find out some information from a nurse that just got off at Janesville regarding a nurse who had saved my life."

"You must mean Beth," said the other lady as she leaned forward to more directly look at Walter. "We know Beth and she certainly is a wonderful person. We think she will be a wonderful nurse. We know she cared for wounded soldiers at that dreadful battle at Gettysburg."

"Her friend Florence saved my life at Gettysburg and I am on my way to Pennsylvania to find her."

"You fought at Gettysburg?"

"All three days," Walter replied, "for the 6th Wisconsin regiment as a member of the Iron Brigade. I was injured the third day and lay unconscious for three days. Florence saved my life. We got separated and I have been trying to find her. Beth told me something that makes me think that Florence and her two friends were hurt, possibly abducted or are very sick. Beth said Florence and her two friends were going to Harrisburg to visit a wounded Wisconsin soldier which was me. But they never got there. Florence has an aunt that lives at Chambersburg, Pennsylvania which is on the rail line between Hagerstown, Maryland where the nurses had been training and Harrisburg where I was.

"Beth said the remainder of twenty-four nurses returned to Madison. Nothing has been heard from Florence and her friends. I am fearful something bad happened on the way to visit me in Harrisburg," said Walter.

"That is a very sad story. Do you have Florence's aunts address?" asked the lady by the aisle.

"You won't believe this, but it is true. My mother and father bought a tract of land adjoining their property north of Antigo, Wisconsin. There were two lakes on this property and on the bank of the larger lake was a large, beautiful log house that no one had lived in for two or three years. On a closet shelf I found an envelope that was addressed to Florence Porter, my Florence, from her aunt in Chambersburg, Pennsylvania." Walter produced the envelope and handed it to the nearest lady.

"My word," exclaimed the other lady. They both read the letter and looked up at Walter.

"You mean Florence lived near your mother and father?"

"That appears to be true. That part of Wisconsin is very sparsely settled and apparently Florence and her mother went to Antigo by a different road than my family did. We didn't even know there was a house in that vast forest."

"Today you met Beth on the train and she is a friend of Florence, you have been very lucky finding information about Florence," said the lady by the window.

"Wait, there is more." He told about Florence's mother at Sparta and his efforts to find Florence.

"That certainly sounds like when you find Florence you will find her mother," said the lady by the window.

"You have very strong feelings for Florence, but I detect your meeting Beth has shaken you and awakened emotions within you that you have not been able to deal with, am I correct?" said the lady by the aisle. Walter was silent. He felt his face flush as he looked at the aisle in front of him.

"You are very perceptive, are you a mind reader?"

"No, I am not a mind reader but I can read what is on your face," said the lady by the aisle.

Walter now felt like he didn't want to visit with these ladies anymore, so he released his hold on the hand strap and moved to the rear of the car and secured another strap. Apparently Walter showed he was taken aback by Beth. He didn't appreciate being told that it showed. Walter could see the two ladies in a serious discussion. They leaned their heads together and seemed to be disagreeing with each other. Walter chose to ignore them and watch the landscape. It was getting near dusk on a beautiful fall evening.

"Beloit," called the conductor. The train slowed and engine bells began clanging as the train pulled into the station. Walter could see the two ladies get up and prepare to leave the car and probably the train. The ladies came near Walter and he made room for them to pass, except they didn't, at least not right away.

"We are very sorry that we over stepped into your private thoughts. We want to apologize and sincerely hope that you, the war hero, can find your sweetheart, the lifesaving nurse. We want to wish you the very best in your search. Thanks for your service in this terrible war. We can tell you are a proud man and we bet you were a great soldier. Goodbye," said one of the ladies. Each lady reached up and patted Walter on the shoulder and then they were gone.

Walter returned to his seat and shortly the train began moving toward Chicago. Several stops were made and the car Walter was in was nearly full all the time. Finally the train pulled in to the station among several trains that were arriving and departing. This was a busy station. Walter shouldered his rucksack and made his way off the train.

PITTSBURGH

Walter consulted with the ticket agent and he recommended he go to Pittsburgh. He could find a train to Chambersburg from there. That train departs Chicago at 6:10 a.m. on track fourteen so Walter purchased his ticket. Walter got a sandwich at the eatery and took a walk around the station and bought a Chicago newspaper and sat on the end of a waiting room bench.

Walter read the paper and found an article about the sad state of affairs of the families of soldiers serving in the war. The article was about a group of mothers appearing before the Illinois State Legislature. This group was asking for about the same thing that Mrs. Freiburger had asked the Wisconsin Senators for in Madison earlier today.

Traffic in the large Chicago train station began to slow down around 10:00 p.m. Walter stretched out on the end of the bench with his head on the rucksack. He used the newspaper to cover himself and proceeded to try to sleep. He still could not understand the emotions he felt for Beth. He concluded he was so happy to learn about Florence he was overwhelmed with positive feelings for Beth. A few minutes later he admitted that he thought she was very pretty, nicely dressed and he thought her braided hair pulled into a bun was very attractive. He felt guilty for having these feelings for Beth. He did think that the long absence from Florence must have lessened his warm and strong feelings for her.

Walter got on the 6:10 a.m. to Pittsburgh. This was a long train with twenty-one cars, mostly passenger cars The engine seemed longer than the one that took him to Chicago. Once the train cleared the city, Walter was impressed that they were traveling at a higher rate of speed than yesterdays train. Walter realized that this train ran between two very large industrialized cities and very likely was of higher quality than most tracks.

The train stopped at several stations but went right through others. Apparently another train picked up and dropped off passengers at those stations. Walter's car was never very full and the passengers kept changing. No one needed to sit with Walter, which was fine with him. He was in a thinking mood anyway. "Toledo, Toledo, ten minute layover," called the conductor. Walter took his rucksack and went looking for coffee and a donut.

Walter boarded a different car when the train pulled out. This car had more passengers and an elderly man sat with Walter.

"Going far?" the man inquired of Walter.

"Pittsburgh and then on to Chambersburg," Walter answered.

"Going to fight for the Union?" asked the elderly man.

"No Sir, I already did that for two years. I was wounded at Gettysburg and a pretty nurse saved my life and I am going to find her. Where are you headed for?" inquired Walter.

"Gettysburg," was his reply. "My brother was killed there and I want to see his grave," replied the elderly man. Both men were silent for some time.

"What regiment did your brother belong to?" Walter inquired.

"The 107th Ohio, Joe had twenty more days and he would have been discharged. He was desperate to get home to his family of wife and four children ages eight to sixteen. Got a cannonball fragment full in the chest and died instantly. I got a look at the letter the army sent his wife. He is buried where he fell at the south end of cemetery ridge," the elderly man said and then he was silent. He had a strange look on his wrinkled face like he had to do something distasteful but he knew he had to do it.

Both sat in silence for several minutes. "What regiment were you with?" asked the elderly man.

"6th Wisconsin, Iron Brigade. Our commander was Lt. Col. Rufus Dawes, I Corps under General Joe Hooker," Walter replied.

"I have heard of the Iron Brigade, black hats and tough as iron," the elderly man said with a smile. "An article in the Toledo newspaper told that you black hats charged into some rebels from Mississippi and killed a bunch but also took several hundred prisoners, including their General. I guess you guys captured their flag also. Did that really happen?" the elderly man asked.

"That happened on the first day after several hours of heavy fighting. Commander Dawes told us to fix bayonets and on his signal we went over the wall and chased those rebels into a railroad cut and trapped them. Truth be known, we were low on ammo but Commander Dawes is an outstanding leader. We suffered loses that day, at least one-fourth of our regiments were killed or wounded," Walter emphatically relayed.

"Were you injured on the first day?" asked the elderly man.

"On the third day," replied Walter. "Our regiment was in a support position as we had suffered great loses in the first two days. We got the signal to move up just as some Confederates reached the rock wall we were fighting from. I was shot in my right shoulder as I moved up and woke up three days later in a hospital tent with this beautiful, kind nurse tending to me. She saved my life and I am going to find her. I am afraid something bad may have happened to her," Walter told the elderly man.

"Do you think she is at Gettysburg?" asked the man. Walter told him what happened in his efforts to find Florence. He produced the letter from Florence's aunt.

The man looked at the address and said, "That town is just west of Gettysburg. I am planning to go through Chambersburg on my way to Gettysburg. Maybe we could travel together."

Walter thought that would be a good idea.

"If we are going to travel together, we should exchange names."

"Charles. Charles Sullivan," the elderly man replied.

"Walter, Walter Rounds," answered Walter. The two men

shook hands and seemed happy for the alliance they formed. They both liked the other and enjoyed each others company.

"What did you do for your livelihood?" asked Walter.

"Was in the lumber business. Had a big sawmill and planing mill and made flooring. Sold it a few years back. New owners have reduced output, shortage of hardwood these days."

"My family is also in the lumber business. My mother and father have a hundred thousand acres of forest land, mostly maple, oak, cherry and a fair amount of white pine," said Walter.

"Are they logging it?" asked Charles.

"My father is in the process of planning to develop a large scale wood drying, planing and milling operation in northern Wisconsin. Any day now, work on a railroad spur will start so finished flooring and other products can be loaded on rail cars and shipped to dealers."

"That sounds like the set up I had. Seventy-five men worked there and the mill ran two shifts of most departments," explained Charles.

"I talked to a man from Milwaukee who told me that his company was developing a new band saw to break down logs into boards. They said they are trying to develop a band saw with blades on the front and back so the saw can cut on the back track as well as the forward cut. Have you ever seen or heard of that kind of a saw?" asked Walter.

"I have not. We used circle saws with the top saw on the head rig that we used to cut large diameter logs. I expect that band saws would work fine once the correct filing could be determined," said Charles.

"I have heard Father talk about a fire hole," said Walter. "Apparently there is a large smokestack associated with it."

"That is where all the scrap wood, sawdust and slabs are burned to produce steam to dry lumber in the kilns. The steam was used to drive steam motors to operate saws, planers and blowers. It was also used to heat the mill and the hot pond."

"What is a hot pond?"

"In the winter the logs are frozen and hard to cut. If logs are put into the hot pond for awhile they thaw out. The pond also lets dirt fall off before they are sawed," explained Charles.

"Cleveland, Cleveland. Ten minute layover," announced the conductor. Walter bought a sandwich and headed back to the car. The train got rolling again heading for Pittsburgh, southeast of Cleveland. Walter felt sleepy so he dozed for an hour or so. By now it was late afternoon and it looked like it would be dark by the time they reached Pittsburgh.

"How are you planning to go to Chambersburg,?" asked Walter.

"From here I will take the train to Somerset, switch trains and go to Breezewood, switch again and take that train to Chambersburg. And then on to Gettysburg. It will take most of tomorrow, I think," explained Charles. "I am going to get a hotel room at Pittsburgh," Charles said. "You are welcome to share the room as my guest."

Walter thought about the offer and responded, "I have soldiered for two years and have gotten used to adjusting to sleeping conditions. I will meet you at the train to Somerset. It may sound strange not to accept your generous offer, but that is just the way I am. I am looking forward to continuing our quest."

"Young man, I admire your determination. I can tell you are concerned about one thing, finding your angel nurse and I hope you can. You are a man of high moral standing and you value the friendship and love with this exceptional lady, I will do whatever I can to help. See you at the ticket agents window in the morning."

Walter got a meal at the eatery, bought a Pittsburgh newspaper and settled on the waiting room bench. The newspaper was full of articles about the steel mills. Producing steel for gun barrels, other gun parts and steel rails dominated the news. Steel for bridges was in high demand, but there was a great shortage of good workers. With many men fighting the war, there just was not enough workers to produce war goods as well as materials needed by all.

An editorial called on Washington, D. C. and the State of Pennsylvania to reduce the draft in Pittsburgh and the surrounding area. Workers are desperately needed to keep the Union supplied. The editorial also suggested discharging soldiers early if they had experience in the steel mills and associated industries. The editorial also bemoaned the plight of the soldiers dependents. It called for an increase in vouchers so families could get more food, clothing, fuel and medical supplies since the main breadwinner is unable to support their families adequately. The article spoke against the idea of a truce with the Confederates. The message was that all had been accomplished would be lost, many thousands of men killed and wounded for naught. Recent events at Vicksburg and Gettysburg have seriously weakened the Confederate forces. We need to press forward and support President Lincolns efforts to win this great and terrible war.

Walter had not been able to follow events about the war after Gettysburg. He did not know where the 6th Wisconsin was located or if they were in any battle. He did know that the burden of the war is wearing many people down. Everyone wants the war to be over.

Walter claimed the end of a bench, put his head on the rucksack. Tonight he took the pistol out of his rucksack and placed it in his belt. He felt somewhat uneasy and did not know why. He covered himself with the newspaper and fell asleep.

TRAIN TO SOMERSET

During the night Walter felt someone grab his left arm. He was instantly awake and saw four men standing near him.

"We need you to work for us," said the man who had grabbed Walter's arm. Walter felt an immediate fear, he was outnumbered. These men looked tough, and he put his hand on the pistol.

"I can't work for you," said Walter.

"You didn't understand me, we need you to work for us," said the ringleader. Walter threw back the newspaper and pointed the gun at the group as he rose off the bench.

"I told you I can't work for you and I meant it, now get out of here and leave me alone."

The four toughs had surprised looks on their faces but they did leave the station. Now what? thought Walter. No sleep the remainder of the night. He wondered if they would hire him out to work in one of the steel mills. Seems like a strange idea. Those four looked like hoodlums and ruffians, not businessmen. Anyway, he will be glad to get out of Pittsburgh. Walter went to the eatery to get some breakfast. He kept the pistol in his belt but kept it covered with his jacket. He kept an eye peeled for any trouble.

After breakfast, Walter saw the ticket agent window was open so he went and purchased a ticket to Somerset. "8:17 a.m., Track Eleven," said the ticket agent.

"I spent the night on the bench against the wall. During the night four toughs woke me and told me they wanted me to work for them. Do you know what that is all about?" asked Walter.

"There is such a shortage of workers for the steel mills that some workers will highjack men to work with them and then they will get paid a bonus by the mill," said the ticket agent.

"You mean they would get a bounty for turning me in to the steel mill?" asked Walter.

"That is correct and one of them would stay with you so you don't leave. They are fairly successful. You being a young man in good condition would bring an extra fee," said the agent.

"Are there any local vigilantes groups around that challenge any men to see if they have served in the military?" asked Walter.

"You bet there are. In some areas they are very aggressive. They look for defectors and draft dodgers. They have some governmental power and they can be very aggressive. How about you? Are they after you?" asked the agent.

"I served two years with the 6th Wisconsin and I was discharged. I was injured very seriously on the third day at Gettysburg. I am on my way to find the beautiful nurse that saved my life. I think she is in Chambersburg and that is where I am headed.

The ticket agent reached his hand through the window, "Thanks for your service." As he shook Walters hand, "The 6th Wisconsin, huh? Our paper told that you guys charged into some Mississippi regiments and captured hundreds including their General," the ticket agent said enthusiastically. "You Iron Brigade troops are really something. When the rebels see your black hats lining up to fight them they are ready to retreat," added the agent.

"How do you know about the Iron Brigade?" asked Walter.

"You guys were in our Pittsburgh paper several times. It sounds like your Commander Lt. Col. Dawes is really a bulldog of a fighter."

By now other customers arrived, so Walter moved away from the window. And true to his word, Charles showed up and bought his ticket to Somerset.

Walter relayed his incident with the four men during the night. He patted the pistol and said, "Good thing my father insisted I take the pistol with me. Things sound pretty desperate around Pittsburgh." Walter showed Charles the newspaper and suggested he could read it on the train.

Time to board so the two men climbed aboard and took a seat. The train moved slowly through the outskirts of Pittsburgh sounding its whistle for each of the many crossings. Finally clear of the city, the train picked up speed but not as fast as the train from Chicago yesterday. The terrain was more like small mountains and the train ran in the valleys usually by a river or a stream.

Charles read the paper and he said, "Sounds like the shortage of manpower is really putting a crimp in the steel mills."

"Do you think Washington, D. C. and Pennsylvania will reduce the draft for Pittsburgh and other important manufacturing cities?" Walter asked Charles.

"Something certainly needs to be done or we will lose our ace in the hole, our ability to keep manufacturing goods while blocking the Confederates from replacing their munitions, food and men. It sounds like the winds of war are finally blowing in the Unions favor, at least just a little bit. Gettysburg put a dent in the armor of the Confederates but they are still one heck of a tough army, but so is the Union army," said Charles.

His voice was of a man who saw the big picture and realized that the North was at a critical point of the war. There is growing opposition to the war from the home front and some politicians in Washington, D. C. States and their Governors are facing tough times too. War is very expensive in manpower and money. Life on the home front needs to be made more tolerable to families. Day by day, the end of this terrible war is drawing to a close, thought Walter.

NEWS ABOUT FLORENCE

Walter and Charles talked about the lumber industry. Walter had many questions as he explained what he thought his father and mother planned to do with their huge forest north of Antigo. There was a middle-aged lady sitting on the seat across the aisle from Walter. He spoke to her when he came into the car and said 'hello'.

"Did I hear you say you were from Antigo?" asked the lady.

"That is correct, why do you ask?" replied Walter.

"Antigo, Wisconsin," asked the lady.

"That is the one," Walter reassured her.

"I am from Green Bay, Wisconsin and my daughter Beatrice was in a nursing program at Hagerstown, Maryland. When the battle of Gettysburg started, she and other nurses went to take care of wounded Union soldiers. Her friend Florence, tended a wounded soldier from Antigo," said the lady.

Walter could not believe his ears.

"That was me," explained Walter excitedly.

"Are you on your way to be with Beatrice?" continued Walter.

"Yes, I am. Beatrice, Rebecca and Florence were all injured by a runaway team of horses and wagon at Chambersburg, Pennsylvania. The three of them are very good friends and were leaving Hagerstown because the hospital was overrun by injured soldiers from Gettysburg. They were going to Harrisburg first so Florence could visit you. Florence had an aunt living in Chambersburg so the three girls were going to visit her and spend the night. They walked to the address and found that a tornado had hit the town in June and destroyed dozens of homes including the home of Florence's aunt. The three of them were at a loss of what to do.

"The train to Harrisburg had left and they were standing on the street near a store when all of a sudden two dogs got into a fight which scared a team of horses that began running toward the girls. The runaways turned to go up the street and the wagon slewed around and hit all three girls. They got knocked down and the heavy rear wheel ran over all of them. My Beatrice finally wrote me a letter telling me what I have told you."

"How are the girls, now?" asked Walter, barely able to speak.

"All three girls are in serious condition, but are apparently improving. Beatrice had a skull fracture, concussion and both legs broken. Florence had a broken pelvis, several broken ribs and her left leg was broken. Rebecca has a broken shoulder, broken jaw, concussion and a damaged kidney," explained Beatrice's mother.

"Where are the girls now?" asked Walter.

"Beatrice gave me the address. Apparently it is a home made into a makeshift hospital," said Beatrice's mother as she dug the letter out of her purse.

"The address is in the letter, which I just got three weeks ago. I couldn't leave because my husband was very ill. He has since improved but I could not leave him until just a few days ago. I went to Pittsburgh and spent two days with my sister who is sitting next to me," added Beatrice's mother.

Walter read the letter and re-read it. He is very happy that he knows where Florence is and that she is alive and being cared for. Hopefully he will see her yet today. He notices the landscape is definitely more mountainous which means slower travel up some grades.

Charles is amazed that Walter is talking to the mother of one of the injured girls. Considering that the accident happened about the middle of July, it is now about the middle of September which means that was about two months ago. Charles mentioned that to Walter and wondered why there was such a delay.

"In the letter Beatrice mentioned that she was so injured that it was about a month later before she could write. A nurse wrote to Florence's mother earlier and she arrived within a few days."

Walter handed the letter back and explained how he had gotten Florence's aunts address and that is why he was going to Chambersburg. He was hoping the aunt would know some news about Florence and her mother since Walter was certain she was with Florence.

"Somerset, Somerset. Ten minute layover," announced the conductor. Walter got off to get a cup of coffee. As he moved toward the eatery he was approached by two men.

"Are you a soldier?" asked one. Walter was immediately on the defensive. What do these two men want. Are they vigilantes, he wondered.

He stepped back a step, "Why do you ask? " said Walter.

"Just answer the question," demanded the same man as he stepped closer to Walter.

"No," was Walters answer.

"Are you a draft dodger?" asked the second man very aggressively.

"Who are you men and why are you asking me these questions? You have not shown me any identification indicating you can legally ask me any of these threatening questions," said Walter.

"Answer the question, are you a draft dodger?" demanded the second man. Walter put his right hand on the handle of the pistol which was under his jacket.

"You failed to show me some identification that allows you to question me in this manner. Now step aside as I am on a time schedule."

Walter moved to the right to get around the man. The closest man grabbed Walter's left arm and Walter produced the pistol and growled, "Let go of my arm."

The man immediately let go of Walters arm and stepped back.

"Take it easy man, don't shoot," the first man said weakly.

The three men stood facing each other and finally the two men backed up and went to leave.

"Two years with the 6th Wisconsin Regiment as part of the Iron Brigade I Corp. under General Hooker," said Walter.

"You fought at Gettysburg then?" the second man asked.

"Yes, and I was wounded on the third day," said Walter.

"Sir, we apologize. We did not realize that you were a soldier in a great regiment," added the first man.

"I will buy you coffee," offered the second man. Walter put his pistol away and hurried to the eatery. The second man was true to his word while the first man hurried to the train to urge the engineer to wait for the Gettysburg soldier.

The train rolled out of Somerset and continued east. It was just past noon and the train had more passengers than before the stop. Mountains continued but on two locations wagons hauling coal were seen and the tracks crossed the canal and Walter could see a barge being pulled by mules. The barge was loaded with coal.

Walter visited with Beatrice's mother and found her name was Eloise VanDenHuvel and she lived near the Fox River in Green Bay. Her husband owned a transportation company that received and shipped cargo on packet ships on the Bay of Green Bay and Lake Michigan. The Fox River was an important immigration route for new arrivals coming to Wisconsin. Many Europeans came via the Erie Canal, through the newly dug Welland Canal around Niagara Falls, through Lakes Erie and Huron. Then into Lake Michigan and then into the Bay of Green Bay.

"Do you know if any of Rebecca's family is with her?" asked Walter.

"The letter from Beatrice did not mention anyone," replied Eloise.

The train made stops at three different towns and finally the conductor announced, "Breezewood, Breezewood, end of the

131

line." By now it was late afternoon and the small group approached the ticket agent. They were hopeful the train would leave yet that afternoon.

"Four tickets to Chambersburg."

"Leaves 7:40 a.m. tomorrow," announced the ticket agent. Disappointed, tickets were purchased and the length of time to Chambersburg was requested.

"Four and one-half hours, mountains," replied the agent.

"Is there a hotel nearby?" inquired Eloise.

"One block to the right, serves food also," replied the agent, seemingly afraid to offer anything but the minimum information.

The four rented rooms at the hotel and inquired about the meal schedule. Walter and Charles decided to walk to the river and watch barges being loaded with coal. Horse drawn wagons, loaded with coal were driven up on an elevated bed beside the barge. A movable chute was placed so coal could be shoveled into the chute, slide down into the barge. From time to time the chute was moved as the wagon got empty. The sides of the ramp were very high and the horses were double tied to avoid any runaways. A man working nearby volunteered that this was anthracite, or hard coal, more valuable than bituminous, or soft coal.

LAST LEG

Bright and early the four travelers had eaten breakfast and were at the train station when the train pulled in, bell clanging and steam hissing. The engine made its chug . . . chug sound as it slowly pulled into the station. Eloise and Walter's faces shone with excited anticipation and wanted this last leg to start soon.

The agent was correct. Slow going with many long grades that required slow speed. The tracks ran beside the river which is also part of a canal system. Several barges were seen, some empty on the side of the canal closest to the train. Loaded barges were being pulled on the opposite side. Mules were the source of power walking on a tow path. The tracks passed through a gap in the Tuscarora mountains was information the friendly conductor offered.

Walter asked the conductor, "Do you know much about Chambersburg?"

"Son, I live there. What do you want to know?"

"There are three injured girls at a make shift hospital. Can you give us directions to it?" asked Walter, hopefully.

"Do you mean the three nurses that got run over by a runaway team of horses?"

"Those are the girls! One is this ladies daughter and one saved my life at Gettysburg," added Walter.

"Those poor girls are the talk of the town. Everyone feels terrible for them. When you get off the train, turn left and go two blocks and you will come to the Harrisburg Pike. Follow that for one block and you will come to our hospital located on the right side of the Pike."

Walter was full of expectation. He was about to see Florence, the wonderful angel that had dominated his thoughts and actions since is awoke from his injury at Gettysburg. He knew she had been very seriously hurt. Will she look beat up? Can she walk? Will she remember me? Have I been in her thoughts at all? The train rolled on.

133

All at once, the train passed through an area where many, many trees were blown down. Tops were blown off many which left debris and branches every where. In a short time the train passed through the path that the tornado had taken. This was the first time Walter had ever seen the effects of a tornado.

REUNION

Finally, around noon, "Chambersburg, Chambersburg. Ten minute layover," announced the conductor. The train stopped and the group of four passengers stepped down. After gathering luggage, they turned left and walked the two blocks to the Harrisburg Pike. There was an underlying fear of what the girls would be like. They all hoped for the best but were braced for anything else.

This group went up the Pike for one block and there it was, the makeshift hospital. They went up to the door and Walter entered first. **There was Florence!** She was sitting on a chair next to a middle aged lady. Walter approached carefully.

"Florence, do you remember me? I am Walter."

Florence looked at Walter with an 'I don't remember' look on her face. Walter knelt in front of her and took her right hand. He looked into her eyes and he could see her searching for some recognition.

"You were my nurse at Gettysburg. You saved my life." Walter detected a slight smile. "After you saved me, I was transferred to a hospital in Harrisburg. Before I left I gave you the plume off my hat." With that Florence had a big smile on her face.

"The plume," she said in a shaky, unfamiliar voice. "Mother, please get the plume." At this time Walter got up and went to Florence's mother.

"You must be Olivia," said Walter.

"Well, yes I am. You are the Walter I read about in a letter Florence sent me. Excuse me, I will get the beautiful plume. Better yet, why don't you come with me and you can see Florence's room."

Walter and Olivia walked down a hallway to a room Florence occupied.

135

"You can probably tell Florence is slow, her recollection is a struggle for her. She has improved. She is battling so many other problems with her body that it seems to be keeping her mind distracted," said Olivia, protectively.

"I think she recognized me and I am very happy for that. She looks beautiful, just like I remembered her," remarked Walter happily.

Olivia found the battered valise, opened it and found the beautiful plume. Olivia handed it to Walter and he saw that it was not damaged.

Walter explained, "Lt. Col. Rufus Dawes traded plumes with me while I was unconscious. When Florence and I were about to part, I gave the plume to Florence and told her I would find her and if she wanted to return it I would probably accept it. I told her it was the second most valuable thing in my life. My life was the most valuable thing and she had saved it."

Olivia found this very touching and reached out and put her left hand on Walter's shoulder.

Walter and Olivia returned to Florence. When Florence saw the plume a wide smile spread across her face. Walter approached Florence and knelt in front of her and presented the plume to her. She held the plume and studied it.

"That was your second most prized possession. Do you remember your most prized possession?" Florence asked Walter.

"My life." After a pause , "and you saved it." With that, Walter rose up and hugged Florence. She reached up with her right arm and hugged Walter back. Florence's left arm and hand remained in her lap.

Walter pulled a chair up close to Florence. He found a chair for Olivia to sit in also. Olivia was a very nice looking lady. Walter could easily see where Florence got her beautiful looks from. Olivia was a lady with grace and charm and had a warm, pleasant personality and Walter immediately liked her.

Walter told how a doctor at Harrisburg had telegraphed the hospital in Hagerstown and was told that her nursing program was cancelled because of so many injured soldiers from Gettysburg. He was told the visiting nurses had gone home to Wisconsin. Walter said he was very sad that he got no news from Florence as he was sure that they shared strong feelings for each other.

Walter told Florence he went to Sparta and found her mother's house and met Antoinette Zimchezk and family. He also talked to the land agent and his plan to possibly buy the house and maybe Olivia would have to put down an address that he could come and find Florence if she accepted his offer to purchase. That plan never developed, but it was close.

Walter told about Jenny from next door and how she wanted Walter to come to her class with his full uniform on, which he did and received great attention. Olivia added that Jenny is a sweet and friendly girl. Antoinette and the family are wonderful neighbors.

"I really wondered if something bad had happened since Florence had not contacted me at the hospital in Harrisburg. When I found out that you, Olivia, left at the drop of a hat after putting your nice house for sale, I was fearful that you had received some bad news and had gone to be with Florence."

"Antoinette told me that you, Olivia, and Florence lived on a beautiful lake up north in Wisconsin. But when the land was foreclosed on you moved to Sparta so a doctor there could help your husband and Florence's father with the health problem he was dealing with. I also found out that your husbands uncle by marriage used to live in Sparta and recently moved to Madison to start a company to build railroad tracks.

"Finally, I went home to Antigo to see if my mother and father could help me find you, Florence. I wrote letters to the University of Wisconsin to inquire whether it was their program and if they knew anything about your whereabouts. They would only now be receiving these letters.

"The very next day my brother Royce, Florence, you met him at that time when he visited me in the tent while I was unconscious. Do you remember what he left with you to give me if I woke up?" Florence had a thoughtful look on her face as she looked at the floor in front of her.

"It was a locket with a picture of your mother and father."

"Absolutely correct," replied Walter, as he reached out and held both hands.

"My mother and father purchased the land your family used to own as it adjoins their land to the east. Father asked Royce and me to ride into the new land, your old land, and report what the tree situation was like. Species, density of stands, swamp land and if the land was level, hilly, rocky or what. We found the beautiful small lake and a flock of scarlet tanagers led us to the larger lake to the east. They also led us to your old house. What a beautiful house and what a setting.

"Royce and I entered that beautiful house and explored the rooms. Florence, in your bedroom closet, I found an envelope your Aunt Azalea sent you and here it is." Walter dug into his pocket and produced the envelope and gave it to Florence. Her eyes got large, her mouth opened as she grasped the envelope. She struggled to open the envelope so Walter helped and then she could read the letter her aunt had written.

"On the upper left hand corner of the envelope was your aunts address here in Chambersburg. I could see that it was on a railroad line from Hagerstown to Harrisburg. I figured you, Rebecca and Beatrice were going back to Wisconsin but you were going to visit me in the hospital in Harrisburg. Since your aunt lived here you were going to stop and visit her and then continue on to Harrisburg. Do I have it figured out correctly?"

Florence responded, "That is exactly what our plans were. The problem was that Azalea's house was destroyed by a tornado and we were contemplating what to do when the three of us got hit by a runaway team of horses pulling a heavy wagon."

Walter continued, "With that return address I packed my bag, got on a train to Madison and on to Chicago. The train from Madison was crowded and I ended up sitting with Beth McLaughlin and we sat together until she got off at Janesville." Florence's face lit up.

"Beth, what a coincidence. She is a very nice person and a very good nurse. It would be fun to see her again."

"Anyway, four days after leaving home with your Aunt Azalea's address I am here. When the train left Pittsburgh, a lady sat across from me and we visited. It turns out to be Beatrice's mother from Green Bay. Her name is Eloise VanDenHuevel and we traveled together and she is with Beatrice at this time in another room. Her sister lived in Pittsburgh and she is here also. Charles is an older gentlemen from Toledo who is on his way to Gettysburg to find where is brother is buried. He was killed fighting for the 107th Ohio at Gettysburg. Charles has been a good friend on this trip."

"You found that letter and you got on a train and came here?" Olivia asked.

"As fast as I could," said Walter. "Since the middle of July I did not have any information about Florence and I was heartsick. This beautiful woman has been the only thing on my mind since we parted and I went to the hospital in Harrisburg. As soon as I saw the address, I knew just what I would do. Since I had been discharged from the army, I really had nothing to hold me back and I intend to stay by Florence as long as she will have me, maybe forever."

By now, Florence looked tired. Olivia said, "Florence needs to lie down. Lets help her get up and walk to her bed." Florence held out her right hand for Walter to hold on while she stood up. Florence made no attempt to raise her left arm. Walter braced his feet, gently pulled and Florence slowly rose to her feet. She paused as she gained her balance. Walter moved to her right side and continued holding her right hand.

Florence slowly took a halting step with her right foot. She slowly lifted and partly drug her left foot. This process continued until Florence stood by her bed. Walter held her right hand as she turned enough so she was backed up to the bed. She proceeded to sit down on the bed and continued leaning to her left. She leaned back and raised her feet on the bed. At last she was lying on her back with her head on the pillow.

"Let's leave her alone for an hour," Olivia said. Walter leaned over and kissed Florence on the forehead just as Florence reached up and held Walters arm. Walter then left the room with Olivia.

WHAT IS NEXT FOR FLORENCE

Walters mind was racing. Florence appears to be unable to easily walk and appears to need assistance. Her left arm is very weak and Florence does not appear to be able to use it. He wondered how her fractured pelvis was recovering. He was very impressed at how good Florence looks. He needs to talk to Olivia.

Olivia told Walter, "Let's take a walk." Out the door they went and walked to the right on the Harrisburg Pike.

"You have had a chance to observe Florence," Olivia told Walter. "Her walking is improving but her left leg is slow to improve."

"What does the doctor recommend about therapy?"

"This doctor is reluctant to start therapy on Florence's left leg or left arm. He wants the pelvis to be fully healed before any therapy begins. He thinks possibly in about one or two weeks. Florence got the cast off her left leg last week. I can tell you that she is much improved over her condition two months ago, just after the accident."

"How have her spirits been?" asked Walter hopefully.

"Greatly improved lately. Getting the cast off her leg and her ribs healing up have been a huge help. I can tell having you here will be a big boost for her morale."

"Is she in much pain?" asked Walter.

"She still hurts in her pelvis but compared with the pain in the beginning it is much reduced. By the time I arrived she still cried from pain anytime she was moved or if she tried to move on her own."

"Today is September 25, 1863. What day did you get here?" asked Walter.

"August 9th or 10th. I got a letter from a nurse on August 4th or 5th and I knew I had to leave immediately to go to Florence. When I arrived and saw her I was shocked. The poor girl had her leg in a cast and it was elevated. Her pelvis was tightly wrapped and she was restricted from any motion. Her ribs were also tightly bound. She had a big bruise on her left arm, left shoulder and on the left side of her head. The other two girls were very seriously hurt too. As you can see this is a makeshift hospital as the real hospital got destroyed in the tornado."

"Where do you stay?" asked Walter.

"I stay right in Florence's room. I sleep in a chair and I help prepare food, clean, make beds and, of course, take care of Florence. It has been very hard for Florence and I am not saying it has been easy for me. Compared to when I got here, things are much improved for Florence and her friends."

"What about your sister? Where does she live?" asked Walter.

"Azalea lives about five blocks from here. She rents an up-stairs of a friends house. Not the best situation but the tornado destroyed her house and nearly everything in it. Azalea was able to get into the root cellar under her house and survived unhurt, however she was trapped there for about half a day. The tornado killed about fifty people and injured another hundred. That part of town was severely damaged.

"With so many men away at war there is very little re-building going on. Things have not been easy for Chambersburg lately. Before Gettysburg, apparently some Confederate troops were here procuring food and horses. Azalea didn't think it was the main body of the Confederate troops. She said it was scary seeing those Confederate troops moving on their streets and pounding on certain doors demanding food. Most people got indoors and locked the doors. Azalea said the sight of the soldiers dressed in gray and carrying rifles was scary. They looked dangerous, like hungry, invading migrants."

"How are Rebecca and Beatrice progressing,?" asked Walter.

"Both girls are getting close to being discharged. The doctor is amazed at how well and how quickly all three women have healed considering the severity of their injuries," said Olivia.

Walter and Olivia returned to the hospital.

"It is time to get Florence up and moved back to her chair. If you will do that I will help prepare supper," said Olivia.

Walter went to Florence's room and found her awake. He leaned over her and looked into her eyes.

"Did you sleep, Florence?" he asked.

"Yes, I just woke up and I am ready to move to the chair in the hallway."

"What do you want me to do?" asked Walter.

"Swing my legs to the edge of the bed, take my right hand and pull me up and swing my legs off the bed. Step back and take both hands and let me pull myself upright. Take my right hand, let me stand for a moment. Then lead the way."

Walter carefully led Florence to the chair in the hallway. He thought she was moving the left leg better than he had seen previously. Florence wanted to walk a few steps past the chair, rest and return to the chair. Walter positioned Florence in front of the chair. He held her left hand as she reached for the arm of the chair with her right hand. She settled on to the chair, looked at Walter and smiled that same beautiful smile that he saw when he awoke at Gettysburg.

About then Charles walked up and Walter introduced him to Florence.

"I can see why Walter came from Wisconsin to find you," said Charles enthusiastically.

"Have you met other people?" asked Walter.

"Yes, I have been visiting with Rebecca and we went for a short walk. Her mother and a sister are on the way from Oshkosh, Wisconsin. Her shoulder and jaw are nearly healed. Her kidney has healed but she still has trouble with the problems caused by the concussion. Her spirits are good and she is hoping she can go home with her mother and sister. She is very anxious to see them."

143

Olivia returned from helping prepare supper. Walter and Charles walked outside as Walter wanted to find out what Charles had in mind. They agreed to share a hotel room and in a couple days or so Charles wanted to go to Gettysburg. Walter wanted to go with Charles to see the battlefield where so many Americans had died. That was fine with Charles as he was happy to visit with Rebecca until her mother and sister arrived.

Mrs. VanDenHuvel and her sister stepped outside so Walter and Charles visited with them. Beatrice was doing surprisingly well. She still has occasional periods where her memory fails her. The skull fracture is apparently healed. She recently got the casts off both legs, and is able to walk, getting stronger each day. They both were planning to sleep in Beatrice's room.

Olivia brought a tray of supper for Florence. She set it on a small folding table that would fit over the chair arms. Olivia stayed with Florence. Walter and Charles got directions to a hotel nearby. They went there and secured a room. Both men stowed their luggage in the room. Walter kept the pistol in his belt covered by his jacket. Chambersburg showed signs of being a prosperous town but the tornado and the war were both having a negative affect. He knew he could be a target with vigilantes looking for draft dodgers and deserters. He didn't intend to be intimidated by any vigilantes but he planned to be careful. Walter and Charles ate at the hotel and then went back to the hospital.

Walter and Olivia sat near Florence and visited. Both of the ladies wanted to know more about Walter's life since Gettysburg. He described his mother, father, Erna, Royce, Ernest and Bertha. He told about Royce wanting to take a walk in the families huge forest and the incident with the huge bull elk. Both ladies had heard the elk bugle when they lived at the lake home. They saw tracks but never saw any elk.

Both ladies were surprised to learn that Walter lived in Philadelphia until Walter was twelve years old. He explained that his mothers parents, the Millers, owned much property in Philadelphia and had bought that very large tract of land north of Antigo around 1839. They were killed in a train wreck and Walter's mother inherited the land. He told that his father was trained as an engineer and had developed a small flooring company but he plans to establish a large sawmill and milling equipment to produce large amounts of flooring. He is about to build a railroad track to the location of the mill. A company from Madison is going to build it. Your neighbor, Antoinette, said your husband's uncle used to live in Sparta and your husband visited him when he was young. Apparently this man moved to Madison and formed a company to build railroad tracks.

"Jack Sanders is my husbands uncle," Olivia said, "and he moved to Madison."

"My father is going to ask the men who are going to build the railroad spur to his mill if they know anyone who used to live in Sparta. I thought that man might know where Florence was. It was a desperate long shot," said Walter downheartedly.

"You were desperate to find out where Florence was. We both admire your determination and I can tell you that we both feel that you will be wonderful help so Florence can recover and go home."

Olivia left to attend to duties in the kitchen part of the make-shift hospital. Walter located his chair so he could sit in front and to the right of Florence. He held her right hand and they both looked into the others eyes. Their smiling faces revealed a deep happiness to finally be together since Gettysburg.

Florence said in a slow halting voice, "I have been hurt so badly that I really could not think of anything. My mind was numb but I am now doing much better. I do remember most of what you and I felt for each other at Gettysburg. Seeing you and hearing your strong voice has helped me to remember."

Walter noticed those few words required a great concentration and effort. Florence seemed to be searching for the

145

correct word and did a fine job on that account but it took her much more time to say those words.

"Florence, you are doing just fine with your words. Let's keep talking so your mind can learn again. I thought about you so much I realize that I must love you," said Walter lovingly.

Walter leaned toward Florence and she leaned toward him and they kissed. Their first kiss! Walter's heart fluttered and he felt his face flush. Florence also felt her heart flutter and felt her face flush. They both were a bit embarrassed but Walter moved in for a repeat performance. This passionate kiss left both a little short of breath but Walter, at least, thought it was the most wonderful feeling he had ever experienced.

Walter and Florence regained their composure. Walter asked Florence questions about her life to get her to talk about herself but also to get practice speaking. Her responses were slow and Walter found himself wanting to help Florence say words at a faster rate. Her pronunciation and use of words was accurate, just slow. Olivia returned and announced it was time for bed. Walter kissed Florence good night and squeezed her hand. They looked into each others eyes as Walter bent over her.

"Thanks for coming to me," said Florence is her slow halting voice.

Walter went looking for Charles and they headed for the hotel. Just outside the hotel a group of four men approached.

"We have been organized to find draft dodgers and deserters. Are you either of them?" asked an older man.

"I am too old," Charles said, "and have been rejected by authorities in Toledo."

"How about you?" asked the man, indicating Walter. Walter didn't like what these men represented but he didn't want any trouble.

"I served for two years with the 6th Wisconsin and was discharged a few days ago," said Walter.

146

"We have heard stories like that before, got any proof?" Walter reached into his pocket, being careful not to show the handle of the pistol. He unfolded the paper and held it in front of the spokesman.

"This is my discharge document. You may look at it but I will not let it out of my hand," said Walter emphatically.

The men gathered around and studied the document in Walter's hand.

"6th Wisconsin? Aren't you part of the Iron Brigade that charged the Confederates and captured several hundred?" asked an older, distinguished man.

"Yes, we did that. If you look at who signed that document you will find Lt. Col. Rufus Dawes name. He was the Commander of the 6th Wisconsin and was a tremendous leader," replied Walter.

"Why are you in Chambersburg?" asked a younger man in the group.

Walter explained being injured and how Florence had saved his life. Florence and two friends were severely injured and now Walter has finally found her. He will stay with her until she is healed. The attitude of the group changed abruptly. They thanked Walter for his service and shook hands. Walter and Charles continued on to the hotel.

THE NEXT DAY

Walter and Charles finished breakfast and left the hotel. The sky was clear and the air had a chill to it as fall was underway. Looking around at the trees, some were showing good color. The two men wanted to see the tornado damaged part of town. It was only a few blocks away and it was very apparent. The devastation was terrible. The path was from west to east and about halfway into the city The tornado lifted and damage was minimum after that.

Walter wanted to find Azalea's house or lot if possible. The sign post for Evergreen Street was visible. They walked down the street looking for any clues, like house numbers on boards strewed around. It was useless. They were about to give up when Walter spotted a root cellar with damaged boards near the opening. The two men studied the remains of the house. Only the first floor remained. The entire house was gone and the floor was covered with boards, broken furniture, clothing, paper and was a genuine mess. Very likely the mess they were looking at was from other homes that were destroyed. The path was about two hundred feet wide and other than that the houses seems to be only slightly damaged. In fact most seemed inhabitable.

Very little effort had been made to reconstruct the ruined homes. In fact there was very little evidence of any clean up effort. Both men pondered why. They finally concluded that with so many men off at war this would be hard work for the women to do. Walter wondered if Azalea would rebuild her house. He also wondered what Olivia and Florence would do for the winter. He should visit with Olivia to see if she has plans.

The men returned to the hospital. Charles went to Rebecca's room and Walter went to Florence's room. She was dressed and ready to walk to her chair in the hallway. Walter's heart fluttered when he saw Florence.

'She is so beautiful' thought Walter. They warmly greeted and Walter helped her up and they slowly walked towards the chair. After a few steps, Walter said, "Maybe we could dance a little."

"We could try it," said Florence.

"That type of activity may be good for all your muscles since you have been fairly inactive since your accident," said Walter.

They stopped and put arms in the proper place and slowly began to sway and dance to an imaginary waltz. Surprisingly they were able to dance quite well. Florence was amazed that she could dance as well as she could. Her left leg even moved better. After about fifteen minutes, Walter suggested they take a break and Florence could rest. While resting in her chair, Olivia arrived.

"We danced," said Florence with enthusiasm.

"What a great idea. How did you do?" asked Olivia with a smile.

"I did very well. My left leg seemed to work better. We are going to dance again today. Do you know if anyone has a Victrola we could use to play waltzes on," asked Florence.

"I will inquire," replied Olivia.

Walter asked Olivia if Azalea had ever talked about re-building her house.

"She wants to rebuild but there are not enough carpenters around. Besides that, materials to build with are very scarce because of the war. This shortage of men is really hurting how we live."

Walter had wondered about offering to help Azalea rebuild but he realized that would not work. With no tools and very little in the line of building materials. He has wondered what the progress is from the doctor. He noticed that Rebecca and Charles went for a walk, apparently her family is to arrive soon and take her home to Oshkosh. They had been here earlier and spent about two weeks with her. She has healed enough to leave the hospital. Charles has enjoyed her company as she reminds him of one of his own granddaughters.

Walter has a deck of cards and he and Florence played smear and sheepshead. Florence is very skillful playing cards. She beats Walter most of the time. She can not shuffle so Walter does that but Florence can deal the cards. Walter is impressed that her mind is nimble and sharp but she struggles to speak. He wants to do everything he can to help Florence heal.

The doctor visits Florence and gives her a check up. He is pleased with things about Florence except the reluctance of her left leg and foot to act as they should. He thought the slow speech would get better. Florence inquired about dancing.

"Dancing would be a fine activity as long as you don't get too wild! Remember that pelvis is not fully healed yet. Walk several times a day and when you are doing that, swing your left arm to try to wake up the nerves. If you are going to be well enough to ride the train back to Wisconsin you need to get stronger," said the doctor.

REVISIT THE BATTLEFIELD

Charles wants to take the train to Gettysburg and look for his brothers grave. He wants Walter to go with him for moral support but also so Walter can see that terrible place when he wasn't shooting at someone and being shot at. Rebecca has gone back to Oshkosh with her family. She plans to continue her nursing program. Charles got very attached to her and he felt he was helpful to her healing.

Beatrice has also has been cleared to return to Green Bay. She left with her mother and aunt to make the long train ride home. She also was planning to finish her nursing training. Charles talked to Walter about asking Olivia and Azalea to take the trek to Gettysburg with them. Walter thought that was a good idea.

"They may not want to see the place where so many men died or were wounded, but I think they should be asked. I will do so if you want me to," answered Walter resolutely.

Walter asked Olivia and Azalea and both showed some reluctance but after thinking about it they agreed to go. Florence would be looked after by the hospital staff. She wanted to go but the doctor said no. The train left Chambersburg at 7:24 a.m. headed for York hauling coal, mail and passengers. It ran through Gettysburg and arrived there at 8:37 a.m. This same train left York and passed through Gettysburg at 4:41 p.m. on the return trip.

The four passengers boarded and they were off with different expectations of what the day held in store for each. Azalea had seen the Confederate soldiers on the streets of Chambersburg and they looked fearful and frightening to her. She had great apprehension because of how mean hearted they looked. To think this nice young man Walter faced those fierce looking men and was able to defeat them at Gettysburg was impressive to her. This thought raised the level of admiration for

151

the Union troops and Walter. She looked at him as he talked to Charles. She had come to realize that Walter had made extraordinary effort to find Florence and he was a wonderful, kind and understanding young man. She could also tell that Florence had very strong feelings for Walter and she really appreciated what he was doing to help her heal. Dancing several times a day, going for walks, doing exercises with her arm and leg, Florence hardly had time to rest.

Olivia was lost in her own thoughts as to what to expect at the battlefield. Florence was attending to wounded soldiers behind Union lines. She could hear the sound of rifle fire and on the third day at 12:30 in the afternoon the cannon fire was unbelievably loud and intense. All at once it mostly stopped. There was a relative quiet for many minutes and then the cannon fire began and a little later the rifle fire got intense. Florence said it seemed to come from the far left and the far right as well as in front of her.

Olivia didn't like the sight of blood. She could imagine the bloody fighting where so many men died or were injured. It must have been very frightening for both sides. Many must have thought their chance for survival was almost nonexistent. The thought of what she might see today made her feel sick to her stomach. She knew she must go and view the grounds where one of the worst battles in the history of civilization was fought.

Her daughter Florence was there during the last two days of the battle. She wondered what effect that has had on her. Maybe her halting speech was caused by her dealing with these men like Walter who had been severely injured. She had soldiers that were too severely injured for her or anyone to save. Watching someone die must affect someone's being.

As the train neared Gettysburg, Walter felt a strangeness that he had never felt before. It was as if what he saw didn't really exist. His mind had gone blank. What was happening? He was about to see the place he had managed to block

152

out of his memory. Now he was forcing himself to dig into his memory and his body did not want him to. He felt sick to his stomach.

The train stopped and many people stepped off. Walter had regained most of his composure. A short distance from the train station was a man with a team of horses hitched to a wagon that had been rigged so people could go up two steps at the back and enter the wagon and sit on the benches on both sides. A sign on the wagon read 'Visit the Battlefield - Donations'.

"Let's take the wagon. Maybe we can ride to the far end and then walk back. It is a long walk," stated Walter.

The wagon filled up and the driver started the team moving. After a few minutes they arrived at the breastworks and rock walls where Walter's Iron Brigade charged down and routed the Confederates and reclaimed a breastworks that happened on the second day of the battle. Walter explained what had happened and the people in the wagon were impressed. They had a Gettysburg combatant among them.

The road the wagon followed was not up by the stone wall and breastworks at all times. The driver told as much as he knew about the battle and since the battle lasted three days it was confusing as to what took place and when. The charge that the rebels made on the last day was explained by the driver.

The wagon lumbered along and Walter recognized the spot where the 6th Wisconsin Regiment waited in reserve on the third day.

"We were in reserve," Walter explained, "because we already suffered severe loses from the first two days of fighting. When the word came we rushed forward according to the plan Lt. Col. Rufus Dawes drew up. The Confederates were beginning to break through and we charged into them with fixed bayonets. That is the place where I was wounded." Tears filled Walter's eyes.

153

The battle had occurred three months before and Walter had fought back any reaction to the memories he held captive. Seeing the place where he nearly lost his life opened the flood gates of his memories. The many friends in the 6th Wisconsin killed in the savagery of fighting in Fredericksburg, Chancellorsville, Antietam, Bull Run and Gettysburg. The many men who will not return home to families, friends and communities. Those who died fighting to preserve the Union and to end slavery. Fighting for freedom but creating serious problems back home. Some people have begun to wonder if all the sacrifice is worth it and support for this effort while at times was failing was being questioned. All of this flashed in Walter's mind. He regained himself and then felt poorly of himself for showing emotions long under wraps.

The wagon continued on and the driver continued to announce locations for various brigades and regiments fought on the first, second or third day. Finally he announced we were on the south edge of cemetery ridge.

"I should get off here," said Charles. The driver stopped and all four got off the wagon.

"Thanks for your service, young man," the driver said as he offered a salute to Walter.

The group began looking for any markers identifying the 107th Ohio or any markers pushed into the ground with a soldiers name on them. In some places the soldiers bodies were laid almost side by side.

"This is terrible," said Olivia with tears streaming down her face.

Walter felt great sadness as he and Charles searched for Joe Sullivan's marker. Azalea and Olivia helped search this ridge that the Union had established breastworks and rock walls on. The ladies stood looking down toward where the Confederates would have advanced from.

"I can picture those mean looking, lean and hungry gray coats slithering closer and closer to this position. It gives some the chills thinking about how dangerous and deadly those three days were," said Azalea.

"Here he is," announced Charles. The others gathered around and stared at the marker. *'Joe Sullivan, 107th Ohio'*. Charles had tears streaming down his face. "Twenty more days and he would have been discharged," said Charles with a deep sadness in his voice.

By now the three others had gathered around Charles and put their arms around him and each other. There was a long silence as each was deep in thought.

"Got a cannonball fragment full in the chest. Killed him instantly. Left a wife and four children ages eight to sixteen. The family is on relief plus they receive a small pension from the army. The three older children have jobs as there is plenty of work. The two oldest are girls and the third is a boy of fourteen. I hope he will not have to go to war. That family has paid enough. Joe had worked in the shipyards building packet ships."

There were many other people visiting the battlefield. Walter noticed a man carried a camera. He appeared to be with a group.

"Should I see if that man could take a picture of Joe's grave site?" Walter asked Charles.

"That would be fine," replied Charles. Walter approached the man and asked if he could take a picture of the grave site.

"Joe was my brother. A picture for his family would be wonderful," said Charles. The man took the picture and Charles gave him his Toledo address. Charles gave the man money to cover the expenses for the picture and sending it through the mail.

"My brother and cousin were killed just to the north of here fighting for the 67th Pennsylvania. We live at Harrisburg and took the train here. My mother and other relatives were very reluctant to come here today, but I think they feel good getting some closure on their loved ones death," said the man with the camera.

The four continued walking north seeing many hundreds of markers for fallen soldiers. They looked down the hill and saw hundreds of markers for Confederate soldiers. They saw three Union cannons that were hit by cannon fire and apparently ruined. It was an amazing thought that about three-hundred-thousand men fought against each other in this valley in front of their view and on this very ridge they stood on.

Finally the exhausted group reached the railroad station. They went to an eatery and got some lunch. The timing was good as the train pulled in, bell clanging, shortly after eating. The group boarded and began the trip back to Chambersburg. Walter has thought about Florence during the day. It would be good if she could visit the battlefield like the group did today. Walter felt bad about not dancing with Florence and exercising her left arm today. They will do the best they can when he gets to the hospital.

On the way to Chambersburg, Walter leaned over the seat to talk to Olivia and Azalea.

"It looks like Florence is making progress toward healing. Have any plans been made when she is discharged?" asked Walter.

"Azalea and I have discussed this many times," said Olivia. "I still have the house in Sparta and we could go there. The one thing we are concerned about is that it will be winter soon and there is only a small amount of coal in the house and very little wood. With the shortage of men, it may be very difficult to keep the house warm. Azalea wants us to stay with her in her apartment, but that would be crowded. Besides it is an upstairs apartment and steps may be difficult for Florence."

The train arrived at Chambersburg and the four tired travelers stepped off. Walter and Olivia went to the hospital. Charles went to the hotel and Azalea went home. Before leaving the train they all agreed it was an emotional day but a very worthwhile, heartrending trip.

Florence eagerly waited for news of how the day went. She was happy to see the two familiar faces and listened to their impression of the day.

"What a tragedy, what a terrible ordeal," said Olivia.

After a pause, "It brought back memories I had hidden away. It was a difficult day," said Walter sadly.

Walter and Florence waltzed while Olivia prepared a meal for the three of them. Florence exercised her left leg and her left arm. Walter took Florence's hands and pulled her to her feet. He looked into her eyes and pulled her to him. They embraced in a very passionate kiss as they held each other close. Walter felt his body reacting in a way he had never experienced before. He could not let his arms release their hold on Florence. She also held Walter very tightly. They kissed again and their bodies began to sway slowly as they held each other very close.

At that moment both Florence and Walter had feelings neither had experienced before. It made them realize their bodies had other emotional needs that were responding to the very special stimulus each was giving the other. They could not hold back any longer.

MR. LINCOLN

It was the first week of November. Two weeks before, Walter had written to his parents and inquired about the possibility of Florence and Olivia coming home with him and spending the winter in his parents home. He said they could have his room and he would sleep on the divan downstairs. He would help pay for any extra expense such as food. His big point was that with such a shortage of men procuring coal or wood to heat Olivia's home in Sparta would not work. Azalea's apartment is too small and apparently there is no other option available in Chambersburg.

Walter explained that Florence needs daily therapy and Walter has been helping her with that. She plans to continue with her nursing program in the spring. Walter urged his parents to allow this to happen. He assured them that everyone would like Olivia and Florence. He told his parents that he had not talked to the two ladies about the possible plan.

The doctor visit involves having Florence perform several different exercises including visiting with Florence and asking questions that required Florence to recall information and process it correctly.

At the end of the exam the doctor declared, "Two more weeks and you can be discharged." Florence had a very big smile on her face and got up and gave the doctor a big hug, thanking him for his wonderful care for nearly four months.

Walter felt this might be the time to visit with Florence and Olivia about all three of them going to Antigo to spend the winter. He knew that as of a few days ago no plans had been made about where the two ladies would be spending the winter after the hospital stay is finished. He had received a letter from his mother telling Walter that, of course, Florence and Olivia are very welcome to stay for the winter. Everyone would be very happy to meet the ladies and they would do whatever they can to make them feel at home.

After the doctor left, Walter got his courage up and brought the subject up to both ladies.

"My family would be very happy to have both of you come and live with them at their home near Antigo," said Walter, enthusiastically. There was a long pause.

"Wow," said Florence. "Mother did you hear that."

"I did indeed," said Olivia. "That is a very generous offer. It is all so sudden. We will have to think about some loose ends that need to be tied up."

"I would need to stop in my apartment in Madison and get my clothes and things," said Florence. "It would be great to visit my classmates at the University," she added.

"I need to stop at my bank in Madison," said Walter. "I also need to buy some winter clothes."

"We should go to Sparta to be sure the house is alright for the winter. I may move back there in the spring," said Olivia matter-of-factly.

"Sounds like you are thinking about coming to Antigo with me," said Walter happily.

Charles is still living at the hotel. He and Walter have become very good friends. He plans to visit Walter at Antigo once the new flooring mill is built. He reads the newspaper out of Harrisburg and he excitedly announced one day, "Mr. Lincoln is coming to Gettysburg November 19th. I am going to see him." Walter heard the news and it stopped him in his tracks as he processed the date.

"I want to go with you. I will tell Florence and Olivia and see if they want to come with us. I think the doctor will release Florence about then."

Walter immediately went to the hospital and relayed the news about Mr. Lincoln coming to Gettysburg. They were both excited about going to see him speak. Florence had a downcast look.

"I hope the doctor will give his approval to go to Gettysburg. I really want to hear what Mr. Lincoln has to say," Florence said excitedly.

"I will seek out the doctor," said Olivia, "and see if he thinks Florence can withstand the trip to Gettysburg."

The doctor thought Florence would be able to make the trip.

"After all, being able to see and hear the President in these trying and terrible times is a special event. I hope my wife and I can go too."

"We will buy you and your wife train tickets," said Olivia.

When Walter heard the good news from Olivia, he kissed Florence and went to find Charles. They needed to buy train tickets as soon as possible. Olivia told Walter to buy a ticket for Azalea as she was certain that she would also want to go. Charles agreed and off the two of them went to the train station.

"Seven tickets for Gettysburg on November 19th," Charles announced to the ticket agent.

"What is the big event?" asked the ticket agent.

"Mr. Lincoln is coming to Gettysburg to speak," replied Walter.

"That is a big event and I will be busy," added the agent.

The morning of November 19th dawned and it found Florence, Olivia, Azalea, the doctor and his wife, Charles and Walter at the train station well ahead of the 7:24 a.m. departure time. There was a crowd! Extra cars were added and there would be no coal cars today. The train pulled in with its bell clanging. The group of seven found seats and were relieved to be able to sit. More and more people boarded the car. Apparently many standing room tickets were sold. Walter offered his seat to a middle-aged lady. The train finally began rolling. The car was crowded and noisy as most people felt that this was a historic day in a very significant event in the history of this young country.

People had mixed feelings about Mr. Lincoln. The war had not gone well and many people blamed Mr. Lincoln for not being able to quell the fighting in Congress. Some felt his choice of Generals was faulty. Many people wanted the Union to seek a truce with the Confederates. This idea was firmly rejected by Mr. Lincoln. That further infuriated a large number of people. The Emancipation Proclamation further agitated other people. In short, Mr. Lincoln was having a tough go of things. But he was respected for his honesty, determination and sincerity of having one Union, The United States of America.

On the train ride to Gettysburg many conversations could be heard.

"I wonder why Lincoln is coming to Gettysburg? To apologize for fifty thousand troops dead or injured?"

"President Lincoln might be here to announce that many of our men will be coming home soon."

"Lincoln just wanted to get away from the mess in Washington."

"I hate the guy but I want to hear what he has to say, after all he is the President."

"I don't think he is going to find many slaves to free in Gettysburg."

Walter kept his feelings to himself, however he did admire Mr. Lincoln as a man that our young country needs at this time. If the states were united under one constitution, each state would be responsible for governing itself within the framework of the constitution. He truly felt that no person should be a slave and Walter definitely agreed with that. Walter looked on Mr. Lincoln as his hero. He hoped to get close to this man today and at least tell him 'hello'. He really doubted that he had much of a chance of doing that, but he was hopeful.

The lady that Walter gave up his seat to found Florence a very easy person to talk to. She was going to Gettysburg to pay her humble respects to the thousands of soldiers in that horrible battle. She had not lost any of her family members, but one of her sons fought there as a member of the Pennsylvania reserves. His brigade was held in reserve and was only called into action on the third day as the Confederates were about to breach Union lines.

Florence was excited. This was the first time she had been around a crowd of people since she was injured. She got caught up in the excitement of the crowd. Many were unsure of what to expect today. Newspapers talked about a parade, gun salutes and speeches. One by Mr. Everett, a well know orator and Mr. Lincoln was to deliver a speech receiving and dedicating the ground which was to be a national shrine.

The train arrived at 8:37 a.m. and everyone left the cars. The parade would be from the Town of Gettysburg to the newly laid out battlefield cemetery. A raised platform was constructed and a speakers podium was present. Walter and the group made their way to the area close to the speakers platform. The crowd was very large, ten to twelve thousand people. Most had come to see where their loved ones had died and hopefully find their grave. Union soldiers were being reburied in the new battlefield cemetery.

The crush of people made movement slow. It was a bright and sunny day, but it was chilly. Being November many people had heavy top coats on which also restricted movement. Walter led the way as he made his way toward the speakers platform. When he was about seventy-five feet away from the platform, he suddenly saw a tall black stove-pipe hat about twenty feet away. It was Mr. Lincoln!!!

Walter could barely contain himself. He held Florence's hand while he pushed toward Mr. Lincoln. Finally, he was there. Several government men surrounded the President. That did not deter Walter.

"Mr. President, could I please shake your hand?" pleaded Walter. This great man had a thin face with many lines and with his black beard looked at Walter with his intense, searching gaze.

"Of course, young man," said Mr. Lincoln. "Let this man and his lady friend come to me."

Walter and Florence moved close to Mr. Lincoln and Walter extended his hand to this tall and very impressive man.

"Walter Rounds, 6th Wisconsin Regiment, Iron Brigade." Walter guided Florence so she could shake hands, if she desired. She shook hands and told the President her name.

"Walter, you have an excellent eye for beauty. This young lady obviously means a great deal to you. Why is that?" asked the President.

"I was injured on the third day a short distance from here. I was unconscious for three days and when I awoke this beautiful nurse was tending to me. She saved my life," said Walter, enthusiastically.

"6th Wisconsin, you are the soldiers who charged into the Confederates and captured many on the first day. My Generals have very high regard for all Wisconsin regiments," added Mr. Lincoln.

"Mr. President, I want to tell you to continue on the path you have laid out for the people of this country. Your burden is heavy and you face many obstacles but you must continue. Thank you for your service, Sir," Walter proudly stated.

"Walter, it is I who must thank you for your service, thank you, Sir," said the President as he extended his hand to Walter then to Florence.

"Thank you for your service, Florence, and also for saving this mans life."

"Florence and I and many others are anxiously awaiting your words," said Walter.

Walter and Florence looked around searching for Olivia and the others. Finally they were found a few feet away. They slowly made their way to where Florence and Walter stood.

"Did you speak to the President?" asked Olivia excitedly.

"We shook hands and spoke to Mr. Lincoln," responded Florence enthusiastically. "He is a very impressive man. He has intense searching eyes and he is so tall, especially with the stove pipe hat on."

The group was excited for Walter and Florence. Much back slapping and hugs took place.

"I can see why you were such a great soldier. You saw what you wanted and you went and did it," said Charles with a congratulatory tone in his voice.

About that time, one of the men surrounding Mr. Lincoln approached and spoke to Walter.

"Sir, the President has asked me to obtain your name and address and that of your lady friend." Shocked, Walter stood with his mouth open.

"Of course." Walter stuttered, unable to understand why. The man wrote down the names and addresses and was gone. He offered no explanation of why Mr. Lincoln wanted that information. Walter happily noted that Florence listed her address as the same as Walter's at his parents home near Antigo, Wisconsin.

The parade participants arrived at the grounds where the speakers platform was located. The first speaker told how work on the cemetery was progressing. Soldiers were being interred in their new location as fast as possible, however, work was far from complete.

Edward Everett, a famous orator of the time was the main speaker. He spoke for nearly two hours and the people assembled grew restless, got colder and were happy when Mr. Everett was finished speaking. President Lincoln was introduced and began speaking in a high pitched voice. Only the people relatively close to the speakers platform could hear what any of the speakers said.

Walter and the group could hear Mr. Lincoln just fine. They hung on every word and in about two minutes he was finished and returned to his seat. The audience realized that he had finished his very carefully prepared speech. Walter, Florence and those around began applauding. The applause grew louder and more intense, whistling and shouting added to the overpowering sound of appreciation for the words spoken by Mr. Lincoln.

Those that heard Mr. Lincoln's speech, realized a powerful message was delivered at a time that it was indeed needed. People looked at each other with mouths open and looks of 'that was some speech'.

Slowly, the crowd began to disassemble, many went to look for resting places of loved ones, others took in the panorama of the immediate battlefield. Olivia had packed some sandwiches so the group found benches and sat down and ate.

"I wish I could remember what Mr. Lincoln said in his speech," said Azalea wistfully.

"I can remember all of it, every word of it," said Florence. *Four score and seven years ago our Fathers brought forth, upon this continent, a new nation, conceived in liberty, and dedicated to the proposition that all men are created equal.* Florence continued repeating the entire address. The last few words were repeated at Walters request. *From these honored dead we take increased devotion to that cause for which they gave the last full measure of devotion - that we here highly resolve that these dead shall not have died in vain - that this nation, under God, shall have a new birth of freedom - and that government of the people, by the people, for the people, shall not perish from the earth.*

The group made their way back to the train. Florence was beginning to tire. She had done amazingly well up to that point.

Walter said, "Hop on, I will give you a piggyback ride." Florence happily hopped on Walter's offered back. "Giddy-up." Walter galloped a few steps following Florence's request.

Slowly, the group moved closer to the train. Finally they reached the train and climbed into the same car they arrived in. Several people were already in the car. An older woman spoke as Walter came down the aisle.

"I saw you, hobnobbing with the President. Do you know him or something?" asked the lady.

"I don't know him any better than you do. He was elected by us to be the President of this young country. I admire him for what he is trying to do under very trying conditions. I fully support him and I wanted to tell him that," said Walter matter-of-factly.

"Well, you don't have to get all huffy about it. I was just jealous and wished I could have done what you did. You are young and I am old. You are the hope of this country and I am like yesterdays mail," said the lady with a mischievous smile.

"Margaret Poullette, State Senator, District 8, State of Pennsylvania," said the distinguished lady.

"I heard you mention the 6th Wisconsin. Are you from Wisconsin now?" asked Margaret.

"I have been in Chambersburg for about the past two months but I am about to leave and return to Wisconsin."

"Why not stay in Pennsylvania, we need young people with courage and it looks like you have plenty of that," said Margaret.

"Are you planning to run for a United States Senator any time soon?" asked Walter inquiringly.

"I have thought about it, but I can do good things for the people in my district if I remain a State Senator. Of course, I need to get elected and that is no small task. There is always opposition and the lies they can tell. It is disgusting but that is the way the game is played," Margret replied with a twinkle in her eye.

Walter could tell this lady was a high quality person and most likely did a good job of developing legislation to help the people in her district.

"One last thing. Some day I hope you decide to be part of what Mr. Lincoln said today, Government of the people, by the people and for the people. May I remind you to never, never back down from what you stand for. Your greatest asset is your reputation. It looks like you are off to a fast start in your quest to do good for mankind."

LEAVING CHAMBERSBURG

The train pulled into Chambersburg and everyone stepped down. Walter and the group met for a few minutes on the platform. The doctor and his wife thanked all of them for the invitation and great company on the trip to Gettysburg. He pronounced Florence completely healed and could leave the hospital.

Walter walked Florence and Olivia to the hospital. On the way, Walter gently asked if the ladies knew where they wanted to spend the winter.

"With you," said Florence.

"Do you agree, Olivia?" asked Walter hopefully.

"Yes, I do, if you are sure it is alright with your parents," answered Olivia.

"I am sure it is alright. They will be very happy to meet both of you and to have you stay with them for the winter," said Walter emphatically.

Plans were made to leave for Madison the next morning, as the train leaves Chambersburg at 8:43 a.m. That means Olivia and Florence need to pack up all their possessions. Walter and Charles could help get it to the train station.

Walter returned after supper and helped Florence pack. She and Olivia would eat breakfast and then Walter and Charles would carry the valises and two boxes of Florence's things to the train station. Olivia had about the same amount of baggage and Walter and Charles would carry that to the station also. Walter and Charles' baggage would be the last to go.

Morning arrived with plenty of excitement. Florence was leaving her home of the last four months. She was very thankful that she was healthy again. Olivia was very happy for Florence and was looking forward to meeting Walter's family and living with them for the winter. Expenses at the hospital and hotel were paid. The four people met at the train station and Azalea was there too. Finally the train pulled in, baggage was loaded and the four climbed aboard after goodbyes. Florence and Olivia both had mixed feelings as the train left Chambersburg behind. Thankfulness and happiness were words to describe their feelings. Florence still could not comprehend that Walter found out where he thought she was, dropped everything to come to her. What a wonderful guy!

Shortly after the train left, Walter produced some paper and pencil and asked Florence to repeat the speech that Mr. Lincoln gave yesterday. He would write it down and put it into his rucksack right along with the copy of the United States Constitution.

"Why do you carry a copy with you?" asked Florence.

"Because Mr. McBeth, my history teacher from Antigo, made us make an abbreviated copy so we would always have it. We studied all the amendments and debated many. The right of free speech was a real stickler. We got so involved that at times we shouted at each other. In the end we came to realize that the 'framers of the constitution' were very astute when they battled it out forming the Constitution. It is a wonderful document for all of us to live by."

"The Constitution is a well thought out document," said Olivia. "Walter, you seem to be very patriotic. Did that come from fighting in the war?"

"Partly. My mother was raised in a family that respected and upheld the Government of the United States. Remember that I lived in Philadelphia until age twelve. Mother's parents, Grandfather and Grandmother Miller seemed very interested in what went on in government. On two occasions they took Mother, Erna, Royce and me to visit Independence Hall.

"The first time Grandfather took great pains to explain how representatives of the thirteen colonies met and eventually agreed on a Declaration of Independence and the Constitution of the United States," explained Walter.

"You mean to say you visited the hall where both those documents were written?" asked Florence.

"Absolutely. The men met and worked in the *assembly room*. My grandparents were very knowledgeable about the entire process. They seemed to really understand the problems that needed to be overcome," said Walter.

"Wasn't the Liberty Bell part of Independence Hall?" Charles asked.

"Yes it was. When we visited, it was in the belfry, but because it was cracked it was not rung anymore. It did have a very important inscription on it that Grandmother Miller insisted that we commit to memory. *Proclaim Liberty throughout all the Land, unto all the inhabitants thereof.* We had to write it and recite it for Grandmother Miller," was Walters proud reply.

"I had heard that the famous inscription on the Liberty Bell was taken as a strong message by the abolitionists wishing to end slavery," Olivia said.

"Grandfather Miller took us to Independence Hall for some special event. I don't remember what it was, but it was held in the room used by 'fugitive slave trials'. That was not why we went there. While there, Grandfather showed us instruments used by surveyors Mason and Dixon, to establish the Mason-Dixon line between Pennsylvania and Maryland."

"I think I just got the answer to the question I asked earlier," added Olivia.

The train rolled on toward Pittsburgh. The day was clear and the bright sun showed on the November landscape as the train passed through it. Walter felt happy to be headed for home. He was especially happy that Florence and Olivia would spend the winter with him and his family. Walter was very thankful that his feelings toward Florence were as strong as when he was recovering at Gettysburg. He was thankful that Florence appears to be completely healed. Her slow speech was back to normal and apparently her mental capacity was like it was before the accident.

Florence could tell Walter was very happy to be with her. She admired his determination to find her and once he did he worked tirelessly to help her heal. She had great admiration for this young, energetic and caring man she loved.

"Pittsburgh, Pittsburgh, thirty minute layover," shouted the conductor. The train stopped and the four travelers stepped down. Walter and Charles went to the baggage car to claim baggage for the group. It was early evening and the tired travelers headed for a nearby hotel and booked rooms. They met in the hotel dining room at 7:00 p.m.

Once seated, Charles made a proposal.

"I would like to buy dinner for everyone. This is my last evening being with the three of you. You are like family to me. I am going to miss all of you and hope to see you again sometime." Walter noticed a slight glisten in Charles eyes and he reached out and put his hand on his elderly friends arm and smiled.

"We will miss you also," the other three said in unison.

The meal arrived and everyone was in a relaxed happy mood.

"Meeting President Lincoln and hearing his powerful speech is something I will remember all of my life," recalled Florence. "When we have children, it will be a great honor to tell them that we personally met President Lincoln and heard his amazing speech at Gettysburg. I am sure history will call it one of the greatest speeches anyone has ever made."

"I entirely agree with you, Florence," Charles added, "and I am very happy to find my brothers grave. It gives me closure in my old age. The picture that the photographer will send will help Joe's family also. It was especially meaningful to have the two of you, and Azalea with me when we discovered Joe's grave. I felt the strength flowing from you as I stood over Joe's grave remembering things we did together. Death is so final. Joe and thousands of other brave men who died did what President Lincoln said, 'They consecrated this land.' We must see that these men have not died in vain."

Charles was silent, as was the rest of the group. This elderly man was very wise and had powerful emotions and feelings that he didn't wear on his shirt sleeve.

After supper, Walter inquired if there was a Pittsburgh newspaper for sale.

"They went like hotcakes," the hotel desk clerk said, "but the newspaper promised to print more copies of this mornings paper and include it with tomorrows paper. It should be here by 5:30 a.m." Walter thanked the clerk and asked.

"Did the paper cover President Lincoln's speech at Gettysburg?"

"It certainly did, and it was apparently some speech," answered the clerk.

"I heard it and it indeed was a powerful speech," said Walter.

November 21, 1863, the group of four climbed aboard the train bound for Chicago by way of Toledo. True to the agents word, today's paper arrived at 5:30 a.m. along with a complimentary copy of yesterdays paper. It contained a picture of the President in the crowd greeting people. Walter and Florence looked at the picture of this very distinguished tall man with his black stove pipe hat. They looked close and both exclaimed at once, "That's us!" Sure enough the picture showed the President shaking Florence's hand with Walter right beside her. The caption read, *President Lincoln greets some of the huge crowd at Gettysburg.*

There was another picture of the orator Edward Everett and a large picture of the President giving his speech. Under the picture was the text of the Presidents speech as close as the reporter could duplicate it. The commentary on the speech followed. It told about *Mr. Everett's two hour long speech that most people had given up on even though it was a great speech, just too long. President Lincoln got up to speak and in two minutes he sat down again. The crowd was stunned. In those two minutes, the crowd of up to twelve thousand people heard one of the most powerful speeches of all time. In a short time after his speech, members of the audience who had heard his speech, many could not because of the size of the crowd, realized what they had heard and began to applaud, louder and louder with whistles and shouts. Below is a facsimile of President Lincoln's speech.* The reporter did a credible job of reporting President Lincoln's address at Gettysburg.

"Someday after the war," Walter told Florence, "we will visit Philadelphia and Independence Hall. If possible we will go to Washington, D. C."

"You seem certain that we will be together for a long time," said Florence with a twinkle in her eye.

"A guy can dream, can't he," said Walter as he put his arm around Florence.

"You need to be careful. There might be someone else," said Florence, with a nod of her head as she shyly looked at Walter.

"Bring him on. I will battle to the death. Oops. That is going to far if I die. Anyway, any challenger for your attention will have a serious fight on his hands. I would not let you go without fighting for you," said a boasting Walter with a big smile on his face.

"That is pretty big talk. Any plans to back that claim to me that you want to share?" said Florence as she leaned closer to Walter and smiled.

"A few years ago my father told me to always respect girls and ladies and don't ever push them into doing something," said Walter with a serious tone in his voice.

"Your father sounds like a very wise man. I am looking forward to meeting him. You have been a perfect gentleman around me and I am confident our friendship will continue," said Florence with a serious tone in her voice.

"I love you," Walter whispered. "You haven't known me for very long. I want you to be sure about me. I know I don't have any doubts about you. I want to prove my love for you everyday for as long as it takes to make you feel that I am the one for you." Walter gave Florence an extra tug on her shoulder and pulled her towards him.

Olivia, sitting behind these two love birds had overheard much of their conversation. She smiled to herself and thought, 'what a gentleman. Florence you are indeed a lucky girl.'

"Toledo, Toledo. Twenty minute layover," sang out the conductor.

"Well, this is where I get off," said Charles. "It has been a real pleasure to meet all of you and to invite me to travel with you. You have been a kind, friendly family for me. Walter, send me a letter when your father and your siblings get that big mill running. I want to come and see it and meet your family. Maybe you will have a bride by then," as he winked at Florence.

Goodbyes were said and Charles retrieved his luggage from the baggage car. Charles stood on the platform and waved as the train began moving, heading for Chicago. Florence went and sat with Olivia at Walter's urging, suggesting an empty seat by a lady might invite an unwanted guest.

"Besides, I doubt if anyone would bother me," said Walter.

Walter settled in and watched the Ohio landscape roll by. It gave him time to reflect back on the past two years with the 6th Wisconsin Regiment. With winter coming on it brought back memories of the past two winters, both spent in Virginia where winters were not as hard as he experienced at Antigo, but never the less they were cold and miserable. Cold rain was the worst. It stole your body heat and turned the ground to mud. That kind of weather caused great sickness with the troops and many Civil War soldiers died without ever seeing combat.

Walter was impressed how poorly some regiments were prepared for bad weather. Lt. Col. Dawes insisted on preparing campsites that were organized to keep men out of the mud and as dry as possible. He realized that disease, despair and being uncomfortable was more of a dangerous enemy than the Confederates. On many occasions the 6th Wisconsin did seek shelter in barns and buildings during inclement weather.

Of Walter's two year stint, the 6th Wisconsin only fought in five big battles. There were many skirmishes with scout parties. Serving picket duty was dangerous, lonely and could be deadly. Both sides had snipers that could shoot from a great distance and pickets were an easy target. The enemy could make the shot and easily slip away. Walter was shot at three times while on picket duty. He took great pains to select a position that offered protection but allowed a good view of the surrounding countryside assigned to be watched over.

One occasion he was beside a boulder with a fallen log leaned up against it. Walter hunkered down with his body behind the log and also behind the boulder. He scanned the area and used a spy glass to inspect anything suspicious. All at once, a bullet struck the tree trunk very near him. Walter could tell the shot came from his right so he got behind the boulder and peeked out, searching for the shooter. As he scanned the hill across the valley he saw a puff of smoke from a gun shot. He ducked down behind the boulder, a split second before the bullet hit the boulder.

Walter knew it would be safe to look above the boulder and try to spot the shooter and return fire. He located the spot where he saw the puff of smoke. He used the spy glass and he found the shooter busily reloading his long rifle. Walter adjusted his sight, leaned over the boulder and fired. Amazingly, Walters shot hit the Confederate, but did not kill him. Walter saw the man limping as he went up toward the top of the hill. Walter reloaded and was going to try another shot but his target was in a very thick grove of trees and the distance was about five hundred yards, so Walter did not shoot.

The other two times he was shot at, Walter was in a thick stand of trees and the shooter hit trees instead of Walter. Because it was so thick, Walter could not locate the shooter. He maneuvered around so he had a large tree to hide behind.

Leaving your picket location or coming to it were dangerous times as you were unprotected while you moved. Walter moved like a stealthy Indian, rarely giving any shooter anything but a fleeting shot. This kind of movement was insisted on by Commander Dawes. Walter smiled to himself as he thought about how Commander Dawes instructed his troops about how things were done and insisted on precise performance.

Pickets were established around the campsite to warn if enemy troops were advancing on the main body. Both armies generally knew where the other troops were, but deception was widely used. One trick used by the Confederates in a different battle was to make some hasty breastworks, take some wagon wheels and axles and lay logs that were painted black over the axle to look like cannons. The Union troops saw the cannons and didn't advance. The Confederates left a few token soldiers behind to show themselves occasionally and fire their rifles at the Union troops. The Union troops held their position for two days. Meanwhile, the main body of the Confederates had a two day head start once the ruse was finally discovered.

Walter thought back about the terrain that the 6th Wisconsin fought in and traveled through for his two years of his enlistment. Parts of Virginia and West Virginia were mountainous but covered with trees. Travel was generally in the valleys which meant a river of some size ran in the valley. The Rappahannock, Potomac and Shenandoah were the big rivers and crossing them required using boats, crossing on bridges or even railroad bridges. The 6th Wisconsin fought in Maryland and traveled in it and it was less mountainous. Once the 6th Wisconsin was commissioned it remained in Virginia, West Virginia, Maryland and Pennsylvania during Walter's enlistment.

The train rolled closer to Chicago. At last it slowed and passed through Gary, Indiana. Smoke from the steel mills was very prevalent. Even a blast of sparks from the blast furnace could be seen. Walter wondered if there was enough manpower to produce and deliver enough iron and steel needed during these war years.

The train pulled into the Chicago station and it was nearly dark. Walter inquired as to when the train to Madison left. "9:12 a.m." replied the ticket agent. Walter purchased three tickets. He had collected all the baggage as they were headed for a nearby hotel. Rooms were reserved and plans to meet at the hotel dining room were made. Supper was eaten and coffee and tea were served.

"What are the plans when we get to Madison?" inquired Walter curiously.

"I would like very much to visit the University Nursing School and see some of my nurse friends," said Florence. "I hope Rebecca and Beatrice are able to be back in the program. If would be nice if we could meet at a restaurant and catch up with everyone. I also need to go to my apartment and get my belongings."

Walter and Olivia both noted the excitement in Florence's voice. They both knew the tremendous ordeal she had been through and now she was happily looking forward to seeing her nursing school friends and visit the familiar surroundings of the University Hospital.

Florence was intending to continue her nursing training. Some reservations had crept in as she was concerned if she had recovered from her injuries to carry out the rigors of the nursing program.

ON TO MADISON

The next morning, November 22, 1863, the threesome arrived at the train station and found the train to Madison. Walter took the luggage and boxes to the baggage car. They boarded at 9:12 a.m. The engineer gave a short blast on the whistle and they slowly left the station. The train moved past manufacturing facilities. A spur of the railroad led to a distant slaughterhouse. Several cattle cars were on the track leading to the facility. Pens with cattle and hogs were barely visible. It was apparent that this was a major meat processing city. Apparently animals from Iowa, Illinois, Indiana and Wisconsin are processed at this giant stockyard.

Finally, the train was out of the city and headed north toward Wisconsin. All three riders were deep in their own thoughts. Florence reflected back on her terrible accident when Rebecca, Beatrice and she were hit by the runaway horses and wagon. All three girls saw the wagon slewing into them but they froze and didn't make any attempt to get out of the way until the very last second. All three tried to get away but Florence remembers that she really did not know where to go. The store building was directly behind them. The way the wagon slewed at them left no avenue for escape.

When the wagon hit, she remembers the terror and then she had no recollection until she woke up in the hospital. The doctor and nurses were swamped because Rebecca and Beatrice were very seriously injured also and all three were at the same makeshift hospital. Florence remembers that when she looked around, her vision and thought process was flawed. She could not quite realize what she was seeing. She looked for a familiar face and found none. She also saw that she was in an ordinary room. She wondered where she was. She had no recollection of what had happened so she could not process where she was at all.

She went to speak and ask what had happened but she could not speak! She remembers looking at those working on her and was completely puzzled as to what was going on. She only knew that she felt great pain. That was that last thing she remembered until she awoke several hours later. When she awoke she found bandages around her chest, a very heavy bandage was around her pelvis and there was a cast on her left leg. She realized that from the bandages position she must have serious injury to her trunk. She could breathe alright so in her clouded mind she realized she must not have punctured lungs.

From what a nurse told Florence, she and her friends were run over by a wagon pulled by runaway horses. Florence's friends are in the hospital also and both are badly injured. The doctor came in and explained Florence's injuries and told her what they planned to do in the next few days to help her heal. Florence asked the doctor if someone could write to her mother and ask her to come quickly. She remembers that she could not recall the address but said it was in a notebook in her luggage. The nurse found the address for Olivia and sent a short letter to Florence's mother.

Florence was in tremendous pain, she could not process her thoughts as well as before, her speech was slow and unsure. She had serious reservations about her future. She wanted to contact Walter Rounds but did not know his address or even where he was. She wanted her mother to be by her side. Florence was very depressed.

Finally, her mother arrived and she was immediately happy and her spirits were uplifted. She was slowly healing. Her mother spent her entire day with her each day and they talked and later her mother helped her get out of bed and to do rehabilitating exercises. Her mother didn't have any idea how to contact Walter. Florence was able to visit with Rebecca and Beatrice. She enjoyed these talks and it helped to build her spirits. Day by day her health improved to the point where she could go and sit in a chair in the hallway.

Then one day, Walter walked in! She felt like she could get up and run to him! Walter beat her to the punch. Now her spirits really soared. Walter had found her. He was just as handsome and polite as she had remembered. The next days went by in a blur. She was very, very happy. Walter danced with her daily and always kissed her hello and goodbye. Walter was such a gentleman. He never spoke a cross word to her even on some days when she was not feeling good. What a guy. And on the night after visiting Gettysburg with Charles, mother and Azalea, Walter was very passionate, and so was she. What a memorable, wonderful time.

Now we are all headed to Wisconsin, faraway from the reminders of the terrible days at Gettysburg. But also away from the wonderful day at Gettysburg when she and Walter met President Lincoln. Hearing that powerful speech at Gettysburg was the highlight of a wonderful day. The four months spent at Chambersburg are cloudy but happy as she improved day by day.

The train rolled into northern Illinois. Fewer and fewer homes and more open fields. Olivia was deep in her own thoughts. When she received the letter telling of Florence's injuries, she panicked, packed two valises and listed her home in Sparta for sale. She took trains to Chambersburg and immediately sought out the hospital. What a shock to see Florence looking so forlorn. They hugged as tight as they could with all of her injuries. Florence's spirit immediately improved and her outlook picked up. She told her that Aunt Azalea's house had been destroyed by a tornado in June. No one seems to know where she is now but Florence did not think anyone had actually searched for her. Inquiries were made, and low and behold, she was found living in an upstairs apartment a few blocks from the hospital. They were reconnected after having been out of touch for a few months. Work with Florence continued each day. It was noticeable that the hospital staff seemed short handed. Olivia asked is she could help with the kitchen in exchange for her meals and would they allow her to sleep in Florence's room. That was happily approved.

Walter arrived! He was everything Florence had said he was. What a kind gentleman. Olivia could tell immediately that he was strongly attracted to Florence. When he explained all he had done to try to find Florence, Olivia was very impressed. To think he found a graduation card from Azalea in our old lake home and then he immediately left for Chambersburg. Florence had her prince charming come to her to love and support her as she healed. What a beautiful story. Florence is very much in love with Walter and he must love her very much also.

Olivia thought about the prospect of her and Florence spending the winter with Walter's family by Antigo. We are both uncertain of what to expect. Walter tells us it will work out just fine. His family is very anxious to meet us as are we to meet them.

We are going to Sparta before going to Antigo. Olivia thinks she will keep the house for now. She knows that she and Florence can move back there in the spring. Olivia really wants to visit the lake house again and she knows that Florence wants to also. She hopes it will be alright with Walter's parents. It is so exciting thinking about that house, the flock of scarlet tanagers and how Walter found the letter with Azalea's address. We loved that house and the beautiful lake. When we stop in Madison, we are going to take Florence to meet her nurse friends. If there is time, Olivia would like meet Jack Sanders, her husbands uncle.

The train crosses into Wisconsin at Beloit. The conductor announces, "Beloit and a ten minute layover." Walter goes and gets a cup of coffee for all three. There are a large number of passengers ready to board the train. Walter inquired if there was some special event going on.

"Big day at the Capital, protesting the slow response to legislation passed to provide additional vouchers to help families who have the breadwinner fighting in the war," said a lady by the coffee counter.

"We plan to have thousands of women and children protest at the Capital. We mean business! Winter is coming and we need help since most of us have much less income now that our husbands and fathers are paid less than most earned before," said the woman with her voice full of determination.

"Good luck. Thousands of families are badly in need," said Walter encouragingly.

The train pulled out of Beloit with some empty seats, but not very many. Walter knew the next stop was Janesville. Beth McLaughlin, Florence's pretty nurse friend, crossed Walter's mind. He finally remembered how Beth had affected him a couple months ago. He felt ashamed to think that he was even attracted to her. Perhaps, if Florence was not in the picture, but she is, so stop even thinking about Beth. Anyway, he did enjoy the time they spent together on the train from Madison. Maybe he was vulnerable since he was going to find Florence. Get her out of your thoughts!

The conductor announced, "Janesville, ten minute delay." The train pulled in and the platform was crowded with women and children. Many of them holding signs. The car began to fill so Walter gave up his seat and stood in the aisle. Some people moved over so a child could sit on the seat with them. Finally, the doors were closed and the train began to move.

The car was full to over the seating capacity and it was noisy. Walter was irritated which surprised him. A lady standing by Walter struck up a conversation with Walter and he was uncharacteristically short with her. In a few seconds, Walter realized he was not polite to the lady and tried to apologize but she didn't seem interested.

Walter was shocked. What happened to get him agitated, he thought. Did that crowded railroad car make him upset? Did the high pitched voices get to him? He remained quiet except for an occasional chat with Florence and Olivia. He wondered if they had observed his rude behavior. He certainly hoped they hadn't.

Walter remained deep in thought all the way to Madison. Was this behavior left over from the five battles he and Royce had fought in? Walter had heard many stories about other soldiers that had gone berserk. Others became reclusive and many became abusive and could be very dangerous if they had a weapon.

Walter remembers a young soldier from Appleton who was in Walter's squad for several months. His name was Leroy and he, Walter and Royce made meals together and all three got along great. They supported each other and were the best of friends. Walter had noticed Leroy seeming to withdraw from him and Royce. Walter had that happen in two other friendships earlier in his life and really didn't think too much about it.

Over several months, Leroy pulled away more and more. He seemed to stabilize and for the rest of the time, up until Gettysburg, their friendship resumed but was never as close as several months earlier. Leroy was also more ready to argue and seemed unwilling to compromise. Walter wondered if he was being affected by the terror, mayhem and death he had seen in the two years he spent in the 6th Wisconsin Regiment.

Walter had to admit that his first combat at Bull Run was pure terror! He did not want to show himself from behind the breastworks of logs and dirt. A soldier about six feet away got shot in the head and the back of his skull was blown away. The man was instantly dead and the sight of his shattered head reappeared many times in his memory. Finally, he realized his job was to shoot the enemy before they overran our position. He stuck his head above the breastworks, picked out a target and fired. His shot was true and the rebel soldier disappeared.

He reloaded and shot again. Finally that battle was at a lull and we regrouped, got more ammo and helped any wounded. Dealing with the dead would have to wait.

Finally, it was dark. Flares were fired to light up the night. Royce, Leroy and Walter hunkered down and talked like schoolboys after a baseball game. They all agreed that they were scared. All three had seen the soldier with his head blown apart. That could have been us! All three of us were excellent shots and all of us had hit several Confederates.

That night I could not sleep. I was shaken from the experience of that day. I had killed men. Many of our 6th Wisconsin troops were killed or injured. Death and dying were all around us and it was playing tricks with my mind. Royce, Leroy or I could have been killed or injured. Why not? Was it just plain luck?

I had never been much of a religious person. Mother had gotten me to attend Sunday school and church. Erna continued on but Royce and I dropped out at the first opportunity. It was unclear to me what or who God was. Maybe we gave up too early. The soldier who had the back of his head blown away led prayers for a small group nearly everyday. Apparently God must have had other plans for him rather than to continue to live and hope he can go back home.

Walter now was worried, would he be mean to Florence? Not take good care of her for the rest of their lives? He mulled this thought around and finally concluded he may be jumping to conclusions, maybe the wrong ones. He made up his mind to be especially careful of how he acts around Florence and Olivia and also to everybody else.

The train arrived in Madison around midday. The crowd of mothers and children headed for the Capital. Walter could tell that those people were mad. The program was to increase vouchers but no vouchers have become available. Shortly after Walter's train arrived, another rolled in and hundreds of women and children got off and headed to the Capital. In the distance, cheers and chants could be heard as these angry mothers and children were not to be denied! It would have been interesting to observe what was going on, but the travelers knew they had other plans. First thing is to reserve hotel rooms in a nearby hotel. They quickly found out that there was only one room left. Walter said, "We will take it." The room was paid for and sleeping arrangements could be worked out later. The main task at hand was to visit Florence's nurse friends at the University. With the luggage and boxes stored in the hotel room, the threesome went to State Street and headed to the University. There were a number of students on State Street and Walter noted they were nearly all female.

Olivia had attended the University also wanting to be a history teacher. The University of Wisconsin was founded in 1848, the same year Wisconsin became a state. Previously it was a territory and much wrangling went on trying to decide on the boundaries.

"Just think, this state and this university are only fifteen years old. Not even as old as I am," said Florence.

"In one of my classes was a young man by the name of John Muir," Olivia said. "He was an interesting student from north of Madison. He was very bright but was shaggy looking. We sat near each other and he was friendly. He left school and went to California and he said he wanted to explore the Sierra-Nevada Mountains. I expect to hear about him again. It is funny but he had an aura about him of greatness, similar to Abraham Lincoln."

Walter was approaching a place in Madison that he was very familiar with. In the distance he could see the stone arch built over the main entrance to Camp Randall, where Walter took his training to be a soldier in the 6th Wisconsin Regiment. The sight of the stone arch was an emotional time for him. This is where his military training began, along with many thousands of soldiers to be, mostly from Wisconsin.

The University Hospital was finally reached and Florence was very excited, actually her face was slightly flushed in anticipation of seeing her old friends and classmates. They entered and the lady at the reception desk took one look at Florence and jumped up and came around the desk and gave Florence a giant hug.

"Welcome back, Florence," said this very friendly lady. About then Rebecca came into the reception area and let out a little scream and shouted over her shoulder, "Florence is here."

Shortly, three or four other nurses came running and gave Florence a greeting hug. Florence was totally overcome by this show of welcome.

"We have been so worried for so long we are just happy that you are better and are here with us," said one of the nurses. About then a tall man in a white coat came in and came to Florence, wrapped his long arms around her,

"Welcome back, Florence. We felt so sorry for you when we learned of your injuries. When Rebecca and Beatrice returned to class we knew you were on the mend. We hoped you would stop in and see us and most of all continue your studies," said Dr. Steiner, the director of Nursing.

Olivia and Walter stood back and admired the outpouring of love and friendship shown toward Florence. They realized then, these nurses are a close knit group of ladies. Olivia thought that the time the nurses spent attending the wounded at Gettysburg and the tragedy of that terrible battle really drew these twenty-seven together with a very strong bond. Walter was impressed with the tremendous show of love and compassion toward Florence.

Florence asked about Beatrice and was told she had returned to her class work but had suffered a setback about two days ago and has not returned to her class work again. Florence inquired if as many nurses as possible could meet at *Smokey's* for a get together and a meal.

"Better make reservations because most of us will be happy to get together," said another nurse.

Smokey's was an eating place just down State Street and was a nurses hangout. Doctors and interns frequented this place also. The food was good and service was great. Since it was early afternoon, Olivia thought she and Florence could try to find Jack Sanders and visit with him. She reminded Walter that he was her husband, Ronald's uncle and was a very nice man. His address was on Mifflin Street, not far from the Capital.

Just as Florence was saying her last goodbyes, Beth McLaughlin came to greet Florence. Walter immediately felt strange! As Beth and Florence hugged, Walter was happy to see her, but could not deny he had a confusing feeling about Beth. In a few minutes, Florence and Beth came over and introductions were made to Olivia and Walter.

"Walter and I met on the train a couple months ago, when he was on his way to find you, Florence. I would say that you are one lucky girl to have such a young man so determined to find and help you," said Beth as she reached out and put her left hand on Walters arm.

Walter felt warm. This was an uncomfortable situation that Walter found himself in. He sincerely loves Florence but somehow Beth has worked her way into his thoughts and feelings. Beth was pretty but so was Florence. Something about her was affecting Walter and was interfering with his feelings for Florence. Olivia looked at Florence with a look of concern. 'Look out Florence, Beth could be a threat' might be what she meant to say.

Walter was intrigued by the feelings he was getting for Beth. She certainly was not making a play for him, but she was friendly, very friendly. He was fascinated by her voice and her body expressions as she spoke. Walter had never been around a girl or lady that seemed to draw him to her like Beth has done. First on the train to Janesville and now. Florence

187

was easily as good looking as Beth. Her large eyes and beautiful smile were captivating. Walter knew very little about Beth and that was a cautionary flag flying in Walters mind. That was about the only thing he was concerned about other than he was loyal to Florence. Walter thought that the best thing for him was to get away from Beth.

Walter visited briefly. And then went outside. He could not risk Beth touching him on the arm. That turns his knees to mush. That girl has cast a spell on Walter and he liked it, but he was very afraid to where it might lead. Something about Beth scared Walter. For whatever reason, Walter thought of a species of spider that he had studied in school. The male knew he wanted to mate with the female. He courted her for hours and he mated with her. When the courtship and mating had reached a certain point, the female spider killed the male spider and ate it! Some instinct drove the male spider. Maybe he didn't know the female was going to kill him. Whatever, the drive was strong.

Walter knew he had much to learn about women. Maybe he is acting like the male spider and unlike the spider, he knows that if he continues being attracted to Beth, it will kill his life with Florence and he could not let that happen.

Olivia and Florence said goodbye to Beth and went outside to where Walter was.

"Are you alright?" Florence asked Walter. "You look a little strange."

"I am fine," Walter lied and he could tell by the expression on Florence's face that she did not believe that for a minute.

"Beth is one of my friends in this class and she is very happy that you found me and helped me to heal. She told me that she thought you were one of the most polite, kind and considerate men she has ever met," said Florence as she came to Walter and put her arm through his bent arm and looked into his eyes and smiled.

188

Walter melted. There was that beautiful smile when he awoke at Gettysburg. Thanks to Florence's help, Walter was heading in a direction that he understood a little and in a direction away from something he was completely bamboozled by.

The trio headed down State Street and eventually inquired as to where Mifflin Street was located. It was very near and the house number 514 was located. Olivia rapped on the door and an large older man answered. It was Jack Sanders. He and Olivia held out arms toward each other and hugged. Jack welcomed everyone to come into his house.

Jack was a very friendly, outgoing man. He had an ever present smile and was very pleased to see Olivia and Florence. Olivia had written a letter to Jack telling of Florence's ordeal. Jack was very pleased to see that Florence had healed very well. Coffee was made and Jack produced a cake pan with a chocolate cake in it. This hit the spot as the lunch period came and went with no one eating anything.

"Walter, did you say your name was Rounds?" asked Jack.

"That is correct. My parents are Edward and Alice Rounds and they live near Antigo," said Walter.

"I know your mother and father!" said Jack, somewhat amazed. "My company built a railroad spur to your parents property, in fact part of the crew is still up there finishing up. Your parents are very nice people as are Erna and Royce. I did not meet the two younger kids, or you, but it looks like you are right up there with the rest of the family."

"Mother wrote to me and told me that she had met you and that you had actually had some meals with them."

"Your father explained what he and your mother are planning with that flooring mill. It sounds like a large operation, able to produce huge amounts of maple and oak flooring. It sounds like many jobs will be available once the war is finished. Apparently our company will be back up there building tracks so boards can be moved into the kilns and then to be milled and loaded on cars for shipment," said Jack.

"Sounds like you are very involved with fathers planning for the mill. There is much work to do to build everything and get the entire operation running," added Walter enthusiastically.

Jack and the two ladies reminisced about Olivia's husband, Ronald and things they had done together. Jack had moved to Madison before Olivia, Ronald and Florence moved to Sparta. Florence had met Jack but had very little contact with him. Olivia had visited him often in the early years of her marriage to Ronald.

Walter still was troubled about his feelings for Beth. He thought she was very friendly, maybe too friendly. Actually she seemed to be a flirt and maybe Walter liked the attention. Walter concluded Beth was probably not interested in him but just enjoyed flirting with him and many other guys. Walter had to admit that he did enjoy the attention but he needed to get her out of his mind. After all, he knew almost nothing about her and he has deep feelings for Florence. The image of the male spider flashed through his mind. 'Oh, yah, I have been acting like that spider'. He was done with Beth! He would not be rude but he would remember she was like a slippery slope that could take him over the cliff and to his doom. Pretty Florence looked at Walter and gave him a beautiful smile that melted Walter. Somehow Walter thought that Florence had been able to read his thoughts about Beth in the past few minutes. Walter smiled at Florence and felt like a heavy weight had been lifted from him.

SMOKEY'S AND MORE

The afternoon turned into early evening and it was time to go to *Smokey's* and meet with Florence's nurse friends. Jack was invited and he happily accepted. He was a regular at the restaurant. The group walked in and many of the nurses were there already and they gave a cheer and clapped hands to welcome Florence and the others. *Smokey's* was crowded and many men were wearing the uniform of the Iron Brigade. Walter realized that they were the trainers from Camp Randall. He recognized Sergeant Thurston, one of the main trainers he served under when he and Royce were inducted over two years ago.

Walter made his way over to the Sergeant who saw him coming and met him with an outstretched hand.

"Walter Rounds," he loudly proclaimed. "What a wonderful surprise!" The Sergeant loudly announced, "Guys, guys, this is Walter Rounds, he and his brother Royce were among the very best soldiers I ever trained. He fought all the way through Gettysburg from the beginning of the war." The Blue Coats gave a cheer and clapped and several came and shook Walter's hand.

Walter recognized a fellow soldier from the 6th Wisconsin and went to him. Sergeant Jones and Walter shook hands. The Sergeant was from Stevens Point and lost a leg at Gettysburg. He pointed to his wooden leg from below the knee of his left leg. "Cannonball fragment took it nearly off on the third day." Walter noticed the Sergeant spoke softly and kept looking around the room like he was looking for someone or something. The Sergeant did not seem quite right but not seriously off beat.

Walter asked if the Sergeant had a family. He said he had a wife and two children ages eight and six. Walter inquired whether they were having any problems getting the vouchers for food, clothing, medicine and fuel.

"Things are very tough for them. I send all I can and they get some vouchers but the extra ones from the State have not shown up yet. Apparently there was a big protest at the Capital today. I hope that will get the vouchers going as things are getting desperate and with the winter starting it could get to be very serious."

Walter sensed that the Sergeant was close to deserting to go to his family. Walter thought that 'would make the situation worse'. He could see that this soldier, and many like him, were very worried about things on the home front and it was distracting him from his duties as a soldier.

Sergeant Thurston approached Walter.

"Lt. Col. Rufus Dawes was at Camp Randall last week," the short stout Sergeant said. "He spoke to the troops assigned to the 6th. What a dynamic leader! His presence and words really energized the troops and the trainers. He is very optimistic that the war will now swing in the Unions favor, but the north must keep pressuring the Confederates to keep them from getting re-supplied. He praised the record of the 6th and told the recruits that they would have a great legacy to uphold."

Florence was having a wonderful time with her nurse friends. Walter could see that there was tremendous friendship between the members of the group. Walter saw that now both Rebecca and Beatrice were there so he approached both and greeted each of them. They were very happy to see Florence and thanked him for helping her to recover and join them.

Olivia and Jack were engaged in talk as they sat at a table off to the side. They seemed to be enjoying each others company. Walter did not see Beth among the nurses. She must have had to work a shift or else she went back to Janesville. Anyway, Walter was glad that she was not present.

The group ordered food and when it arrived the tables were pushed together and the group of nurses gathered around. Walter was asked to eat with the group but Olivia and Jack stayed at their table. Florence glanced at them and had a sly little smile on her face. Walter observed that and wondered if Florence knows more about Jack and her mother than she had ever told him.

Finally, the party broke up and everyone went their separate ways. Most of the army trainers had left, but not all. Three had held back and Walter had wondered if they had friends among the nurses group. Sure enough, three of the nurses did not leave but joined the soldiers at their table.

Florence and Walter joined Olivia and Jack and headed for State Street.

"Jack has invited me to stay at his place tonight," Olivia said as they neared Mifflin Street, "and I have accepted his invitation." Florence had an amazed look on her face and looked at her mother with a look that said, 'really mother'.

"How are Walter and I going to get along without you?" Florence smiled.

"You two will just have to get along without me," Olivia responded.

Walter detected a sly glance at Florence and he wasn't sure but he thought he saw Olivia wink. Olivia and Jack split away and went to Jack's house. Florence grabbed Walter's arm with both hands and they continued on State Street toward their hotel. They looked at each other and grinned as they hurried to the hotel.

"Did your mother stay with Jack for their desires or did she do it to allow us some very special time together?" Walter asked later as they lay in bed.

"Mother is still interested in men," said Florence with a smile on her face. "She has not dated anyone since Father died but she has hinted that she would like to. She has whispered to me on occasion that she thinks that man is something special or that one makes my heart skip a beat."

"Your mother is an attractive lady," said Walter, "and I don't blame Jack for wanting to be in her company. Do you think they are in bed together?"

"Silly you. Of course they are. The way they were looking at each other at *Smokey's*, I could tell those two had strong feelings for each other and good for them."

"You look beautiful with your hair spread out on the pillow," said Walter as he rolled over and kissed Florence with a long passionate kiss that Florence eagerly returned.

Some time later they bathed and dressed and waited to hear from Olivia. There came a knock on the door and there were Olivia and Jack.

"I need to freshen up, so Walter, why don't you and Jack go down to the restaurant and have coffee. Florence and I will be down soon," said Olivia with a guilty look on her face, but a look that said 'I am glad I did it'.

Jack and Walter did go down to the hotel restaurant and had coffee. Walter liked Jack. He was easy going, friendly and was easy to talk to. Small talk was all they could talk about. Walter had a strange feeling about what was happening. Jack seemed nervous. What could be happening? Walter felt a sixth sense and it seemed to be warning him, 'change of plans'.

Olivia and Florence joined the men for breakfast. More small talk while they ate.

"Walter," Florence finally said. "Jack has invited Mother and me to spend the winter in Madison with him." Walter sixth sense was right on. Thinking about events of the past week of two, Olivia must have thought about the possibility of something like this happening. On the train from Chicago, she had said she wanted to look up Jack. That seemed innocent enough.

"Wow!" said Walter. "Are you going to accept his offer?"

"The second semester of my nursing program starts in January. I could continue my studies," said Florence as she put her right hand on Walter's extended arm. Walter was stunned and remained quiet.

"So you are going to accept Jack's offer?" said Walter.

"I can see you are having some difficulty accepting this change of plans," said Florence.

Walter sat looking at his coffee cup. 'Does this mean our relationship is going to end?' Walter was very confused. Why hadn't they brought that up before now? Walter could feel a strange feeling coming over him. Were his war memories causing that or was he just having trouble processing what the beautiful lady he loved had just told him. Anyway, Walter was shocked and just sat there for some time.

"I am sorry. I am trying to figure out what all of this means. It is very sudden and I guess I feel hurt that you have made the decision without giving consideration of how I might feel about it," said Walter sadly. Florence got up and came to Walter. Olivia had a shocked look on her face as Florence put her arm around his shoulder and put her other hand on his other arm.

"Walter, my best friend, I can see that I have hurt you," said Florence with tears beginning to flow down her face. "I was wrong to not have discussed this plan with you. It came about suddenly and I have to admit that I didn't give your feelings enough thought," said Florence as she bent over Walter and wiped her eyes.

"I am very sorry that I reacted the way I did." Walter stood up and held Florence, and with a consoling tone in his voice said, "I temporarily thought that you and I might be finished. I could not possibly be happy about that."

"Jack offered his home to us for the winter," said Olivia. "We thought Florence could continue her studies for the second semester and I could try to find a job here."

"No, the plan is good and it makes perfect sense. I was just caught unaware and I am afraid I handled it poorly. I had hoped both of you could meet my family and maybe you still can," said Walter with a compromising tone to his voice.

"I need to take some responsibility here," explained Jack. "I suggested that these ladies could spend the winter with me. I have been able to buy and procure enough coal to heat the house for the winter. Your plan to invite Olivia and Florence to live with your family was excellent. I just thought Florence could get started working on her nurses class for the second semester."

Walter had time to process this wonderful offer and he felt sheepish about the way he responded. He deeply loved Florence and he had to realize she had a life and a career of her own and he had no right to prevent her from seeking happiness. He was just hoping that her happiness included him.

"Walter, I am very sorry for the lack of regard for your feelings," Olivia said. "Of course, you would be hurt and I apologize for that. For just a few moments we forgot how much you have shown you love Florence. I hope you will forgive me. Of course we want to meet your family. Maybe we can do that after we go to Sparta." Walter got up and went to Olivia and gave her a hug.

"Of course, you are forgiven," said Walter emphatically.

SPARTA

Today's plan is to go to Sparta. Olivia had to take care of the house and some other business there. Jack was invited and he accepted since he used to live there also. Luggage was rounded up and the foursome headed to the train station. "Train to Sparta leaves at 9:51 a.m.," said the ticket agent. Walter bought a Madison newspaper because they had about an hour before departure. The paper was full of the protest by the families at the Capital yesterday. Several pictures and many interviews plus a report on what went on were in the paper.

The families were angry! The newspaper did a good job of reporting the temperament of the approximately seven thousand in attendance. Many ladies spoke about the hardships the war was causing their families in their communities. With winter around the corner keeping their families warm, clothed and fed were front and center to the legislature and Governor Solomon.

"The program has been approved to get the vouchers to our families **Now!! No more excuses!!!** That was a direct quote under a picture of Ann Freiburger of Antigo.

"Hey, I know that lady," said Walter. "We rode on the train together two months ago and she convinced me to go with her to testify to the Senate about the need of vouchers for food, clothes, medicine and heat. She is very passionate and is a fighter." Also in the paper, was an article stating President Lincoln declaring the last Thursday of November as Thanksgiving Day. Walter thought for a while and said, "That is today, maybe someday it is will as big a holiday as Christmas, at least in the United States."

The train arrived that would take the group to Sparta. There were several groups of mothers and children that boarded also. Walter visited with the lady across the aisle.

"I saw several articles and pictures and events at the Capital yesterday. Have you been following what that is all about?" asked Walter.

"Indeed I have. In fact, my daughter and I were in attendance and we are hopeful that the vouchers will be available soon, very soon. Governor Solomon spoke to the crowd and he assured us that the program for vouchers is ready and within a week all counties will have the vouchers and families can begin picking them up. He was very apologetic and claimed he was working closely with the program but it was more complex than was originally thought. He did offer the Capital for anyone needing to spend the night. No beds or blankets, but a warm building. My family and I spent the night there as there were no trains going to Sparta until now. Actually, in the evening Governor Solomon and several others brought sandwiches and cookies for those of us spending the night in the Capital. That gesture was very much appreciated," said the lady.

"Sounds like Governor Solomon is trying to get help to the families and that is certainly needed in these trying times," said Walter sympathetically.

"My daughter just whispered to me that she is pretty sure that you visited her class dressed in your soldier uniform."

"I did visit Jenny Zimchezk's class in Sparta back in September," said Walter.

"Yes, yes, that is my daughter's class, too. She was very impressed by you and your uniform. She also told me that you were trying to find the nurse that saved your life. You knew she lived in Sparta at one time and was trying to locate her."

"Well, here she is. Florence Porter, on her way to Sparta from Chambersburg, Pennsylvania where she was in the hospital," said Walter proudly as he introduced Florence to the lady and her daughter.

"You are quite well known in Sparta as the reason this Gettysburg war hero was in town," said the lady. "There was an article and pictures of this soldier in our newspapers when he visited my daughters class."

"Is your husband in the army?" Walter asked.

"No, he is not. He had an accident when he was young that injured his right foot so he struggles to walk. The main reason for being deferred is that he works with Jenny's father building barrels and they are essential for the war effort."

"I know Abner and Antoinette and they certainly are wonderful people. But if your family has the main bread winner, why were you at the protest rally?"

"Our family is fine. but I know many families that are in dire need in our community. I wanted to go to represent the families that could not go. One reason is they could not afford the train ticket. I was happy to try to help out," answered the lady.

"Julie, my daughter was given permission to miss class to attend the rally provided . . . What did Miss Nichols ask you do to?" teased Julie's mother. Julie had an embarrassed look on her face.

"I have to give a full report to my class."

"Miss Nichols certainly seems like a wonderful teacher," Walter told her. "I bet she really makes your class work on arithmetic tables, spelling, history and being good citizens. A few days ago President Lincoln gave a tremendous speech at Gettysburg and Florence, her mother and I heard it and it was a very powerful. Florence and I got to meet President Lincoln and shake his hand. He has a very difficult job and I wanted to tell him to continue in the direction that he is going."

Walter excused himself and went to the baggage car, found his rucksack and retrieved his copy of President Lincoln's speech and brought it back to his seat.

"Julie, this is exactly what President Lincoln said. Why don't you and your mother read it. You can see it is short. In fact, it only took President Lincoln two minutes to read it."

Julie and her mother read the address. Julie struggled with some of the words but when they finished they leaned back in their seat.

"Why was President Lincoln at Gettysburg?" asked the Mother.

"It was to dedicate the Gettysburg War Memorial which included the Gettysburg Battlefield Cemetery," answered Walter.

"What a powerful message. This just happened last week?"

"Yes, on November 19, 1863. There were about twelve thousand people in attendance and it took a short time for people to absorb what he said and then we gave the President a tremendous ovation. Florence was recovering from a terrible accident at Chambersburg, Pennsylvania which is only a few miles from Gettysburg and we knew we needed to go back to Gettysburg."

Julie and her mother whispered and then Julie leaned in front of her mother.

"Would you please come to my class," Julie asked Walter, "and read this address? My classmates would really want to see you again. If you could bring Florence along that would be great. If you could, we could go to my school as soon as we get to Sparta."

"I don't want to interfere with Miss Nichols and the lessons she is presenting," said Walter emphatically.

"That is alright, we can out vote her," Julie said with an impish smile. Walter consulted with Florence, Olivia and Jack. Olivia and Jack planned to go directly to her house so they had no objection if Walter and Florence stopped at the school. Florence said she would be happy to go with Walter to Julie's class. Walter, however, could feel a small anxiety creeping in and it scared him. What was happening? He sat quietly for a few minutes before giving Julie an answer.

"Yes, Florence and I will be happy to come to your class if you are sure Miss Nichols would approve."

The train passed through the tunnel and Florence grabbed Walters arm.

"I always get scared when I go through this tunnel. The sound of the engine is weird and even though I know it is not dangerous, it still scares me every time," said Florence with a sound of fear in her voice.

The train pulled into Sparta and many passengers stepped off and on to the platform. Julie made sure that Walter and Florence followed close behind after Jack and Walter retrieved the luggage. Walter carried his rucksack, one box and one valise.

"We must look like some transients," Florence remarked.

"Well, maybe we are at the moment," replied Walter haughtily.

Julie was excited. She skipped ahead and stopped once in a while to urge the followers on at a faster pace. Her excitement and actions put smiles on Walter and Florence's faces.

At last the little procession reached the school. Julie waited by the main door.

"Bring your luggage into my classroom," said Julie barely able to catch her breath. They went to her classroom door and she opened it and went in to talk to Miss Nichols. Walter and Florence looked at each other with hopeful but unsure smiles. The door opened and it was Julie and Miss Nichols.

"Of course, you two are welcome," said Miss Nichols, her voice full of enthusiasm.

All at once, a scream was heard from inside the classroom and a very energetic girl pushed past Miss Nichols and came running to Walter. It was Jenny Zimchezk. Walter knelt down and the two hugged.

"I have been hoping you would come back and I was praying you would find your nurse, Florence," said Jenny almost overcome with excitement.

"This is Florence," said Walter as he introduced her to Miss Nichols and Jenny.

"Come in and put your luggage down. Julie wants to tell the class something," said Miss Nichols.

As soon as Walter walked through the door, the students stood up and clapped and cheered. Florence was very impressed. Julie explained, "I met Walter on the train and recognized him from his visit to the class in September. Last week President Lincoln was at Gettysburg to dedicate a cemetery and memorial park in honor of that terrible battle. Walter and Florence, sorry I should have told you who she is, she is the beautiful nurse that saved Walter's life. She was badly hurt and is just now coming to Sparta from a town near Gettysburg."

The class cheered and Florence blushed.

"Walter and Florence got to meet President Lincoln," Julie continued, "and shake his hand. Both of them. Imagine that, shaking hands with President Lincoln!"

"After another man spoke for two hours, the President was asked to speak. He spoke for two minutes . . . two minutes! And then sat down. His speech was so impressive that it took the twelve thousand people gathered there several seconds to realize what they had heard. People began clapping, cheering and whistling. Walter has a copy of that address that he let me read on the train. I thought you would want to hear it so that is why Walter and Florence are here. OK, Miss Nichols?"

"Absolutely, Julie."

Walter and Florence walked to the front of the class. Both were very nervous.

"I am very happy to visit you again, especially as you can tell, I found Florence. She was very seriously hurt by runaway horses pulling a wagon and that was over four months ago. She battled back and now is as good as new." Many of the students cheered and clapped.

"We were hoping to get close to the speakers stand and, all at once, there was President Lincoln a few feet from us. I greeted him and asked to shake his hand. This man is impressive. He is very tall and besides that he was wearing a black stovepipe hat. He has an intense, searching gaze. Florence and I shook hands with the President and he asked for our names. I told him I fought at Gettysburg and was seriously injured a few feet from where we stood. I told him I fought with the 6th Wisconsin Regiment and he knew a great deal about the 6th. I wanted to tell him to continue on the path he had laid out for the people of this country. I thanked him for his service and he said thank you but, it is I who needs to thank you for your service and you also, Florence. We were both very impressed with President Lincoln."

Walter produced the paper with President Lincoln's address. *Four score and seven years ago our fathers brought forth, upon this continent, a new nation, conceived in liberty, and dedicated to the proposition that all men are created equal.*

Florence recited the next two paragraphs as she did this from memory. The students listened with their mouths agape. *Now we are engaged in a great Civil War, testing whether that nation, or any nation so conceived and so dedicated, can long endure. We are met on a great battle-field of that war. We have come to dedicate a portion of that field, as the final resting place for those who here gave their lives that the nation might live. It is altogether fitting and proper that we should do this.*

But, in a larger sense, we can not dedicate - we can not consecrate - we can not hallow - this ground. The brave men, living and dead, who struggled here, have consecrated it, far above our poor power to add or detract. The world will little note, nor long remember what we say here, but it can never forget what they did here. It is for us the living, rather, to be dedicated here to the unfinished work which they who fought here have thus far so nobly advanced. It is rather for us to be here dedicated to the great task remaining before us - that from these honored dead we take increased devotion to that cause for which they gave the last full measure of devotion -

Walter read the final paragraph and reread the final words. *That we here highly resolve that these dead shall not have died in vain - that this nation, under God, shall have a birth of freedom - and that government of the people, by the people, for the people, shall not perish from the earth.*

The students sat there, Miss Nichols was silent. Finally, the students clapped and cheered. The students came out of their seats and gathered around Walter and Florence. Many shook hands but mostly they wanted to be near this Gettysburg war hero and his beautiful nurse. Many reached out and touched both persons.

"Could the class borrow your copy, Walter," asked Miss Nichols, "so each student can make their own copy."

"Absolutely. I could stop in tomorrow and pick up my copy," said Walter enthusiastically.

"I will write it on the blackboard and each student can copy it." Walter had titled the speech. 'President Lincoln's speech at Gettysburg'. Miss Nichols thanked Walter and Florence and also thanked Julie for convincing them to visit the class.

Walter and Florence left the school and proceeded to Olivia's house. The weather had turned cold and there was snow on the ground. As they approached the house, they could see smoke coming out of the chimney. That was a very reassuring sign that there may be heat in the house.

Next two days Olivia took taking care of things in Sparta. Walter and Florence visited the Zimchezk family next door. Antoinette was thrilled to meet Florence. Jenny had told her about both of them coming to class and telling about hearing President Lincoln's speech. She proudly showed us her copy of the President's speech at Gettysburg. Walter explained what had happened to Florence and thanked Antoinette for finding the information that he had asked about. Antoinette was impressed that Florence was going to continue her nursing studies in the second semester.

Sunday morning arrived and the foursome headed to the railroad station to board the train to Madison. Olivia and Jack made the house ready for winter, heavy winter clothes were brought out of storage and it was a good thing because it was cold.

The trip to Madison was uneventful and Florence got scared going through the tunnel like always. When they arrived at Madison they headed to Jack's house where they will stay for a few days. Walter needed to visit the bank where his army pay had been deposited. He planned on drawing out about half of it. The plans were to go to Antigo on Tuesday. Florence and Olivia would visit there for a few days before returning to Madison.

VISIT TO THE FAMILY

Tuesday dawned bright, sunny and cold. Olivia, Florence and Walter bade Jack goodbye and made their way to the train station to board the train to Antigo. Water sat alone and Olivia and Florence seemed to be engrossed in a mother-daughter discussion. Walter wondered what changes he might find at home. His father seemed to be moving toward his goal of building a large lumber mill to produce large amounts of hardwood flooring and other wood products.

Walter thought about what Olivia and Florence would do. He doubted that they would care much about the current lumbering operation. One thing that would interest them would be a visit to their old lake house. Around Madison there is only a few inches of snow. More than likely it is deeper in Antigo, many miles to the north. If snow isn't too deep we could ride horses right to the house. We would need to watch out for branches, though. Maybe he could take a horse and handsaw and cut off any branches that would be any problem. Walter smiled at his good idea.

The train continued north through Portage, named for the portage between the Wisconsin and Fox Rivers. Apparently it was a very important water route from Fort Howard in Green Bay and another one in Prairie du Chien, called Fort Crawford where the Wisconsin flows into the Mississippi River. Those were important waterways to go from the Great Lakes to the Heartland, before railroads were developed like they are now. This allowed settlers to obtain land and make developments west of Milwaukee and Madison in the years before Wisconsin became a state.

The train continued north and arrived at Stevens Point. "Stevens Point, twenty minute delay," announced the conductor. The threesome stepped off the train and went to the station lunchroom for something to eat. Walter saw a familiar face and he approached the man.

"Ted Liskau," Walter announced as he held out his hand to shake.

"Walter," Ted replied. "I thought I would never see you again. Are you still enlisted?"

"No, I got discharged this past fall. I have been near Gettysburg helping Florence recover from a serious accident involving a runaway team of horses and a wagon. She is the nurse that saved my life. What have you been doing? I think you were going to help on your fathers farm."

"I did, but there was an infection in my stump and I had to go to the University Hospital in Madison to clean it out and get it to heal properly. I spent two months there and am just on my way to Merrill now."

"What are your plans?" asked Walter.

"Not sure. I found that a one-armed guy is not able to do most farm chores," said Ted resolutely .

"What about Matilda, your lady friend?" inquired Walter.

"She is very supportive and helps with work around the farm. Between us, we do alright. I feel that she would like to do other work. We are planning to get married in the spring but that depends on how my stump heals. We are short of money since I have been in the hospital."

"What is your address?" asked Walter as he produced a pencil and piece of paper. "I will try to keep in touch."

Walter took two twenty dollar bills out of his wallet and put them in Ted's shirt pocket.

"Here is a very small loan that you can repay when things in your life are going good." Ted looked at Walter with a look of thankfulness.

"Old friend, I really appreciate the loan. I will pay it back," said Ted as they shook hands.

"Better yet, Ted, help someone else who seems to be up against it. That would be the best repayment I can think of," as he gave Ted a hug.

The journey north continued. Walter had sent a letter to his mother telling her that the three of them would arrive about Tuesday so they were right on schedule. Walter would have to rent a horse and carriage from the livery to go from Antigo to his parents home.

"Wausau, ten minute delay," announced the conductor. The threesome stepped down and Walter retrieved their luggage. The ticket agent informed them the train to Antigo leaves in twenty minutes. Tickets were purchased and cars for that train were located. It was mid-afternoon by the time the train rolled out of Wausau. Walter hoped there would be enough light to get to his parents home today.

There were only a few riders in their car. Walter leaned against the window so he could visit with Olivia and Florence in the seat behind him. By now the outside temperature was close to zero degrees and the temperature in the car was barely above freezing. All three riders realized they did not have enough clothes on. Welcome to winter in northern Wisconsin.

The train pulled into Antigo in late afternoon. Walter rounded up the luggage and his rucksack and the threesome headed to the livery about three blocks away on the edge of main street. On the way there, they went past the courthouse. There was a line of mothers and children waiting to get into the building. Walter saw Ann Freiburger talking to ladies at the end of the line. Walter told Olivia and Florence who she was as they approached the line of ladies and children.

"Ann Freiburger, it looks like you have succeeded in your efforts to get vouchers for families," said Walter.

"Walter, great to see you. Is one of these ladies the nurse you were looking for?" asked Ann excitedly.

"Yes," Walter said, "The taller lady is Florence, the person who saved my life. The other charming lady is Olivia, Florence's mother."

"Ladies, ladies, this is Walter, the Gettysburg war hero who lives north of Antigo. He helped convince the Senators to install the voucher program in the state. Let's give him a hand," said an enthusiastic Ann.

"Hold it," said Walter as he raised his hand. "Ann is the one who deserves all the credit for organizing the meeting with the Senators. I am just happy that the families are getting some voucher help. Good luck everyone."

The livery was the next stop. A two-seat carriage was approved, the single horse hitched up and off they went. Walter would feed the horse and return the rig in the morning. The snow was not so deep that the buggy could not go through it. By the time it was getting nearly dark they arrived at Walter's parents home. Several lanterns were lighted in windows and on the wrap around porch. Royce and Erna had been watching as they knew when the train from Wausau was supposed to arrive.

As Walter drove up by the porch, Royce, Erna, Edward and Alice came out to greet the travelers. After greetings were exchanged, Royce offered to take care of the horse for the night.

Olivia and Florence were very impressed with the large, spacious looking house. Olivia commented about the large wrap around porch as she thought it was elegant. Florence was impressed with how well this beautiful house fit into the lay of the land and the large oak trees that seemed to protect the house.

Olivia and Florence immediately liked Walter's family. Olivia and Alice were close to the same age. From what Walter had told Olivia and Florence, they both felt very comfortable in her presence. Walter's family was equally impressed even though Walter had not written as much about Olivia and Florence as he had been able to tell the two guests about his family.

Royce returned from caring for the horse. Alice and Erna began preparing the supper. Walter and Royce showed the visitors around the house. A bedroom upstairs had been prepared for them so their luggage was carried there also.

Olivia was very impressed with the spacious house and the well planned rooms.

"Who designed the house?" asked Olivia.

"We all helped but in the end Mother did most of the planning," said Royce.

"Mother got many ideas from her parents home in Philadelphia," added Walter. Olivia and Florence unpacked and came downstairs a few minutes before supper was ready.

The seven hungry diners took seats around the large table. A platter of juicy steaks was passed around as was the rest of the fare. Walter has been very generous of his praise of his mother and sisters culinary skills.

"I asked Mr. Peroutka for seven of his best steaks," Erna announced, "because Walter's nurse friend, Florence and her mother Olivia are coming for a visit. Olivia and Florence immediately perked up.

"We know Mr. Peroutka. He is a wonderful butcher and his shop is stocked with great meats. The smell of smoked meats in the store was wonderful," said Olivia.

"Mr. Peroutka indicated that he thought he knew you, Olivia," Erna continued.

"Well, yes, we know Mr. Peroutka," commented Olivia. "Florence and I stopped at his butcher shop on several occasions.

"Mr. Peroutka said a few years ago, Olivia and Florence used to stop in on a regular basis but only in the summertime," Erna told the group. "Mr. Peroutka said that it must be the same people because they used to own a beautiful house north of Antigo on a lake, and he thinks it would have been east of our land."

The steaks were indeed wonderful. After everyone had eaten their fill, Erna brought out an apple pie for dessert. Small talk continued. Inquiries were made about Florence's health. Edward had been quiet.

"Florence, our family owes you a debt of gratitude for all you have done for Walter. He has spoken very highly of you and whatever our family can do for you, please let us know."

"If it is possible," Florence asked, as she looked at her mother after a pause, "for Walter or Royce to take us to visit our old lake home, that would be a wonderful gift."

"I think Walter could do that soon, maybe tomorrow. What do you think, Walter?"

"The weather seems to be warming somewhat. I need to go ahead and cut any tree branches that might interfere with travel on horseback," said an anxious Walter.

"I really want to visit this wonderful house," said Alice. "I think Erna and Edward want to visit also. I would guess Ernest and Bertha would want to visit it too, but we will do that on another day. Tomorrow is for Olivia, Florence and Walter to visit the wonderful house that holds many memories for those three."

A VERY CLOSE CALL

The next day dawned warmer, but cloudy. Royce and Walter saddled up three horses after breakfast. Walter found a hand saw and all three saddled up and headed to the lake house. Royce held up a compass to Walter as he sat in the saddle.

"You might need this if it snows hard," said Royce with a big brother smile. Walter took the compass and scoffed at the thought that he, a war veteran, would need a compass to find his way back home or any place at all.

The threesome started for the lake home. They could follow a logging road for about a mile. The next mile or so was through the thick forest looking for the easiest way to the lake home. At the appropriate distance they came to the blue line, the line of blue marked trees that indicated the boundary of the original sixty thousand acres. So far Walter thought they were headed toward the lake home.

It began to snow. Light at first but then heavier and heavier. Walter called a halt and took the reins of Florence's horse and she took the reins of Olivia's horse. Walter expressed concern over the snowfall which was very heavy now. Visibility was only a few feet.

"We have got to turn back," as Walter called a halt, "this snow is really something." Florence and Olivia did not object as both of them had concerns about where they were in this vast forest. Walter turned the little convoy around and followed the tracks they had just made. The problem is that in a few minutes the tracks were covered and it was impossible to see beyond a few feet.

Walter estimated that about a foot of snow had fallen in twenty minutes. He knew the wind had been out of the southwest which was the direction they had to go to get back home.

Walter dug out the compass that Royce had wisely given him. He clutched it tightly and looked at the compass. The group was heading northwest! The wind had switched and was now blowing from the northwest instead of from the southwest. Walter picked out a tree southwest of their position. He rode his horse there and took another compass reading on a tree to walk to. It was slow going, stopping every couple minutes or less.

Florence and Olivia were scared and besides that, they were now wet and cold. About two feet of snow had fallen by now and there was no sign of a let up at all. Walter was beginning to get worried, too. The horses were having some difficulty walking.

After several compass sightings on trees, Walter found a tree from the blue line. He was encouraged because the logging road was only about three hundred yards away, if he was where he thought they were. Walter now headed west as he thought that route would put them on the logging road.

Walter continued to shout encouragement to Florence and Olivia. Both of them sat on their horses with their heads down. They made no effort to see where they were going as they completely trusted Walter and the horses.

The wind was stronger and the snow blew almost horizontally. By now the snow was two and one-half feet deep and Walter's horse had difficulty plowing through the snow. Walter was really concerned. If the horses could not plow through this snow they would be in very serious trouble. By now the wet snow had soaked everyone and all three were cold and getting colder. All had cold fingers and hands. Walter told Florence to wrap Olivia's horses reins around her wrist so Olivia's horse didn't become lost.

As the three struggled, all at once they heard a steam whistle! Walter thought, I must be delusional, there are no trains around here. All at once, the whistle blew again. It must be the steam engine that father uses to saw logs and run other equipment. The whistle seems to be coming from directly west of the three strugglers. Walter encouraged the two ladies.

"Father and Royce must be coming to rescue us with the steam tractor." About then there was another blast heard from the whistle, closer this time. Walter judged the sound to be about one hundred yards away. Suddenly the snow stopped and Walter could see the steam tractor. It was right in front of them about seventy yards away. Walter urged his tired horse on but the snow was too deep. Walter's feet dragged in the snow so he knew the horse could not go on.

Walter traded horses with Florence. That was a struggle for both people as the cold was making movement difficult. Florence's horse had enough energy to break trail toward the steamer. Several whistle blasts were heard which indicated the Royce and Edward could see the three struggling toward them.

Royce jumped out of the steamer and broke a trail toward the three strugglers. In about ten minutes the horses could follow Royce's trail to the steamer. The exhausted, cold riders reached the steamer and all three were helped into the cab where there was some warmth.

Royce took the reins of the three horses and began to lead them toward home on the tracks that the steamer had made. Edward welcomed the group and gave all a heavy blanket that Alice had sent. The warmth felt wonderful. Edward began to maneuver the steamer to get it turned around. The snow was at least two and one-half feet deep and even this huge tractor had difficulty getting around in that much snow.

Finally, turned around, the steamer followed its tracks toward home. Walter put his arms around Florence and Olivia as they huddled near the fire box in the steamer. He noticed that all three were having difficulty talking and moving. All three had very cold fingers and all were shivering. By now the outside temperature was well below zero.

All three knew that had Edward and Royce not come with the steam tractor, very likely would all have died. What a violet change in the weather. 'If Royce had not given me the compass we surely would have died,' thought Walter. 'We would not have had any idea where we were and where we had to go to get back home.'

All three of the freezing explorers noticed a strange feeling in their thought process. It was slow and their speech was sluggish as well. They were greeted by Alice and Erna and the wet clothes were removed and replaced with dry, warm clothes that Alice had put in the oven of the cooking range.

"Watch out for the buttons, they may be very hot," warned Alice.

The warm clothes felt wonderful. The three huddled around the warm cook stove in the kitchen. Erna had made some elk stew when she knew Royce and her father were going to try to find these three. They ate the warm stew, huddled around the stove with blankets over their shoulders. Slowly their bodies began to return to normal as did their thought processes.

"My, look at that snow!" said Olivia.

"I know I have never seen it snow that hard and pile up like that any time in my life," Edward said, emphatically.

"Looks like we can put the buggy and wagons away and get out the sleighs. Work around here will be considerably harder now, lots of shovel work."

That evening, when the family and guests sat down for supper Walter asked if he could ask the blessing.

"Dear Lord, We thank you for being rescued by my father and Royce. Florence, Olivia and I owe our lives to you and our rescuers. Amen." Once again Walter thanked his father and Royce for saving their lives.

"Yes, yes, you are our saviors," Florence said. "Thank you." Olivia echoed Florence's words.

"Thanks to Royce for giving me the compass," added Walter, "we were able to head in the right direction. The message is, don't go in these huge woods without a compass!"

RELAPSE

The meal finished and dessert offered, the group sat around the table enjoying conversation. Discussion about the lake house was interesting as Florence and Olivia told of some of the things that happened there. Both ladies were very good at catching fish. Mostly they used cane poles with a bait of some kind and fished from shore. A bait called a 'spoon hook' was very good for catching pike. The pole had a length of heavy line as long as the pole. The spoon hook is cast out and retrieved in various patterns.

The lake had large numbers of good sized pike and many were caught. The action was exciting and many of the pike caught were of the larger size. Many were released but throughout the summer fish were eaten often. A boat was available but Florence was not comfortable in it and both ladies preferred fishing from shore. Sometimes they went barefoot into the water.

Walter suddenly began to grimace and make strange whimpering sounds. Florence looked at him with a questioning look. "Walter, what is wrong?" Walter continued to grimace and whimper. Everyone looked on in shocking disbelief. What is wrong with Walter? This thought went through every ones mind.

Florence got up and went to Walter and put her arms around his shoulders. Walter stopped grimacing and whimpering and looked up at Florence with a look of 'why are you standing there with your arm around me?'

Just like it started, Walter reverted to his old self. Everyone looked at him and it seemed like he had no idea that anything had happened. He looked around at everyone and saw that each one was looking at him with strange expressions on their faces.

Walter looked up at Florence.

"Why is everyone looking at me so strangely?"

"You must have had a bad dream," Florence told him.

"I don't think I was sleeping so how could I have been dreaming," Walter responded.

"Do you remember anything about the dream?"

Walter was silent for some time. He sat at the table with his head tilted forward and his downcast eyes toward the middle of the table. He had his hands clasped and he had a distant look on his face, like he was on a faraway journey.

"We were at Antietam," he finally whispered," and our regiment was charging across a cornfield. I got my feet tangled up in the corn and fell down. A soldier, running beside me, was shot and killed and he ended up falling on me. I was frightened. The rebel gunfire was terrible. I decided to lie where I was and pretend I was dead. I lay there for hours and near dark I pushed the dead soldier off from me. I looked around and tried to see where my regiment was. There were many unarmed troops helping injured soldiers from both sides.

"I asked a soldier where the 6th Wisconsin was and he indicated a grove of trees near a church. I picked up my musket and made my way over and around the hundreds of dead soldiers from both sides. I could tell that both armies had gone back and forth across that cornfield several times that day. In some places the dead were two or three bodies deep. It was a terrible loss of life. I was able to return to the 6th Wisconsin and, in confusion of the battle, I was not missed."

Walter could tell by the looks on peoples faces that a very serious event had just taken place and he was responsible for it. Apparently it had something to do with battlefield fatigue and it was very scary. Walter had experienced several smaller events that were troublesome but none of them lasted very long and in a short time everything about him returned to normal. This event was clearly much more serious than anything before. Walter was scared, as were his family and guests.

What caused him to act like he did? Did getting wet and very cold trigger some strange reaction in his body? Walter knew he had never been as cold as he was today. Maybe he was not entirely warmed up. Walter decided he should lie down and sleep.

Walter invited Florence to go with him and they went to Ernest's room and got under the blankets with their clothes on. They snuggled together and Walter looked into Florence's eyes with a pleading look.

"What is wrong with me?" Walter wanted to know.

"Just get some sleep," Florence told him. "Things will be better after you get some rest." Florence cuddled up to Walter and held him close. Walter responded by holding Florence close and giving her a kiss.

Walter fell asleep in a few minutes. Florence could not sleep as she tried to understand what was going on with Walter. She was very worried that whatever happened could happen again, maybe it would never go away. Florence knew about battlefield fatigue. She understands that it affects some soldiers, but not all. Those that are affected seem to be affected in a variety of ways. She had heard stories of returning soldiers going berserk and harming people around them. The most common story is a complete change of personality, becoming untrustworthy, deceitful and argumentative. Many returning soldiers begin to drink heavily which leads to issues with the family, friends and in many cases the collapse of the family finances. Many returning soldiers can't hold jobs and their lives are a mess. Florence is frightened. Is Walter about to show a personality completely different from his kind, helpful, friendly self who is very willing to share his love with her.

As Florence lay next to Walter while he slept, she was heartbroken. When she thinks about how hard he worked to find her and help her heal, it brought tears to her eyes. She is worried that any thought of life together may be in jeopardy.

Florence has great respect for Walter as a person and for the great promise he has of doing wonderful things for mankind. Those thoughts seemed to be fading away.

Downstairs, the family and Olivia are recovering from being stunned by what they saw Walter doing.

"It must be from things that Walter experienced in the war," said Royce dejectedly. "One day after Antietam, Walter told me about what he told us today. He had been acting depressed so I questioned him about what was wrong. He looked at me with a beaten down look and quietly told me the same thing we heard today. What he didn't tell us was how guilty he felt and how much like a coward he felt. He said he let me down and all the other soldiers in our regiments. He remained in this depressed state for about two weeks and finally he was just like his old self."

"Seeing and hearing Walter was one of the very worst events of my life," Erna said sadly. "Can he get over it or his life ruined?"

"The Confederates didn't kill him at Gettysburg but they may end up succeeding after all," said Royce.

"Walter is very strong,' Alice told the group. "We need to give him time and love and then he can put this behind him. We all need to really support Walter and give him time to heal."

"Walter has much to offer all of us," Edward added. "He is very caring and unselfish. We don't know what the future has in store for any of us. Walter seems to want to help those who need help and we should do all we can to help support him."

"When I found out what Walter had done to find Florence, I could barely believe it," Olivia said. "He then spent all this time with Florence, helping her to heal. That man is a special person and is a hero to Florence and me. Yes, I agree that Walter has much to offer. He is kind and understanding and he really believes in this country. He and Royce have proven that. We should love Walter and try to help him help others and pray that he can overcome whatever is causing him to be burdened like he is."

All the people in the Rounds house that night went to bed with heavy hearts. Walter slept soundly in his clothes under the covers. Florence remained with him and slept very little as she carefully watched over Walter. She had gotten over her crying about fear for Walter. She resolved to stand by Walter and learn all she could about what was causing Walter to act irrationally. She would be his constant companion and try to help him in any endeavor. She had decided not to pursue her nursing training at this time. She hoped her mother would understand.

A NEW DAY

Morning arrived and it was warm, at least for a winter day. Snow had already begun to melt as the temperature was well above freezing all night long. Walter woke up and that rousted Florence. It was mid-morning and all the other members of the house had been up, eaten breakfast and were sitting around the table waiting for some news about Walter.

Walter and Florence greeted each other warmly. They continued to snuggle and kiss and each looked into the others eyes, searching for answers.

"How do you feel?" asked Florence hopefully. There was a long pause.

"I feel strange. My mind seems confused. I had several dreams and some scared me. We need to talk about us. Will you marry me?" Walter asked with a hopeful tone in his voice.

Florence was taken aback!

"You want to marry me? We have only known each other for a few months. What would we do?"

"I don't know," replied Walter. "I just know that I need you and your love. I don't know where our life will lead us but I believe with you as my wife we can do anything we want in this world. Besides, I want us to have children, soon."

"You are kidding me, right?" said Florence with a happy grin on her face as she hugged him.

"No, I am not kidding and I will more formally ask you after I ask your mother for her blessing. There is more to this. I am afraid my war experiences will overwhelm me eventually. I could be terrible to live with, maybe even dangerous. Even during the war, I had some episodes that scared me. I have had several since Gettysburg, but the worst by far was last night. I had talked to Lt. Col. Dawes about these episodes and asked if he knew anything I could do to overcome them. He said group therapy may help. He said he has some memories that haunt him too.

"The one thing that scares me is that these episodes are closer and closer together. It seems like my brain is broken and can not fix itself. I know it is a very serious problem for many returning soldiers. One more thing, if we marry I would like to have us start trying to have a baby as soon as we are married. I love you with all my heart, but I could not possibly do anything that would make your life unhappy and sad. If you say no, you will still always be my loving friend and I would not try to hold you or keep you from doing what you want to do with your life. There, I have said what is in my heart and I imagine it has scared you. This is all very sudden and I don't expect an answer right away."

Florence has been sitting on the edge of the bed as was Walter. They had turned toward each other and they held each others hands.

"I don't doubt your love for me," Florence finally told him. "I hope you don't doubt my love for you. I would be very happy and proud to be your wife, Walter Rounds. Trying to have children soon is wonderful news. If your war memories continue to haunt you, I will stand by you and try to help you deal with them. Between us, we will deal with that problem if it comes up again. Walter, you have so much to offer the people, you must continue."

"When should I ask your mother for her permission for your hand in marriage?" Walter asked Florence.

"Let's go down, eat some breakfast and see if the opportunity presents itself. You must be starved." The two reached out for each other and embraced in a powerful, tightly held hug and both enjoyed a long passionate kiss. When they separated, they looked into each others eyes as they held each others hands. Walter was ecstatic.

THE PROPOSAL

Walter and Florence went downstairs wondering what the five people sitting around the table were thinking.

"Good Morning, you two," said Edward.

"How do you feel this morning?" asked Alice with a motherly tone.

"I am as good as new, just very hungry," said Walter with an excited look on his face.

Erna jumped up and headed for the kitchen.

"Eggs, bacon and potatoes alright for breakfast?" Florence answered, "Whatever you are willing to make is fine and yes, that menu sounds wonderful."

Royce had carefully studied Walter's face and finally asked, "Any idea what caused last nights episode?"

"A contributing factor may have been that all three of us had gotten very wet and cold," Walter answered. "I could barely speak or walk. I may have gotten my body dangerously close to shutting down. I think all three of us were very close to serious trouble. Florence and I think that played a major part in last nights relapse.

"That certainly sounds plausible," added Edward. "Losing body heat is very dangerous. The strange thing is that after that terrible snowstorm, today is very warm. The snow is melting and settling, just like a spring thaw. It would not surprise me that these sixty degree temperatures will melt most of this snow by tomorrow night and then we will have mud."

Olivia had remained silent in the few minutes since Florence and Walter had joined the group. Florence could see her mother was concerned, maybe about several things. Her main concern would be for Florence's future. Would she return to Madison and resume her nursing program? Would she feel that Florence should look after Walter? If that is the case, what will they do to make a living? Then what about her own life? She had planned to return to Madison and spend the winter, at least, with her husbands uncle, Jack Sanders.

"Breakfast is ready," Erna announced. "Come and help yourself. Florence and Walter complied and returned to the table with the wonderful breakfast. Edward and Royce left the house to undertake some job they had to do. Alice and Erna were busy in the kitchen. Breakfast was finished and it looked like a good time for Walter to approach Olivia to ask for Florence's hand in marriage.

Walter invited Florence and Olivia into the living room. Olivia was seated in a stuffed chair as Walter approached her, got down on one knee.

"Please, may I have your permission to marry Florence?" Walter asked Olivia. Olivia looked shocked! She put her hands up to her open mouth. Nothing was said for several seconds.

"I don't know what to say, this is all very sudden."

"Say, yes!" said Walter cheerfully. Another long pause as Olivia looked over to Florence and her eyes queried. Is this what you want? Florence had a happy look on her face and she nodded her head yes.

Olivia's mind was racing. If she said yes it doesn't mean they have to marry. Even if Olivia said yes, Florence could still change her mind. Finally, she really admired Walter and thought he would be a wonderful son-in-law. She had reservations about his battlefield memories.

"Is this what you want also?" Olivia asked Florence.

"Yes, it is," replied Florence cheerfully. Olivia finally smiled and looked directly into Walters eyes.

"Yes, permission granted." Walter jumped up and hugged Olivia and thanked her.

"I will try to take very good care of Florence and I know she will take good care of me. We love each other very much." Walter went to Florence and gave her a hug and kiss.

He said he had to leave but would be right back. In about two minutes, he returned with his right hand behind him. He got down on one knee in front of Florence, took her left hand.

"Florence, will you marry me?" Florence had a beautiful smile on her face.

"Yes, Walter I will marry you." Walter stood up.

"I don't have a ring, but I will give you my second most valuable possession until I can get a beautiful ring for you." With that he pulled the plume from behind his back.

"I hope this will show my commitment to our marriage."

Walter and Florence thanked Olivia again and went into the kitchen and told Alice and Erna the news about the marriage. Both ladies were very excited about the news of a new member in the family. Alice especially showed great happiness and gave Florence a big hug as did Erna. Both hugged Walter too.

"When is the big day?" asked Erna excitedly.

"First things first," said Walter happily. "We have not discussed anything about a ceremony like when and where and all the other things that need to be planned. Stay posted as we hope to have news soon."

Walter and Florence retreated to Ernest's room.

"We have some planning to do," said Florence.

"We want a church wedding, don't we?" asked Walter hesitantly.

"For sure we want to be married by a minister, don't we?" said Florence equally hesitantly.

"How do you feel about the wedding held here in this house or out on the lawn?" offered Walter.

"You're thinking, maybe get a minister to come here and perform the ceremony?" asked Florence with a surprised tone in her voice.

"That would be alright if that is what you think we should do," said Walter carefully.

"Let's go down and ask our mothers for their input since we don't really have any preference at this time," said Walter searchingly.

Both mothers were sitting at the big dining room table enjoying a cup of coffee. Florence and Walter joined them and asked if they had any preferences as to the kind of ceremony and where to have it. Both mothers liked the idea of having the ceremony at or in the house with the minister coming here.

"What minister would we try to get to perform the ceremony?" asked Walter hesitantly.

"Olivia and Florence, do you have a minister in mind from Sparta or some other place?" Both ladies looked at the other with looks that said neither of them had a minister in mind and that is what they told Alice.

"What about the lake house?" Walter all of a sudden asked. Both Florence and Olivia, drew in a breath and put a hand up toward their mouth.

"That might work," Florence said excitedly. "We need to really think that through. I would love to be married in that house." No decision was reached and the group went on to other things.

The temperature had risen to sixty-eight degrees and there was a strong breeze from the south. The snow was melting and settling. Apparently there had been a very violent collision of cold and moist air that caused the terrible snowstorm. Within hours this warm dry air pushed into the area as cold air left. It was amazing how in a little more than twenty-four hours more than half of the snow had melted or settled.

"We may be able to go to the lake house by Saturday," said Walter to Florence.

"That would be wonderful," she responded. "Maybe my mother, Bertha and Ernest could come along. Maybe the rest of your family could come too."

"Hold on. We don't have that many saddle horses," said Walter wistfully.

"How many saddle horses are there?"

"We have five." Nothing was said for a few minutes.

"Five of us could go there and I could bring the horses back, pick up the other four people if everyone wants to go," said Walter enthusiastically.

"We would have to do that same kind of trip to get back home, or some of us could walk on the trail that the horses make," offered Walter.

The afternoon was spent discussing wedding plans. Walter wanted to get married as soon as possible. That would rule out the lake house since there was no way to make plans to use the house in the winter because of all the snow. Walter could sense that Florence and Olivia wanted the ceremony at the lake house. Walter picked up on the little fact that there temporarily was a disagreement on where the wedding ceremony would be held.

Neither side had dug their heels in, yet. After all, the idea of a wedding was only a few hours old. Walter was more or less clueless about what goes into planning a wedding and a possible reception afterward. He decided he had things to do outside and asked to be excused. Florence and the two mothers were happy to tell Walter that they would try to get along without him. Walter said he was sorry and, as he turned to leave, the ladies winked at each other and smiled. Walter suspected that they were happy to see him leave.

Walter seemed like his old self. He is usually not a worrier but these war memory episodes have him very concerned. He is worried that they may become more frequent and maybe more violent. Then again, maybe not. The uncertainty is scaring Walter. He does not want Florence to pity him on this issue but he knows he needs her strength so he can deal with this problem. Because the episodes are occurring more often, Walter is afraid the time will come that he will be unable to function around other people. He wants to have children before he is either unable to or that he has passed on.

BIG DAY

Friday dawned cloudy but still warm for December 2nd. The temperature was sixty-two degrees and in the open the snow had mostly disappeared. Walter could see that snow remained in the woods as the tree trunks blocked the rays from the sun. Today, Walter and Florence were going to Antigo to pick out an engagement ring for Florence. That was one errand. Stopping at the post office to pick up any mail was another. Finally, Bertha and Ernest need to be picked up from school and taken home. Very likely a stop at the general store would be required as well.

Walter consulted with Edward and Royce. Should he use the cutter or the two seat buggy? After some discussion, the buggy was chosen. Alice, Edward and Erna had lists of items from the general store. Olivia asked if she could ride along.

"Of course," said Walter cheerfully. "It might be a little crowded on the way home but we will make it."

The threesome loaded into the buggy and away they went. The road was muddy but firm underneath. The first stop was at a jewelry store on Fifth Avenue. The jeweler pulled out several trays of engagement rings. Florence was radiant as she looked at the rings. From time to time she asked questions of her mother, Walter and the jeweler. She got it down to three rings, all of which had matching wedding rings.

"Oh, dear, I just can't decide," said Florence with a voice of happy exasperation. Finally, a set of rings was selected, a beautiful diamond with several smaller diamonds around it. Olivia and Walter both agreed that ring was beautiful.

"Now it is my turn," said Florence.

"We want to look at men's wedding rings." The jeweler brought out trays of men's rings. This was easier. The first ring that Walter picked up was the one he selected. A down payment was made, the ring fingers were measured and the jeweler said he would have the rings properly sized right after lunch. Florence's face beamed. Olivia put her arm around her as did Walter.

"See you after lunch to pick up those rings," said Walter as the threesome left the jewelry store.

Next stop was the post office. The post mistress retrieved the mail for them. Walter sorted through the dozen or so letters. The very last one was addressed to Mr. Walter Rounds and Miss Florence Porter. The return address said A. Lincoln, Washington, D. C. Florence and Walter looked at each other with their mouth agape and eyes wide open as they both drew in a breath. Florence showed her mother the envelope and her reaction was similar.

Carefully, Walter used his pocket knife and opened the envelope. He gingerly removed the letter and opened it with Florence and her mother looking over his shoulder. Two twenty dollar bills were included so Walter removed them so they could read the short letter, written in a powerful, beautiful hand. *Dear Florence and Walter, I have an important task I want to discuss with you. Please come to the White House at your earliest convenience. Show this letter at the front door. Hope to see you soon. Thank you. Abraham Lincoln, Washington, D. C. November 24, 1863.*

Florence and Walter looked at each other with mouths wide open with questioning looks on their faces.

"What could the President want to talk to us about? What important task?" Both were exhilarated!

"Imagine that! President Lincoln wants to meet with us," said Florence questioningly.

"We should go Sunday," said Walter matter-of-factly. "It will take three days to get there, I think. That would put us there late Tuesday. We would be able to meet with the President on Wednesday, if he is available," added Walter.

Walter and Florence left the post office in a daze. The postmistress smiled at them and said, "Have a nice day."

Olivia wanted to stop at Peroutka's meat market so that was next. When Mr. Peroutka announced;

"Well, if it isn't Olivia and Florence. Oh, who is the young man following you? Now I get it. Walter is being nice to you ladies because you are so beautiful."

Mr. Peroutka was indeed a jolly, friendly man. Olivia and Florence were pleased with the welcome by this well known butcher. Olivia perused the meat displays. Apparently she and Alice had discussed Olivia purchasing steaks for Saturday's supper.

"Please select nine of your best steaks and wrap them up." said Olivia with a friendly twinkle in her eye.

"They are for a special occasion, Florence and Walter are getting married and we are going to celebrate that news with some of your famous steaks."

"When is the big day?" inquired Mr. Peroutka. Florence answered sweetly, "We have not set a date yet, but we will, happily."

"I have a beef loin that has aged for over two weeks," Mr. Peroutka told Olivia. "If you give me a few minutes, I will bring it out so you can view it. If you approve, I will cut it exactly like you want, excuse me please." Olivia and Florence looked in the display cases. 'What else would go with the steaks,' Olivia mused.

"A bottle or two of wine would be nice," Florence said after a few minutes. "and maybe a special cake or pie for dessert."

"We need to go to the bakery and liquor store," Walter said. "Both of those stores are nearby. Let's tell Mr. Peroutka and stop at those stores." Olivia informed Mr. Peroutka of their plans and he understood.

The threesome selected three bottles of wine that each picked out. This is entirely new for Walter. The bakery was easier as there were very few choices. A yellow cake was purchased and put in a box. The bakery also makes candy so Walter selected two pounds of assorted chocolates. These items and the wine were picked up and taken to Peroutka's and permission was sought and received to leave them with the butcher so they could pick them up when they were ready to leave for home. The steaks were cut and ready.

Next stop was the general store. The team was hitched and they went into the store. The store was crowded with ladies, most of them young to middle age. Walter noticed some of them were carrying official looking papers. The clerks were not able to keep up with filling orders. So Walter picked up a box from the pile and the three began filling their order themselves. A lady stopped Walter and showed him what she had in her hand.

"This is the voucher that you and Ann Frieburger made possible. I want to thank you very much," said the lady as she gave Walter a hug.

Walter blushed and stammered, "You are welcome. I hope it will help your family. I also hope your husband and the other soldiers can come home soon."

The items on the list were picked up and presented to the clerk. Payment was made and Walter went to the hardware portion of the store to get several bolts and nuts for Edward.

"Heard your father put a rail spur up to his property," said the owner. "Must have big plans."

"What ever he is planning, he will need many men,' answered Walter. "With the war on, manpower is very hard to come by so he will probably not be able to build the business as soon as he would like."

The items from the general store were locked in the boot of the buggy and the three went for lunch at a lunch room on Fifth Avenue. The group met two ladies on the way and both waved at Walter and thanked him for helping with the voucher program.

"Apparently these vouchers were sorely needed," Olivia said after passing the ladies. "It is wonderful, Walter, that you helped convince the 'powers that be' to help these families provide for their children while the father is off to war."

After lunch, the steaks, wine, cake and candy was picked up from Mr. Peroutka. He included a small package of sausage slices to eat on the way.

"Keep me in mind when you make your wedding plans."

"Oh, Mr. Peroutka, we will not forget you and I bet we will remember you tomorrow evening when we eat these wonderful steaks." All three bid goodbye and added these items to the boot on the buggy. It was time to head toward the school and pick up Ernest and Bertha. They would have a valise with extra clothes that they would have taken to school.

All their errands completed, Walter headed the horses north toward home.

"See what Walter gave me?" said Florence excitedly as she extended her bare left hand toward Bertha and Ernest. Bertha took one look and shrieked

"You two are getting married!" Florence shook her head and her eyes said she was very happy. Ernest appeared noncommittal but did offer a congratulations as did Bertha.

The back seat was crowded as Olivia, Ernest and Bertha sat back there. Florence pulled the letter from President Lincoln out of her purse and carefully handed it to Ernest.

"Take very good care of this but go ahead and read it," said Florence proudly.

"A. Lincoln, does that mean Abraham Lincoln?" asked Ernest curiously.

"Open it up and look," said Walter as he hurried the horses along.

"It is Abraham Lincoln," screamed Bertha as the letter was unfolded. Both read the letter.

"What does the President want to talk to you about?" asked Bertha.

"Is this some secret plan to win the war?" said Ernest proudly.

"How did he know where to send the letter?" asked Bertha.

"Remember we heard the President speak at Gettysburg on November 19th. We met him and shook hands with this great man. Later he had one of his body guards come to us and get our address," said Walter matter-of-factly.

"Are you two going to go?" asked Bertha excitedly.

"We have to. We have been asked by our President. Remember, government of the people, by the people and for the people. We are people," said Walter with a patriotic tone in his voice.

The horses continued north on the muddy road. In the open, the snow had all melted but there was some left in the woods. Olivia offered the bag of sausage slices that Mr. Peroutka had so generously sent along.

"The directions were to eat these on the way home, so help yourself," said Olivia.

The little party was nearly home and it was near dusk. Walter pointed out a faint star directly in front of them.

"That is the north star and we can head right for it. Look to the southwest and you can see a bright star like object. It is a planet because it moves. I don't know which one it is, maybe Venus, Mars or Jupiter. The stars and planets were comforting companions when Royce and I were fighting."

THE LAKE HOUSE

Saturday, December 3rd dawned clear and still warm for this time of year. Plans were discussed about visiting the lake home. Everybody wanted to go so proper clothing was put on. Alice and Erna packed a lunch of sandwiches, pickles and oranges newly purchased from the general store. The five saddle horses were brought around. Olivia, Florence, Alice, Erna and Walter would go first. Walter would lead the four rider-less horses back to pick up Edward, Bertha, Royce and Ernest.

Walter led the way using a handsaw to cut any overhanging branches. The first group arrived at the lake house and the response from Alice and Erna was one of awe.

"What a beautiful house and such a nice setting," said Erna. Olivia and Florence were overjoyed to see their old house.

"This is like finding an old friend," said Olivia.

The group rode up to the front of the house and dismounted and entered the house. Walter gathered up the reins of the other four horses and headed back home to pick up the last four riders. In about half-hour they arrived at the lake house also. The same feeling of awe was felt by this group. Walter accompanied the late arrivals into the house.

"This is certainly a spacious, beautiful home," said Edward approvingly.

"Wait until you see the upstairs," said Bertha to the late arrivals. "The rooms are wonderful and each one has a dormer." After some time, Erna broke out the lunch and all gathered around the old table.

"It is wonderful for Florence and me to return to this house with so many memories. It was a very sad day when we had to leave. We are very happy that such a wonderful family owns this house and property. This lake, and all the other lakes, make this a fisherman's paradise," said Olivia.

"Are there more lakes than this one and the smaller lake to the west?" asked Royce.

"Heavens yes, up over the hill behind the house there are several in a chain. Those are all at least as big as this lake. To the northeast are two more nice lakes. We have never fished any of those lakes. The fishing on this lake is so good we had no reason to fish the other ones."

"Also, the Wolf River runs through north of here. That certainly is a beautiful river, but it looks dangerous," said Florence emphatically.

"We saw a mountain lion walk between this lake and the house one day in the fall three or four years ago. The woods are full of many different animals," said Olivia.

"Walter come with me," Florence said and rose quickly. The two of them quickly went up the stairs to Florence's old room.

"Take that picture off the wall, please." Walter complied and presented the picture to Florence.

"Turn it around and lean it against the wall," Florence directed. Walter could see several sizes of paper wedged into the corner of the back of the picture. Florence bent down and deftly retrieved the papers. She turned them over and several beautiful pictures were revealed. Walter looked on as Florence spread the pictures on the bed.

"These pictures are really something," said Walter breathlessly.

Florence and Walter looked at the pictures before them.

"Florence, these pictures are spectacular, you are very talented," said Walter enthusiastically. A picture of a doe and two fawns drinking in the lake in front of the house included the beautiful trees, water and deer. Another picture was of a flock of scarlet tanagers, a third was of a pack of wolves, one black and two mottled light color and two gray. Another was of a horse pulling a sulky, another showed a pileated woodpecker, one was of a large bass jumping out of the water catching a dragonfly. The last picture was of the small lake west of the lake house.

"Where did you learn to paint like that?" Walter asked with an inquiring voice.

"Three summers ago I spent eight weeks attending an artist school in Madison. It was at the University and several artists worked with us."

"Why didn't you continue painting?" asked Walter.

"I didn't think I could make a living at it. I do, however, enjoy painting very much and would love to continue."

The pictures were carefully brought downstairs and spread on the table. Astonishment shown on all faces except Olivia's. She was very aware of Florence's skill as an artist. Olivia has great skill as an artist also.

"I had great encouragement from my mother," Florence said. "All the pictures on the walls in this house were done by my mother." With that information, the Rounds family looked at the pictures in the dining room and living room. All were of beautiful lake and forest pictures. One was a picture of the lake house from across the lake, another showed a large buck deer in a glade with the moonlight shining on it. The picture in the living room showed a man fishing as he waded in a swift flowing river. A lumberjack cutting a large tree down was shown in an upstairs bedroom. In another upstairs bedroom was a picture of children playing on the beach.

"Olivia and Florence," said Alice, "I can see that both of you ladies have great talent and I am certainly impressed. I am sure that the rest of our family is equally impressed. I have some walls in our house that need some pictures. Perhaps we could commission you to paint some for us."

"Oh, no, my talent is very limited," exclaimed Olivia matter-of-factly. "Florence on the other hand has real talent."

"I hope Florence could paint pictures for us," Walter said, "but lets give her a chance to get fully recovered." Edward agreed and the other family members nodded approval.

By now it was mid-afternoon and it was agreed that the group better head for home. After all, they had a celebration to prepare for. Edward will ride one horse and lead the other four with Alice, Olivia, Florence and Erna riding on them. The remainder of the group will walk carrying the basket the lunch was brought in. Walter very carefully carried the seven beautiful pictures that Florence had painted.

THE FEAST

By evening, the celebration began. Erna and Alice had prepared the beautiful steaks by putting them in a special marinade that Alice prepared. These beautiful steaks were the special Peroutka meats that Olivia had purchased. The three bottles of wine were brought out and opened.

"We need to throw the corks away," Royce suggested, "that way, all the wine needs to be consumed."

"Let's just put the corks aside," Alice wisely said. "We don't need to overdo the celebration, besides Ernest and Bertha are too young to imbibe."

"A couple of sips won't hurt Bertha and me," Ernest commented.

"We will just have to see," said Alice with a warning tone in her voice.

The wine was poured and this large group hunkered down in the living room. Small talk prevailed.

"When is this wedding?" Edward asked. "It is the first one in this family and it is very special as are all weddings."
There was a long silence and then Bertha spoke up wishfully.

"I was hoping to be an attendant, but, of course, that is up to Florence and Walter."

"That decision is up to Florence. Whenever and wherever she wants the ceremony is fine with me," said Walter wistfully.

"Mr. Rounds, we have not decided everything yet. There are many factors that need to be decided," said Florence.

Walter rolled his eyes. What factors? I sure have not heard of any factors, thought Walter. He also knew he had told Florence he wanted to get married as soon as possible. Funny thing, Florence never asked me why I wanted to get married as soon as possible. Oh, well, apparently the woman getting married has much more on her mind and many more important decisions to worry about than the lowly groom does.

The wine was mostly consumed in the comfort of the spacious living room. Oil lanterns lit the room with a pleasant warm glow. A crackling fire was in the large fireplace and everyone seemed happy and relaxed. Talk of the wedding didn't fly very far so Edward tried again.

"Tell us more about the invitation to visit President Lincoln." Walter explained the events of the visit to Gettysburg and how he and Florence got to meet the President.

"Dinner is served," said Alice emphatically. She and Erna had slipped away and prepared the steaks to perfection. They were presented on two platters on the table. Also prepared were many mushrooms that Alice had grown in her fruit cellar in the basement. Canned asparagus, potatoes, fresh bread and butter made a meal fit for a king. Erna offered Grace.

"Dear Lord, please provide the family a safe trip and meeting with President Lincoln. Thanks for the wonderful news of a marriage of Florence and Walter and thanks for this wonderful, bountiful meal. Amen."

The platters of steak and serving dishes were passed. The first bites of the steaks produced pleased smiles and many comments about the flavor, tenderness and the degree to which each steak was cooked. The meal was completed and not one bite of steak was on anyone's plate.

"Do you want cake now or later?" asked Olivia. Consensus was that there might be room for a piece of cake. Coffee was served along with the cake. A tray of assorted candies was passed also. Finally the table was cleared and dishes scraped, washed and dried. Walter and Royce helped with those tasks.

The well stuffed celebrants retired to the chairs in the other room.

"What do you think Mr. Lincoln wants to talk to you and Florence about," Edward once again asked Walter. Before Walter could say anything, Erna interjected.

"The poor man is probably so tired of all the vile goings on in Washington, D. C. he probably just wants to talk to two very nice, seemingly friendly people. From what I am led to believe, Washington, D. C. must be a real snake pit now."

"Why do you think President Lincoln wants to talk to us?" Walter asked Florence.

"The President has a task he wants to discuss with us," Florence responded in a clear, strong voice after a long pause. "I have wracked my brain as to what it could be. He sent forty dollars in the letter to cover expenses. Walter did tell the President that he thought he was on the right path for the country and to not give up. He also seemed to know a great deal about the 6th Wisconsin Regiment and said his Generals had high praise for all the Wisconsin regiments. If you are asking me, I think he wants us to talk about ways the Union army could be improved. He may be looking for a view of a soldier in the ranks. After all, Walter, you hailed him and offered to shake hands. He may have been impressed that this young soldier from the 6th Wisconsin had the courage to talk to the President and then telling him to keep going on the path he had chosen for our country. After all, he may be as much impressed by you as I am."

"Don't forget the letter was addressed to you also," Walter added. "What do you think he wants from you?"

"He knows I was a nurse and cared for injured soldiers in the field tents. Maybe he is trying to find better ways to help wounded soldiers."

"From what I remember how Washington, D. C. works," Royce said, "only those elected or appointed have the ability to make changes, increase or decrease spending and make new laws or rules. Walter and Florence, you don't have any power to do any of those I mentioned. What you can do is make suggestions to anyone the President wants you to talk to. My bet is that Walter and you will appear before a committee of the Department of the Army."

"What should I be prepared to tell him if that comes to pass?" Walter asked Royce.

"You will be able to come up with plenty of ideas. Better keep your list to not over six or seven items. I will have a list for you by the time you leave tomorrow," said Royce matter-of-factly.

"I have a better idea," said Walter, "why don't you come with us. I could use my influence with the President, ha-ha, to come and help us." Walter said with a wide humorous grin on his face.

"And how much is that?" Florence wanted to know. Walter held his hand up with the thumb and index finger about one-tenth of an inch apart.

"Just a little, teenie-weenie bit," said Walter to loud laughter.

"Seriously, Royce you definitely should go with us. So should Erna, Ernest and Bertha. I know you two would miss school, but I bet you would have things you could tell the other students. Mother and Father, are you still planning to go to Philadelphia on business? If you are you could go to Washington, D. C. and then stop in Philadelphia on the way home. Of course, we could not go without Olivia."

Ernest and Bertha were excited. They were very young kids when they left Philadelphia and had never been to Washington, D. C.. Finally it was settled. The entire family, plus Florence and Olivia would get on a train in Antigo tomorrow and head to Washington, D. C. Edward had already contacted Amos, a neighbor, to look after things and feed and water the horses. Since the snow had melted off the road, it was decided to take two buggies, one was a two-seater and the other had only one seat. These rigs and horses would be left and boarded at the livery until they returned.

Erna had gotten an atlas and was looking at a route they may take to go to Washington, D. C.

241

"We could go through Gettysburg," said Erna very excitedly.

"Let me see that map," said Royce with a doubting tone to his voice. He studied the map and finally said, "Big sister, you are absolutely correct and I for one would like to stop at Gettysburg." Ernest and Bertha were excited to be able to visit the battlefield that their two older brothers fought on and nearly died. Alice and Edward were also excited at the thought of visiting Gettysburg.

Sunday morning, Alice and Erna had breakfast ready by 4:45 a.m. The eggs, elk sausage and toast hit the spot. Breakfast finished and part of the crew washed the dishes and others made sandwiches to eat later in the day. The horses were hitched, luggage stowed and then they were off. The temperature was twenty degrees Fahrenheit and the road was frozen, but the ruts made when the road was thawed presented challenges to the drivers, Walter and Royce.

The crew arrived in Antigo at 7:15 a.m. with plenty of time to unload passengers and luggage and take the horses to the livery. Alice had already asked Ernest and Bertha if there was one of their friends that could take a note to the principal so he would know where they are.

"Tommy Peterson lives about two blocks from the train station. I could take the note to him," said Ernest helpfully. Alice produced paper and pencil and made a note to the principal stating, *Ernest and Bertha are going to be out of town with Edward and me and will be absent all week long.*

MADISON AND POINTS EAST

Edward purchased the nine tickets to Madison.

"Must be a big event in Madison" said the ticket agent in a friendly voice.

"Not Madison, but further east, Gettysburg and Washington, D. C." answered Edward with a patriotic tone.

"Those are two important addresses regarding this war," said the ticket agent. By now this man had picked up on the fact that two Civil War hero's and their family and friends were off on a mission to visit those places. He hoped Edward would drop a hint of two, but Edward thanked the agent and took a seat on the waiting room bench. Edward thought he had told the ticket agent more than he should have. He could tell by the mans reaction that he was hoping for more information. Edward realized that maybe the letter Walter and Florence have might be about some project involving national security.

Edward invited everyone to step outside for a minute. He cautioned all the group.

"Please do not reveal why we are going to Washington, D. C. Tell people that we just want to visit. Don't mention President Lincoln's name at all. We don't want to possibly jeopardize our country's security. I have already told the ticket agent more than I should have."

The 8:10 a.m. train began loading. Its bell began clanging as it headed for Wausau. There were very few passengers. Walter and Ernest were able to snooze. The group had to leave this train and board the train to Madison. The train rolled along on the southward journey. Many times the Wisconsin River was in sight. Stops were made at Stevens Point and several passengers boarded the car the Rounds group was in. Two young men sat in front of Walter. They appeared to be about eighteen years old. Walter observed them and listened to their conversation . He learned that they were friends and neighbors from a small town east of Stevens Point by the name of Rosholt. They were on their way to Camp Randall, drafted into the Army of the Potomac, 7th Wisconsin Regiment.

Walter debated if he should talk to these young men. What would he ask them? What would he tell them? Walter decided it was best if he did not say anything. Just like Royce and him, they would learn what the Union trainers would tell them. Very likely it is different than what Walter and Royce learned over two years ago. Walter did feel sympathy for these two strong looking, young men that needed to be lucky, as he and Royce were to survive in this war.

The train rolled on. Next stop the conductor announced dutifully, "Portage, Portage, ten minute delay." Walter and Royce got off seeking a cup of coffee. Many people boarded and when Walter and Royce arrived at the seats they had occupied, they found people sitting in them. Since there was no way to reclaim the seats, Walter and Royce grabbed a standers strap and looked straight ahead as the train rolled on toward Madison.

Walter looked over at Florence, comfortably seated by Olivia. Her eyes seemed to tell Walter - nice going, Walter, now what? Stand up until Madison? How was that taste of coffee? Florence smiled and looked out the windows. 'Poor Walter, he really is a klutz, a well meaning one, but a klutz'.

The train began to slow. "Madison, end of the line. Chicago transfers, Track number seven. 10:50 a.m." Edward looked at his watch, 10.30 a.m. it read.

"Twenty minutes to track seven. Do your business and be on time," Edward announced to his travelers. The train was loading and, "All Aboard in five minutes," the conductors voice was heard. Walter had purchased a Madison paper and was looking through it. One picture caught his eye. A railroad baggage cart at the Madison train station was piled high with large bags of vouchers. The caption read, *Family vouchers finally ready. Today thousands of vouchers are on their way to county seats all around the state.*

Walter was confused. About a week ago there was a huge rally at the Capital about the voucher program. A day or two later Walter saw mothers in Antigo lining up to get vouchers. Ann Freiburger has been very instrumental in the program from the start. She must have procured vouchers for Antigo and took them home with her. That lady is really something.

Edward had been watching the time. "Let's get aboard our train." The group began to move toward their train and Walter noticed Royce was not in the group. He was about to tell his father that, when he saw Royce running on the platform. There was a large, older man struggling behind Royce. 'What the heck is going on?' thought Walter. Did Royce do something to make the man run after him? Walter looked at the older man and thought he recognized something about him. He did, it was Jack Sanders!

Royce and Jack caught up with the others. Olivia held out a ticket for the train and they embraced as a winded Jack tried to catch his breath. Jack greeted everyone and now he could meet Ernest and Bertha. Apparently Olivia and Royce had hatched a plan for Royce to run to Jack's house with the note asking him to quickly decide to join the Rounds family, Florence and Olivia on a trip to Gettysburg, Philadelphia and Washington, D. C.. Royce had asked his mother and father if it was alright with them and of course it was.

Walter greeted Jack warmly. They had become good friends in the few days they were together. Walter was happy that Olivia and Jack seemed to have renewed a friendship that apparently was blossoming.

The train rolled out of Madison on the way to Chicago. The little group now numbered ten. Walter thought about his siblings. Erna was a dynamic, determined, lovely person. As far as Walter knows, there is no man in her life. Erna has implied that she wished there was someone like Walter trying to find her. Maybe she should go to Madison, attend the University and develop a career that will put her in contact with other people. After all, Erna was very nice looking, has a beautiful smile and is very intelligent. Her dark brown, curly hair, slim figure and medium height would certainly attract attention. Walter had thought that Erna is Mothers right hand person and the two are very close. Maybe she does not want to leave home.

With Mother and Father planning to develop the large flooring mill, Erna will no doubt be given the opportunity to be part of it. I would think that she would be in a management position. Looking ahead a few years Walter could imagine a very large operation with perhaps one hundred workers or so. Very likely, Erna will be a very important asset to the lumber operation. Walter reminds himself it is Erna's business, not his so don't worry about it.

Royce wants to be a forester. He loves the forest and enjoys working among the trees. Royce also is very intelligent, very dependable and is a wonderful leader. Walter can see him taking over the reins from his mother and father when those two retire. He could see Royce as a very well respected business owner that carefully uses the forest products and sees that the trees are replaced and the company's intrusion into the vast forest is at a minimum. Royce will see to it that the families footprint from the flooring mill will be gentle. Perhaps Royce will meet a lady friend soon, while attending the University the second semester. Royce has unlimited potential plus he is very kind and compassionate. Walter remembers the many long conversations they had in their tent during the two years while fighting in the war.

Walter wondered what is going on. Why is he so melancholy about Erna and Royce. Why not Ernest and Bertha. Because they are younger than him he doesn't have the same feeling about love toward them? That definitely is not true as he loves both of his younger siblings, and very much cares about their future.

Walter wonders about his future. It should be very bright with Florence and him getting married. For whatever reason any thoughts about the future seem to have dark clouds hovering in the distance. Are his war memories causing his mind to act strangely? Walter feels mean tempered all at once.

"No, go away!" Walter says out loud to no one in particular.

"Walter, what is wrong?" said Florence as she put her arm around his shoulder. Walter turned his head and looked at Florence with a blank look.

"I, I don't know," said Walter, sadly. "All at once I said that and I don't know why. Please hold my hand," said Walter with great concern in his voice.

Royce had heard the outburst and came and leaned over Florence and looked carefully at Walter.

"Where were you just now?" he asked Walter thoughtfully.

"I was thinking about my brothers and sisters. I was thinking about the future and I saw dark clouds hovering in the background for my future. I told them to go away," said Walter as he looked wistfully from Florence to Royce. His gaze was fleeting and he had a faraway look on his face.

The train rolled into Chicago in the early afternoon. The speed was slow and the engineer sounded his whistle at all the main crossings. Finally, the engine bell began clanging and the platform and the station came into view. Actually, their train was three tracks from the station. The conductor had already called, "Chicago, end of the line." Edward explained that this engine will be disconnected, put on the round table and turned around. It will be routed around and the caboose reversed. In a short time this train will be ready to head back to Madison.

Tickets to Cleveland were purchased and the ticket agent informed the group, "Train to Cleveland leaves in fifteen minutes on Track 11." The men gathered up the luggage and got directions to track eleven. Luckily it meant only crossing five tracks, that was enough as there was no paved pathway to their train. Baggage was stowed and the train began to roll with the engine bell clanging and several blasts on the whistle were heard.

CLEVELAND

The train rolled east, apparently on high quality tracks as the speed was noticeably faster than from Madison to Chicago. Once again, this train stopped at some stations and went right by others. The car was mostly full and Walter enjoyed watching people. At one stop west of Toledo, three young men got on. They sat nearby Walter. One sat across the aisle and two sat behind Florence and Walter.

Walter thought these young men may have been home on furlough. Their talk confirmed his suspicion. Finally, Walter asked Florence if she minded if he asked these young men a question.

"Heavens, no, go ahead," was her reply.

"What Regiment do you men belong to?" inquired Walter.

"The 107th Ohio," said the larger of the two men.

"Were you at Gettysburg?" asked Walter.

"Yes, we all were there," answered the smaller man.

"Did you know Joe Sullivan?" asked Walter hesitantly.

"We knew Joe," said the larger man. "He was a Sergeant and a top notch soldier," offered the smaller man.

"Got hit by a cannonball fragment right in the chest. Dead before he hit the ground," added the larger man.

"Are you a friend of his?" asked the smaller man.

"No, but I know his brother Charles. We went to Gettysburg together and found Joe's grave."

The third man sitting across from the man joined in the conversation.

"Joe saved my life the first day at Gettysburg. We were under attack by the Confederates and they had us outnumbered. I was reloading my rifle behind the rock wall when this rebel jumped over the wall and was about to stick me with his bayonet when Joe shot him and killed him. He actually fell on me when he died. Joe was as good a guy and as good a soldier as anyone could be," said the soldier sadly.

"We were among the lucky ones. The 107th Ohio suffered big losses," said the smaller man.

"Where are you headed?" Walter explained the stop in Gettysburg and then on to Washington, D. C.

"You look like you could have been a soldier?"

"Two years with the 6th Wisconsin," replied Walter matter-of-factly.

"Aren't you the guys that charged the Mississippi soldiers and captured a bunch of them?"

"Yes, we did," Walter replied. "Our commander told us to fix bayonets and on his signal we went over our breastworks and charged. We trapped them in a railroad cut and that is where a few hundred surrendered."

The conductor announced, "Toledo, twenty minute layover." The Wisconsin crowd got off to stretch their legs and make restroom stops. Edward bought a bag of cookies for the group to eat on the train. The trains engine began clanging the bell as the train slowly pulled out of the station. It was late afternoon and it looked like it would be dark by the time they reached Cleveland.

"Cleveland, Cleveland. Twenty minute layover," sang out the conductor. The travelers stepped off the train. As luggage was being retrieved from the baggage car, Royce went to the ticket agent to inquire when the next train to Pittsburgh would be leaving. "6:20 a.m. track eight." Edward was consulted and it was agreed that they should buy tickets tonight as it might be rushed in the morning.

As the group was headed to the hotel, which was near the station, they were confronted by four men. The leader asked Ernest if he was a draft dodger or deserter.

"What are you talking about?" said Ernest. Walter stepped by Ernest.

"Who are you men and what authority do you have to stop and question this young man. I don't see any badges."

"Just answer the question!" the leader snarled as he stepped closer to Ernest.

"The boy is fifteen and lives in Wisconsin," said a loud threatening voice. It was Edward. He made his way up to Ernest too, and had his hand in his open valise. "I would suggest you men step aside and let us pass. There are no draft dodgers or deserters in this group. There are two Gettysburg soldiers that served this country for two years. Can any of you say that you served in the army for two years?"

The four men backed up and let the group pass. It was evident that they did not appreciate that they were made to back off. Edward stayed at the back of the group with his hand in the valise until they reached the hotel. Rooms were secured and plans to meet in the dining room were made. Edward inquired about the four men to the hotel desk clerk, an older man.

"They claimed to have been given their authority by the draft board. The hotel owner has confronted them about stopping potential customers and harassing them. They were very rude and told the owner, it is none of your business," explained the desk clerk.

The group gathered for supper and before they ordered Bertha said, "Father, you were great standing up to those men."

"If I had been by myself I think they would have taken me away someplace," Ernest added. "Thanks again, Father." Edward relayed what the hotel desk clerk said.

"Apparently, these men do this vigilante work in lieu of serving in the military. A badge or some other identification would be helpful to prevent what happened tonight."

The group ate breakfast Monday morning and made their way to the train station keeping a wary eye out for the vigilantes. The 6:20 a.m. train was able to be boarded as it sat on Track 8. Walter purchased a Cleveland newspaper and looked for news about anything, but especially news of the war and Washington, D. C.

251

News about the war was non-existent. The article claimed that the Department of the Army reported significant gains recently but in the interest of national defense nothing more could be spoken of.

Walter thought that was a significant step in the right direction. Previously, if the Confederates wanted to know about troop movements they just had to read the newspapers. Another article reported that the Ohio voucher program for the families of soldiers was fully implemented and was doing what it was supposed to do. There was an article talking about a shortage of coal due to so many men being in the army. There was a shortage of miners, teamsters and rail hands. A request to the Governor was being considered. One suggestion was to find women to take over any job they could handle which would free men for more physical work. It was suggested that a child care voucher could be enacted to allow capable women to work while someone looked after the children. The article pointed out that a shortage of coal was not the only thing in short supply. Food, clothing, shoes and steel were some items listed.

The train rolled along as the terrain got more mountainous. By late morning the conductor sang out, "Pittsburgh, twenty minute delay." The group got off to stretch their legs and make a restroom stop. Alice and Olivia went to the lunchroom counter to see what could be purchased to be eaten on the train. Ready made sandwiches were selected and put in a bag.

The train finally cleared Pittsburgh headed for Somerset, Pennsylvania. The low mountains on the route were familiar to Walter. This train was headed for Harrisburg and the group would stay on it until it reached Breezewood, Pennsylvania. They would have to get a different train there. That train would then go to Chambersburg, Pennsylvania and if connections could be made, they hoped to spend the night in Chambersburg.

The long train ride was wearing on everyone. Most seemed to be deep in their own thoughts. Somerset was reached and a ten minute delay was allowed. The train continued east toward Breezewood, The scenery was new to all but Florence, Olivia and Walter. Finally, Breezewood was reached by late afternoon. The travelers happily stepped down off the train. Royce, Walter and Jack retrieved the luggage and Edward sought out the ticket agent window. He inquired about the next train to Chambersburg. "Leaves in twenty-seven minutes," replied the agent. Edward purchased ten tickets and joined the rest in the lunchroom. Hot soup and a sandwich was ordered by all.

By the time the train rolled out of Breezewood it was late afternoon. With appetites satisfied the group was in a better mood.

"I sure would like to meet President Lincoln," said Bertha to her mother.

"I imagine everyone here would like to meet him. I know I hope to," said Alice.

"I can't imagine all the details the President must deal with," said Erna. "The war and dealing with all the slanderous remarks by newspapers. Everyone seems to have something to accuse the President about. He needs his own newspaper that prints the truth. Maybe no one would buy it because it seems like people like contrary ideas."

"I would buy a newspaper that told the truth," Ernest said.

"How would you know if it was the truth?" Bertha countered.

"If it was directly from President Lincoln, it would be true!" said Ernest emphatically. "He is an honest, kind and trustworthy man and I believe in him."

The train rolled eastward and several times canals were visible. Mules pulling barges were seen. One was loaded with coal, the others were empty. This type of goods transfer was very old, older than the railroad and is not used at all in Wisconsin. The Erie Canal in New York State is very famous and many immigrants coming to Wisconsin traveled the Erie Canal to get to the Great Lakes. Once they arrived at Buffalo,

New York they could load their belongings on packet ships and sail to places like the Bay of Green Bay, Milwaukee, Manitowoc and other ports.

It was nearly dark as the train approached Chambersburg. The conductor recognized Walter and they visited. This man was very happy that Florence and the other two nurses had recovered and gone back to Wisconsin and he told Florence that. Finally the train stopped at the Chambersburg station and everyone happily got off. Luggage was retrieved and the group headed to the hotel. Florence told the group that the temporary hospital was two blocks away.

Hotel rooms were secured and plans to meet at the hotel dining room were discussed. After rooms were assigned and the travelers settled in, Walter offered to go to Azalea's apartment and ask her to join them.

"That would be wonderful," said Olivia. "Since it is nearly dark, see if Royce or Ernest can go with you." Royce and Ernest were in the same room when Walter asked if they could accompany them to ask Azalea,

"Of, course we will go," replied Ernest, not waiting for Royce to respond.

The three men headed for Azalea's apartment. Walter's knock on the door was responded to by the question, "Who is it?"

"Walter Rounds, Azalea. Olivia and Florence are at the hotel and they were hoping you could join them as they eat at the hotel." The door opened wide and Azalea warmly welcomed Walter with a long hug. Introductions were made.

"I thought somehow Olivia had gotten here ahead of us," commented Royce.

"People do say we look a lot alike." Azalea commented. Azalea inquired about Florence and hoped she was fully recovered.

Azalea happily joined the trio and as they headed to the hotel, Walter explained about the trip to visit President Lincoln.

"You should have seen him seeking out the President. This Walter has courage. I am glad President Lincoln wants to talk to him, maybe wants to make him a General," said Azalea as she put her left arm in the crook of Walter's right arm. As the four returned to the hotel, they entered the dining room.

"Azalea!" exclaimed Olivia and Florence simultaneously. Both got up from their chair to greet Azalea with long hugs. Azalea was ecstatic! Introductions to Alice, Erna, Edward, Bertha and Jack were made. A place was made for Azalea at the table.

Discussion about the itinerary for the next few days was the main topic after supper. Azalea was warmly invited to join the troop of ten on their adventure to Gettysburg, Washington, D. C. and Philadelphia. It was determined that on the trip back to Wisconsin from Philadelphia the group would take a route through Harrisburg. That would mean Azalea would need to take the train from Harrisburg to Chambersburg. She eagerly accepted the invitation to join the group so Walter, Royce and Ernest volunteered to walk with Azalea to her apartment. The three men told her they would be back in the morning to carry her luggage and walk with her to the 7:24 a.m. train to Gettysburg.

GETTYSBURG REVISITED

The 7:24 a.m. train was loaded and the engine began clanging the bell and the train began moving. Overnight, a light snowfall occurred. Even though it was December there was virtually no snow on the ground at Chambersburg. Walter hoped that there was not much snow at the battlefield, but they would know in a short time. Bertha was excited about visiting the battlefield. She was a very good student and her history teacher at Antigo, Mrs. Strandburg had found an eager student in Bertha. Discussions about the Civil War were held nearly everyday. "Mrs. Strandburg realizes that our country is at a very important time and she wants us to understand what is happening." said Bertha one day while taking to Walter.

Bertha very much believed what President Lincoln was doing was right. She made no bones about how she felt about the two big issues in the Civil War.

"Preserving the Union and freeing the slaves, are very important," she told her mother one day.

"President Lincoln is right and I stand with him," Bertha announced to her father one morning.

Bertha seemed obsessed with the government and how laws were made. Women not being able to vote really made her mad.

"I want to be a Senator someday and the very first thing I would do would be to allow women to vote," she announced one morning last fall at the breakfast table. The family soundly supported her and hoped she could become a Senator. She was warned that there were many pitfalls along the way.

The train pulled into Gettysburg and the group of eleven stepped down from it. Walter was relieved that there was no snow on the ground. The group walked to the battlefield cemetery. Many other people mingled around the headstones of loved ones and acquaintances. Many others appeared to be searching for a particular name. The group walked between hundreds of markers and with great sadness, read the names and tried to picture who lay buried there. Walter and Royce walked side by side when, all at once, Bertha ran up behind them and hugged them, one in each arm. She had tears streaming down her face.

Walter and Royce stopped and hugged Bertha. Without a word, she went to her mother and hugged her. She held her mother's hand and wiped her tears with her other hand. Florence, Olivia and Azalea walked together. All at once, Florence began to cry softly and reached out to her mother and her aunt. Erna had joined her mother and Bertha in an embrace as tears flowed.

Ernest stayed a small distance from the group. He carefully studied the names on the markers. At fifteen years of age he seemed quite mature. As the group moved on Ernest fell farther behind. 'What is he thinking?' his father wondered. Finally Edward went back to talk to Ernest, if he wanted to talk. Nothing was said for many minutes as Ernest moved on to another marker.

"Why did these men have to die? What if one of these markers were for you or Royce or Walter? I would not have a father or two brothers. I am the lucky one because I have my father and brothers but look at this grave . . Daniel Taylor, 107th Ohio. Does he have sons or daughters wishing he could return home? What about his wife? What will she do? It is terrible, just plain terrible," said Ernest as he went to his father and they embraced.

"Look at this," Ernest said as he swept his hand over the thousands of markers. "Did these men die in vain?" Edward could see that Ernest was shaken by the sight of so many markers.

"History will judge the results of this terrible war. In the history of mankind, disagreements are common. Many battles have been fought and millions have died. Is it right or wrong?

We who hold life precious have a very difficult time justifying battles. But then we look at what the alternatives are and we must decide, do we fight for what we believe in or not. Just think about President Lincoln, how sad he must feel to make decisions that he know will cost many, many people their lives and disrupt many families. Think of the Commanders that know they are sending troops to certain death but they must do it to try to defeat the enemy. This is hard, Ernest, very hard." said Edward as he held his left arm around Ernest's broad young shoulders.

Walter and Royce had ranged ahead of the group. All at once Walter spotted a marker and pointed. 'Albert Olund, 6th Wisconsin.' Both men moved to the marker and stood looking at it as they remembered this soldier.

"Excellent shot. Was a sniper and volunteered for picket duty. Nice guy. From Milwaukee," said Royce sadly.

"Look over there, Samuel Perkins, SGT. 6th Wisconsin." said Walter. Both men tried to recall this man.

"I can picture a man that was very tall . . Didn't know much about him," offered Royce.

The group gathered and decided to go to the rock wall that protected the Union soldiers. On the third day, cannon fire had damaged the wall in several places. The group moved up so they could see the open field west of the stone fence.

"Imagine, fifteen-thousand Confederates grouping up in that field about a mile away and at least a mile wide. That was after the tremendous fire of two hundred cannons aimed at the Union lines.

"The battlefield was eerily quiet as the fifteen thousand Confederates began advancing toward the Union lines. They were directed by a Confederate officer by the name of Pick-ett. After the war, this event was known as 'Pickett's Charge'. The Union troops withstood that attack. Walter was very se-riously hurt and Royce was injured also. The Confederates retreated and the task of treating the injured and burying the dead was begun," said Jack.

"How do you know so much?" asked Olivia curiously.

"There have been several articles in a Madison paper. Since the Wisconsin soldiers were trained at Camp Randall the paper has printed several articles about the days at Gettysburg."

Edward had checked on the train schedule leaving Gettysburg and going to Hagerstown, Maryland. From there they would take a train to Washington, D. C. The train to Hagerstown leaves at 12:47 p.m. The group made their way to the depot and found the station did not have a lunchroom. The ticket agent informed Edward that there was a lunchroom three blocks away. Tickets were purchased for Hagerstown and the group headed for the lunchroom.

LAST LOOK AT GETTYSBURG

The group loaded on the 12:47 p.m. to Hagerstown. When the train began to move, the group collectively doubted if they would ever return. Walter and Royce were glad to be putting Gettysburg behind them. It was time to move on. Both men were thankful they survived their two years in the army. Their memories are mostly of bad events. When the train finally left Gettysburg behind, Walter looked at Royce and smiled. His eyes told Royce, 'that chapter is our lives is over.'

The train pulled into Hagerstown station at 2:05 p.m. Edward checked on the next train to Washington, D. C. and was told it would leave at 2:37 p.m. Tickets were purchased and the group settled down to wait. Walter sat down by Ernest as he had looked at Walter with a strange look on his face all the way from Gettysburg.

"What are you going to tell President Lincoln if he asks you?"

"I have some things in mind but Royce and I are going to compare notes on the next leg to Washington, D.C." replied Walter.

"I am wondering why you asked the question you just did?"

"Please tell the President to find a way to win the war without killing so many men," said Ernest hopefully.

"If I get that chance I will pass that request on," said Walter as he put his arm around Ernest.

The 2:37 p.m. train to Washington, D. C. was loaded and began to roll. The group of eleven travelers had gotten over the remorse of a Gettysburg visit. The spirits of the group was noticeably more jovial. Bertha was especially happy and her happy face was infectious to the entire group.

Walter and Royce sat together. Walter planned to ask Royce what he would tell President Lincoln if he could talk to him.

"What happened on the third day at Gettysburg after I was injured and I was unconscious?" Walter asked Royce before discussing their upcoming visit with the President. Royce thought for a time.

"Only about ten Confederates made it over the wall." Royce told him. "Our 6th Wisconsin dispatched them, some by bayonet. Our arrival was well timed as a large body of rebels were about to come over the wall, but we showed up on our side of the wall. As one fired his musket he retreated to reload.

"Amazingly after about three volleys we offered the rebs a chance to surrender or retreat and we would not fire on them. They lowered their guns and began retreating down the valley. Both sides had had enough fighting for that day. That is when I went looking for you. When I found you and rolled you over, I feared you were dead. I located a stretcher and got directions to a hospital tent. I got soldiers to help me and we took you to the tent with a surgeon and in a few minutes he removed the bullet. I had to return to our troops but later that day I checked on you and talked to Florence."

Walter thanked him for telling him what had happened while he was unconscious and he also thanked Royce for quickly taking him to the surgeons tent. Walter asked Royce what he would talk to the President about if he were asked. Royce thought for a bit.

"He is not expecting us to tell him how to fight the war," Royce told Walter. "There are some things that common soldiers could tell him or a committee that may help the plight of 'Billy Blue' as they battled 'Johnny Reb'."

"You and I have talked about how terrible the food is, how unsanitary our eating and living conditions are. Many good men died of disease that were aided by terrible unsanitary conditions. Having soap and water available before each meal would be a big step in the right direction," Royce added hopefully.

"Have the troops avoid close contact as much as possible," Walter offered. "Having enlistees take a physical exam would weed out many of those we saw that were not up to the rigors of marching long distances and actually fighting in a battle."

"Men with serious crimes on their record would be rejected," added Royce. "We found they were untrustworthy, were thieves and stole money, wallets and identification of dead soldiers."

"Child care vouchers," brought up Walter, "so wives who are capable could take jobs of men that could move on to jobs that would produce materials that could help fight the war. That would also help on the home front. A child care voucher program would allow women to work while someone watched the children."

Royce said he knew that new immigrants that had not voted were not eligible for the draft. He knows that for some folks that is a sore point back in Antigo. If that policy would be reversed it would help the immigrant fit into the community and also provide needed soldiers.

"We know our troops are fighting in many places," Walter said. "We have heard about Vicksburg, Mississippi and Atlanta and Savannah, Georgia along with the Indian uprising in Minnesota and other western territories. You and I have only fought in the States close to Washington, D. C. There are battles being fought on the ocean ports and big rivers to keep war material, food and clothes from reaching the Confederates."

"We were part of the army of the Potomac and we fought against the top Confederate General, Robert E. Lee," Royce brought up. "Perhaps President Lincoln feels that if General Lee can be defeated and captured the war will be over. Maybe he has no interest in what we think but only wants to say hello and visit for a few minutes."

Walter invited Florence to sit with him. They had not been in close contact for the past days as she and Olivia sat together on the train. He held Florence's hand and looked into her eyes. Walter read her eyes and they were very supportive. Her smile told Walter that she is very much in support of Walter's trying to prepare for what the President may be going to ask them.

"Florence, what do you think President Lincoln will be expecting of you?"

"Maybe he just wants to visit with us. I have been really thinking about what can be done to help injured soldiers differently than we are doing from what I saw at Gettysburg. If my nurse friends and nurses from Hagerstown had not helped out there would have been a very serious shortage of nurses. For certain, I would say that many more nurses are needed but specialized training is needed to deal with the type of injuries we encountered. These nurses need to travel with the troops. Men could be nurses too. Someone needs to make decisions about who gets treated and in what order. I saw three soldiers that were brought to our tent that died within minutes of their arrival. Valuable time was lost while they were removed and another injured soldier was put on that cot. We were short of some medical supplies and ran out of many things because of the staggering numbers of injured. Maybe training nurses could possibly be earning credits toward their nursing degree as they learn while being with the troops."

MR. PRESIDENT

"Washington, D. C. Washington, D. C. end of the line" announced the conductor. The eleven travelers were excited! Finally, they were in this famous city and hopefully they will meet with Mr. Lincoln soon. Of course, maybe he is unavailable. Time will tell. The group stepped off the train and directions to a hotel were sought and received. Walter and the others were pleased that people seemed very friendly. The hotel was a fair distance and it took twenty minutes to walk there. Would there be rooms available? Walter and Edward approached the hotel desk clerk. Edward inquired if five rooms were available. The clerk had a pained look on his face.

"Very crowded tonight . . I find four vacancies only," said the clerk. Walter and Edward huddled.

"Let's see if three cots are available, but before we do that we had better reserve those four rooms, for two nights," said Edward.

Edward said he would take the four rooms. The clerk agreed and then Walter asked about three cots or small beds.

"Indeed, the hotel has three small beds available," the desk clerk said. Sleeping arrangements were agreed on as was a time to meet in the hotel dining room.

The dining room was busy. Unlike other dining rooms on the trip to the east, this room was busy with well dressed men and woman. The group of eleven had to wait for a few minutes as workers reshuffled tables. Alice had looked at the diners and thought many of them were Senators or Congressmen. Edward put is index finger to his lips which told the group, 'just visiting Washington, D. C.'. Bertha was excited as she looked around the room and saw these well dressed, well mannered diners.

After dining, Walter and Royce asked the desk clerk how far the White House is from this hotel? The clerk replied it was about fifteen blocks away and would be a good sized walk for this group. Royce asked the desk clerk if there was any transportation available. The clerk said there were several coaches that departed from the rear of the hotel. If your group chooses that option, just pass through that door and speak to the gentlemen with the uniform on.

Wednesday morning found the group eating breakfast by 6:00 a.m. All wore nice clothes, but compared to the diners in this room the night before they felt underdressed.

"Walter and Florence are here to meet with President Lincoln," Alice quietly said sensing that feeling. "The President could care less what clothes they have on and neither do we. We are proud Americans who are here to support Walter and Florence."

Alice's words made everyone smile. Edward reached over and put his hand on Alice's hand. They looked at each other and smiled. His eyes told Alice, 'Thanks for your uplifting words'.

Breakfast finished, the group followed Royce to the doorway leading to the coach loading area. Royce found the uniformed gentleman he needed to address.

"Eleven to go to the White House," said Royce with a sense of urgency in his voice.

"Your party has business at the White House?" inquired the uniformed man.

"Yes, we do. That man is Walter Rounds, 6th Wisconsin veteran who has been invited to visit President Lincoln. The President also invited Florence Porter, a nurse who saved Walter's life at Gettysburg."

The uniformed man was noticeably impressed.

"Which one is Walter Rounds, I would like to meet him and Florence Porter, too." Royce motioned for Walter and Florence to come forward. They came and stood next to Royce.

"You two must have done some extraordinary feat. Very few young soldiers, or nurses, have been invited to visit President Lincoln. Sir, thank you for your service and Miss Porter . . Thank you for saving Walter's life." Both thanked the man.

"This is my brother Royce and he also fought at Gettysburg and he, too, was wounded," related Walter.

The uniformed man thanked Royce for his service. There was activity in the area of the coach loading. A large three-seat coach pulled by four horses was driven up for the group to be loaded into. Edward inquired what the charges were so he could pay for the ride.

"For you and your group, there is no charge. To have Gettysburg veterans going to meet with President Lincoln is a great honor for this hotel. When it is time to return to the hotel, ask the Chief of Staff to telegraph me and we will be there as quick as we can." Edward thanked the man and shook his hand.

Loading was contemplated. The uniformed man quickly formulated a plan.

"Three to a seat, this young man and the other Gettysburg veteran, please climb up by the driver." Ernest and Royce scrambled up to the high seat. The others sat three to a seat and the journey to the White House began.

As the coach rolled along, the passengers noticed groups stopped and watched as they rolled by.

"These folks must think that we are special people," Alice quietly said.

"Well we are . . . With some important people!" said Bertha with an impish grin.

The White House came into view and the group could see people milling around and some with signs. As the coach got closer they could read some of the signs. 'Stop the war.' 'Mothers against the war.' 'Troops sent home' 'Stop killing' There were about one hundred protestors milling around and being kept back by Union soldiers.

The coach pulled up to a gate and stopped. A Union Sergeant came up to the coach. Walter addressed the Sergeant as he held up the envelope that President Lincoln had sent himself and Florence. The Sergeant opened the letter and read it. He put the letter into the envelope and handed it back to Walter.

266

"Who are the rest of these people," inquired the Sergeant with an unthreatening voice.

"Most of them are my family and Florence's family. We visited Gettysburg yesterday as many of the group wanted to see that famous battleground where Royce and I had fought."

"Florence and I invited them to come with us to Washington, D. C. to see our nations Capital and the White House," answered Walter in comprising voice.

"I suppose you want them to meet President Lincoln when you do?" said the Sergeant sounding a little sarcastic.

"Azalea and I heard the President's address at Gettysburg as did Walter and Florence. We would like to thank the President for his amazing address," said Olivia in an excited voice.

"I know most of that speech," said an excited Bertha.

"So do I," chimed in Ernest.

"What about the rest of you?" inquired the Sergeant.

"We are good American citizens," said Erna. "and I for one really support President Lincoln in his endeavor to win the war and end slavery."

"Alright, alright," said the Sergeant with a smile and a twinkle in his eye. "I am going to pass the word on to President Lincoln, this group will love you to death, watch out, especially for the youngest girl." The Sergeant waved the coach on toward the canopy. He waved and smiled as the coach began to roll.

The driver drove the team up under the canopy near the front door of the White House. Walter got out of the coach and addressed the official that came to meet him. Walter handed the envelope to the man, who opened it and pulled out the letter and read it.

"You came all the way from Wisconsin to meet with President Lincoln?" asked the man curiously.

"Miss Florence Porter was invited also and here she is," added Walter proudly.

"If President Lincoln invited you two, you are more than welcome to follow me. Walter and Florence looked at each other and then back to the others. The man paused by the door.

"All of Florence and Walter's party are welcome too." He announced. "Don't keep the President waiting," said the man admiringly with a welcoming smile on his face. He offered his hand to each member of the group but waited to see if the ladies offered their hand.

The group entered the White House and were impressed by its elegance. "Wowie," said an exited Bertha. A pleasant stylish middle aged lady approached the group. Walter handed her the envelope which she opened and read the letter.

"The President is in today and has meetings until 11:00 a.m. I will show him this letter and he may change his schedule. He told me that he was expecting a young Gettysburg soldier from Wisconsin and the nurse that saved his life. He did not know when you might come, but he was positive that you and Florence would come to meet with him." The lady looked at the remainder of the group.

"What a wonderful show of support for Florence and Walter. The President will be even more impressed when he sees you. Take seats and make yourselves comfortable."

The group settled into chairs and presently a young man and an assistant entered the room carrying a coffee pot and a tray of cups. Coffee was offered and presently a lady dressed as a bakery chef entered with a tray of cookies. In a few minutes the first two men came back and asked if he could pick up the empty coffee cups. They had barely left the room when a man introduced himself as John G. Nicolay, the Presidents personal secretary and asked the group to follow him.

"When meeting the President, the men are to offer their hand in greeting. Ladies could offer their hand or offer a small curtsey. Remember the President has important business with Walter and Florence, but he will want to meet all of you," said the secretary in a kindly voice.

The secretary opened the door that led into the Presidents office. President Lincoln got up from behind his desk and approached Walter with a warm hello and a handshake. Next he turned to Florence and she offered her hand. The group was impressed with how tall and thin this man was. His eyes were indeed distinctive and his gaze was piercing. In a few seconds, the group could tell that this tall, kind man was indeed a special person. The group was immediately taken in by this man. The President welcomed each, and when he got to Bertha, she ignored the Presidents hand and moved in and hugged the President. President Lincoln was noticeably shaken.

"President Lincoln, keep on your plan," said Bertha excitedly.

Finally, all were greeted.

"Walter and Florence, I can see where you two get your strength," the President announced. "Before me, I see wonderful family support. Your coming with Walter and Florence from Wisconsin is proof of that. Now Walter and Florence, we have work to do. This terrible war has affected Americans in many ways. My main goal is to defeat General Robert E. Lee. If we can do that, this terrible war will be done. I have asked you to come here because I want to hear how a tough Union soldier thinks we could help our troops to win the war. We need to be able to take care of our injured soldiers and that is why I have asked Florence to assist with that.

"I get most of my information about our troops from my Generals. I doubt that any of them sleep in a tent with another soldier or prepare their own meals. I doubt that many of them know what happens to wounded soldiers. I want both of you to tell me how we could be a better army and win this war. We could ask the rest of the group to leave or they could stay."

Walter looked at Florence and quickly answered.

"Please let them stay, and Sir, if I could, I would like to ask permission for my brother Royce to be by my side. He and I enlisted together over two years ago and both were injured at Gettysburg."

"Of course. Royce come forward."

Chairs were brought in for the group. The President's secretary also returned with paper and pen to record what transpired. The President began by asking Walters name, address, regiment, brigade and corps he served in when wounded at Gettysburg.

"Walter," the President asked, "what are five or six things our Army of the Potomac could do to improve our chances of winning the war with General Lee?"

"Royce and I wondered if you would want this type of information. We think the most important thing that would help our troops would be to provide soap and water so soldiers could eat meals with clean hands and avoid passing disease among the soldiers. Along with that, avoid congestion as much as possible. Royce and I have concluded that in the two years we served, sixty-five percent of the time was spent in camp. We traveled about twenty-five percent of the time and fought only about ten percent of the time."

"The second most important thing is to recruit people to cook meals and provide them with portable kitchens and better food. More soldiers died of disease, weather and poor food than those killed in battle.

"Number three would be to give enlistees a physical exam. If they fail, they are not drafted. Troops are trained to fight in units. In the regiment, weak, unfit soldiers endanger all the rest of the soldiers.

"The last thing would be not to draft anyone with a criminal record of serious crimes like murder, theft and burglary. We have seen these men steal identification, money and shoes from our dead soldiers.

"One more thing that I read about in the Cleveland newspaper is to consider providing child care vouchers so Mothers could work to keep war materials in production as well as everyday goods on the home front. The shortage of men in most communities has caused real shortages of food, clothes and fuel, like coal.

"Oops. One more thing . . . Consider drafting immigrants that have not voted. In our community, we have many new arrivals. Many people think they should be drafted also. There, now I am finished unless Royce has anything to add."

"Sir, Gettysburg was fought on some of the hottest days of summer. All of our Regiment and many others had to wear our winter uniforms. Thank you."

"Thank you, Walter and Royce. You have told me things that make good sense and they sound like important changes that we should try to make. I can tell that both of you have given much thought to making the plight of our soldiers better. I will do my best to see their implementation is considered by the people both in the army and the government," said President Lincoln with an appreciative voice.

"I hate to interrupt again sir, but my younger brother Ernest asked me to ask you something. Since he is here would you allow Ernest to ask you what is on his mind?" said Walter hopefully.

"Of course, Ernest can ask. Ernest what did you want to ask me?" Ernest slowly rose from his seat and began with a humble voice.

"Sir, we just visited Gettysburg, the Gettysburg battlefield and cemetery. It saddened me to see the markers of all the men that died there. My request to you is to please find a way to fight wars that don't kill so many men. Thank you."

"Ernest, how old are you?"

"Fifteen years old, Sir."

"You are a member of a wonderful family that very much cares for our fellow man. You are a very sensitive young man and you are very thankful that your two brothers names were not on those markers. I am sure you realize how it saddens me to give orders that will mean deaths and injury to hundreds and

271

thousands of wonderful men. We have had many meetings with the army planners. Besides winning battles, our main goal is to prevent such staggering loss of life. We have changed our strategy from the first days of the war. Now we try to get the job done with less troops but they are more highly trained and attacking with coordination from the Calvary. . . Ernest we are improving and I hope this war is concluded by the time you may be drafted," said the President in a fatherly voice.

"Florence, it is your turn next," said the President. Her name and address were recorded and then she began.

"I was on a special nurses program at Hagerstown when the fighting started at Gettysburg. We volunteered and went as near the battlefield as we could and found the army doctors and nurses were overwhelmed. Even with our twenty-seven nurses and others from the Hagerstown hospital, the medical facilities were woefully overwhelmed. I would suggest that more nurses travel with the troops at all times. Possibly, the nurses could be trained as part of their nurses program at some university. The other important thing to consider is to have trained personnel to decide who gets treated and when. Some critically injured soldiers should be routed away from the stream of injured soldiers. In my tent, three soldiers were there for a few minutes and they passed away. It took several minutes, or longer, to remove the bodies and free up a cot for another injured soldier. Several precious minutes were lost for treatment to begin for these men. The Gettysburg battle had many more injured soldiers than we could adequately deal with and our medical supplies ran out or were rationed in order to make do. If there is another Gettysburg-sized event we need to be prepared with more doctors, nurses, tents, cots and very importantly, more medical supplies.

"I would like to add to what Walter and Royce said about using soap and water to clean hands before eating. In our studies we have learned about germs that can cause many diseases. Apparently at many camps or battle sites, water is taken directly out of streams and rivers. We have learned that most germs in the water can be killed by boiling the water for three minutes. Well water is safer but not often available, apparently. If all water in the camps were boiled for three minutes it should prevent diphtheria, dysentery and diarrhea. Even though you can't see these things called germs, they are deadly. Washing hands with soap and water should kill germs on the soldiers hand. Camps should be set up so slit trenches for excrement are away from the camp water source. Thank you, Mr. President," said Florence.

"Thank you, Florence, for your volunteering at Gettysburg and saving Walter's life and many other Union soldiers. Thanks for your comments and I will assure you that I will do all that I can to address your suggestions."

"Walter, Florence and Royce, I hope you can meet with a group of men tomorrow. My aid is negotiating a meeting with the appropriate army officials and the committee on military affairs of the Congress. That committee is made up of several Senators and several Assemblymen. Hopefully, a meeting can be arranged and we will inform you at your hotel. Meanwhile I hope you can visit the Capital and maybe look up your Senators from Wisconsin."

The group thanked the President and left his office. Just outside of the office door were five or six well dressed men who apparently had am appointment with President Lincoln. What a busy schedule for the President.

As the group exited the White House, the doorman was there.

"Finished so soon?" The doorman teased. "Really, the President gave you more time than most groups get. Did you see those men waiting outside the door? Well, here they come, apparently their time with the President is up. The man is very busy."

The doorman inquired if they needed a coach to visit the Capital. Erna stepped up near the doorman.

273

"Yes, we would like a coach," Erna said. As the group waited, the doorman and Erna engaged in talk. Both seemed interested in the other. Bertha wandered past her mother and said under her breath, "Looks like Erna is interested in the doorman."

Finally a coach pulled up under the canopy.

"Wow, they are going to pick us up under the canopy?" said an astonished Ernest.

"Looks like they are," said Royce. The group loaded up.

"My schedule as doorman is finished for today and if you don't mind, I would like to be your tour guide."

"That would be fine with me," answered Erna quickly.

This quickly brought teasing responses from her brothers and sister.

"It looks like we approve, Mr. Doorman," Ernest said.

"The question is where will you ride?"

"I will change my title to footman," said the doorman, "and if you look at the rear of the coach there is a nifty place for me to ride and be a footman."

"Before we go much farther, Mr. Doorman, do you have a name?" asked Edward quizzically.

"Roger, Roger Hammer," answered the doorman with enthusiasm. "Now I will carry out my duties as footman. Mr. Driver, please advance." With that the coach began to move forward and Roger stepped on the footman standard at the rear of the coach. Erna clearly was pleased.

The ride from the White House to the Capitol took about twenty minutes to traverse the distance. The coach came to a stop at the steps of the Capital. Roger offered to help everyone off the coach.

"How about some help for me?" said Bertha looking quite helpless looking down from the drivers seat.

"If you can get your brother to move and get to the edge of the seat, I will hop up there and see that you are safely deposited on the ground." With that Roger climbed up on the coach wheel, working carefully, Roger guided Bertha to step down on to the spokes of the wheel also. In a short time Bertha was safely on the ground.

"That was neat. Thank you," said Bertha with a small curtsey to Roger. She turned and winked at Ernest. Ernest thought 'What a show. . . .Bertha climbed up and down like a monkey before Roger showed up.'

Roger was a good tour guide. He showed the group both Chambers of Congress, but neither body was in session. Next he took the group to find the offices of the two Wisconsin Senators. Neither man was in his office as they were in committee meetings in the building. The office staff of each Senator warmly welcomed the group and asked all to sign in. Looking at the list of names and addresses, both Walter and Royce had put down the 6th Wisconsin Regiment after their names. The sight of the 6th Wisconsin Regiment caused the staff to be very excited.

"Lt. Col. Rufus Dawes was here last week. He is a good friend of the Senator and the two have worked together on the problems of the war. He is an impressive person," said one of the ladies.

By this time it was late afternoon and the group was ready to head to the hotel. With Roger's guidance, the group arrived at the coaches stand and Roger did his footman duties and all got on the coach, including Bertha who happily accepted Roger's help. Erna and Roger were not far from each other during the afternoon at the Capital. This fact had not gone unnoticed by Florence and Olivia.

"Looks like Erna and Roger are an item, at least for this afternoon," said Olivia with a coy smile on her face.

The coach delivered the group to the hotel. Roger, the footman, was thanked by all. Alice approached Roger and invited him to dinner this evening with the group. Roger was amazed! 'These fine folks want me to join them for dinner'.

"Are you sure it is alright with everyone?"

"I can read my family and they approve. Besides that, I can outrank them," said Alice with a twinkle in her eye.

"What time?" asked Roger excitedly.

"7:00 p.m. in the hotel dining room," replied Alice. Erna moved closer to Roger and smiled sweetly at him. Roger turned and departed with the salutation that he would see everyone at seven. Erna sidled up to her mother and whispered, "Thank you."

The group entered the hotel lobby and the desk clerk called out to Walter, Florence and Royce.

"There is a message from the President's office." The clerk handed the paper message to Walter. It was in President Lincoln's sweeping, beautiful hand.. *Walter, Florence and Royce. The meeting will be at 10:00 a.m. in Room 209 on the second floor. Attending will be several Senators and Assemblymen. Several army officials will attend also. All have been provided with notes on our meeting today. Do not be afraid of this group. A Senator from New York will huff and puff but in the end he is a good man so don't let him intimidate you. You may feel some resistance from the army men. They don't like to be told there is another way. There is a General, but the man that gets things done is Lt. Col. Schofield and he will sit in the back row in the right hand corner of the room. He likes to be in a position to 'read the attendees'. Stick to your guns and good luck. Wish I could be there. Abraham Lincoln.*

At 6:00 p.m., Walter knocked on Florence's door.

"Royce and I think that the three of us should meet for a few minutes. Can you come to our room now."

"I will be there in five minutes," replied Florence.

The three settled into a discussion about what we think would do the most good and what chance do we have of getting anything accepted. They are looking forward to the meeting and talked about not becoming flustered and humiliated.

They feel they have great ideas and know that not all of them will be accepted.

"The child care voucher would be a good thing to pursue. That will win points back home and people will think the Congressmen are working for the people," said Walter hopefully.

Dinner at 7:00 p.m. at the hotel dining room was three people short. Olivia, Jack and Azalea were missing. Florence relayed the message that Jack wanted to take the two sisters to a restaurant that he knew about. Roger, the doorman, showed up and fit right in. Bertha was a tease, much to Erna's dismay. Finally, a cross look from Erna made Bertha put on a 'if you say so' look on her face.

Roger was from Rockford, Illinois and came to Washington, D. C. as an aid to Senator Kincaid from that state. The Senator got defeated, but Roger applied for a job at the White House and since President Lincoln is from that state he got the doorman job.

Roger was a happy, smiley man of about 25 years of age. He had attended the University of Illinois, majoring in political science. He had one year to finish a degree.

"Any plans to use that degree when you get it," inquired Edward. Roger squirmed a little.

"Actually, I want to change my major to business. Originally I thought I wanted to be a Senator or Assemblyman. The more I saw of what those jobs are like, the more I realized that I did not want that life style or anxiety.

"I really thought about attending the University of Wisconsin at Madison. There is a Professor there by the name of James O'Brien that has a great reputation in the business world."

"Royce is going to start at the University in Madison the second semester. He is going to be a forester to manage Mother and Father's forests," chimed in Bertha with an all knowing tone in her voice.

"What can you tell us about President Lincoln?" asked Alice with an inquiring tone in her voice.

"He is sitting at his desk right now. He had no visitors scheduled this evening but that may have changed. The President works twenty hours on many days and he eats scant meals at his desk. That man is as kind of person as there is in the world. I have seen him with tears in his eyes after talking to parents of Union soldiers killed in this war.

"He is not only kind, but he is honest in everything he does. He is wonderful to work for and there is no doubt that treating everyone fairly and with dignity is of utmost importance. He has fired workers that failed to treat everyone with dignity and respect. This man has unbelievable weight on his shoulders. There is so much back stabbing, underhanded deals and lack of respect for this great man and it is disgusting."

Small talk accompanied the meal. Roger was quizzed by Royce as to who might be at the meeting tomorrow.

"I am afraid I don't know who might be there. I can tell you that your best strategy is to be well organized, be direct with your recommendations and don't be intimidated by those men. Don't forget, President Lincoln asked you to come to Washington, D. C. to tell him what can be done to win the war. From what I can see of this family, I think Florence, Walter and Royce will do a great job tomorrow. Good luck!"

"Will the family be allowed to be in the room?" asked Alice.

"The answer is 'yes'."

BIG DAY AT THE CAPITOL

Breakfast was eaten early Thursday and a coach was called to take the group of eleven people to the steps of the Capital. Room 209 was located at 9:45 a.m. An aide to President Lincoln welcomed the group and invited Florence, Walter and Royce to join him at the table in the front of the room. A few men had taken seats at the three rows of tables arranged in a semi-circle. By 10:00 a.m. the Congressmen and army brass were in attendance. The remainder of the Rounds group took chairs at the rear of the Chamber. The room was nearly full of people, including several newspaper reporters.

The aide called the meeting to order. Introductions were made. Walter noted who the Senator from New York was. He also located Lt. Col. Schofield sitting in the right rear seat. The moderator reminded the men of the copies presented to them of the testimony at a meeting with President Lincoln.

Florence, Walter and Royce were asked to make additional comments.

"We think the most important changes the army could do," Walter said, "involves the water used in cooking and drinking. Florence is a nurse and has studied about things called germs and she will cover that."

"Deaths due to disease," said Florence, in a clear voice, "poor food, and weather are much greater than losses in battle. Germs are invisible but they cause diphtheria, dysentery, diarrhea, colds and flu. These germs could all be in the water or in their food. We think the very most important thing we could do to protect our soldiers would be to be careful where we procure the water. But it must be boiled for three minutes to kill these germs. This sterile water would be used in cooking, washing dishes and cooking utensils. And very important, men need to wash their hands with this sterile water and lots of soap before they eat. No hand wash - no food."

"The other very important thing that could affect our soldiers," Royce told the group, "is to provide good meals three times a day. Walter and I served for two years with the 6th Wisconsin Regiment and in that period of time we spent about sixty-five percent of the time in camp. Men should be drafted to provide meals for the troops. Appropriate wagons need to be provided. The members of the regiment could be assigned certain jobs that last a week or so. Procuring and preparing firewood, building and maintaining the fires, obtaining water to be sterilized are jobs that could be shared. Procuring food from the army or local sources, washing dishes and cooking utensils are tasks that most men would gladly be willing to do once they knew they would get good food. And the dangers of dying from disease would be greatly reduced."

"How a camp is set up is important," Florence said as she spoke again. "Slit trenches need to be away from the main camp. Care should be taken to prevent runoff from the area into rivers and lakes. Also very important, water should be procured from upstream of the camp. Well water is far safer that surface water. All water needs to be boiled. A large cooking grill needs to be provided so several large cooking kettles with water in them could be boiled at once."

Walter spoke about the possibility of a child care voucher. He explained the shortage of men on the home front is causing a shortage of military materials and everyday goods. Many women could take several of those jobs if they could find someone to watch their children. We would encourage the development of a child care voucher program.

Florence spoke about the need for a trained person to make the decisions about who gets treated when dealing with injuries such as happened at Gettysburg.

"In my tent," she said, "three men were brought in and put on cots but died within a few minutes from their injuries that were too serious."

With that the three signaled that they were finished. The moderator asked if there were any questions that they would like to ask these three people.

The New York Senator thanked the three for their presentation.

"What qualifies you folks to address this body?"

"Florence and I were at Gettysburg," Walter answered, "when President Lincoln spoke on November 19th. We were able to speak to the President at that time. I explained that I was severely injured only a few feet from where we stood. Florence was a volunteer nurse that saved my life. Royce and I fought with the 6th Wisconsin Iron Brigade for two years, ending at Gettysburg. Sir, our President invited Florence and me to come to the White House and meet with him. That is how we are qualified."

Another Senator asked about the child care voucher.

"This could possibly be handled through the county court-house or major city and the funds would come from the federal government with an additional tax placed on liquor and tobacco. The family voucher program that many states are providing the funds for has been very successful and we feel the child care voucher program could be handled in much the same way," Walter explained.

A General asked Florence if she really thought germs were as dangerous as she said.

"In our studies at the University of Wisconsin," Florence responded, "we learned that diphtheria is caused by a germ, the name of which I cannot tell you now. Other germs causes dysentery and diarrhea. We grow cultures in our laboratories of tissue from patients with these diseases. Our instructors have insured us that clean sterile conditions will not allow these germs to survive."

"Statistics of deaths since the beginning of the war shows almost three soldiers die from disease, weather, poor food and accidents for each soldier killed in battle," reported Royce.

"It is clear to me that at this time in history our best chance to avoid theses deaths is to sterilize water, wash hands and utensils with soap and sterilized water. Providing more blankets in winter and perhaps a small folding stool and raincoat could protect soldiers in inclement weather and keep them off the cold, wet ground."

Lt. Col. Schofield said he was impressed by the presentations. He completely agreed with the idea of sterilized water and using soap before eating. We may be entering a phase in the war where our troops will be more mobile. How would we provide sterile water if we don't have long encampments?

"Local wells could be found," Walter replied, "and the water wagon with several barrels could be filled with well water. Hardtack will keep a solder alive when in battle or on the move. It is alright providing it is not rancid or infected with weevils."

The moderator looked at the clock and declared that the meeting was finished.

"Each of you will receive a summary of what was said today." Several men stepped forward and offered hands and said thanks for the presentation today. Lt. Col. Schofield stopped to talk.

"Lt. Col. Rufus Dawes and I are good friends," he said. "I commanded the 24th Michigan as part of the Iron Brigade. He is a wonderful leader, as you two men know. I was asked to come to Washington, D. C. after Antietam. I hope you can get Rufus to join us in Washington." Walter offered that Lt. Col. Dawes is very interested in the politics in Wisconsin and Madison.

The Chamber was filled with perhaps eighty people besides the Congressmen and army brass. The Round's family and friends had plenty of company. Some of the group displayed banners 'Stop the War'. Most appeared to be interested citizens but several could be seen taking notes. After the three presenters were finished talking to anyone with questions, a man with a note pad approached.

"William Lewis, *Washington Dispatch, newspaper for the open minded,"* said the man. Immediately, Walter was on alert. He was wary of this man but politely greeted him. "I listened to your presentation with interest. I get the feeling that the three of you are of the opinion that this war will go on for some time. Our paper very much supports the idea of a truce so this terrible war will end. Do the three of you have a response to that idea?"

Royce looked at the reporter with a stern look on his face. "We are finished here." From his look, Walter and Florence got the message and followed Royce to the back of the room to meet up with the rest of the group.

Bertha ran to meet the threesome. "You were great," as she hugged each of them. The greeting by the remainder of the group was similar.

"Why were you so short with the last person you talked to?" Erna asked Royce.

"He is from the camp of 'let's call a truce and end the war'. That would mean that Walter and I, along with thousands of Union and Confederate troops fought and died for nothing. No Union of all the States in America and no end to slavery. It has been a difficult struggle, but President Lincoln knows that in the end the Union will win." Alice, Olivia and Azalea all clapped and came up and patted the three presenters on the back.

The group had grown by one as Roger, the doorman, had joined them as it was his day off.

"That weasel Lewis is a low-life that has whipped up support for ending the war," Roger offered. "He is not welcome at the White House but he is allowed in. President Lincoln despises the man and what he is promoting but he staunchly defends his right to express his views."

"That is what makes America such a wonderful country to live in," Ernest chimed in.

"The Senate is in session. Do you want to go and watch?" asked Roger.

"I do," said Bertha excitedly.

"Roger, lead the way," Alice said. The Senate chamber was crowded with spectators, but Roger led them to the balcony where there were seats available. Most of the group got seats by the balcony railing and Bertha was one of the lucky ones. It was difficult to hear what was being debated. The group was impressed about how orderly the proceedings were. The Senators were polite to each other and discussions were vigorous and spirited at times. Finally, it was time to vote on the bill that was being debated. The yeas won by three votes over the nays. The group could identify the two Wisconsin Senators. The Senate broke for lunch and so did the group of twelve.

Roger led the way to a lunch room used by the Senate and Assembly pages as well as visitors. It was a cafeteria which was a new experience for some. Food was selected and Edward asked the cashier to keep track of all the meals for his group and he would pay when he came through.

As the group sat together and ate, Bertha asked, "Roger, why are there so many young people in here?"

"Many are pages," said Roger. "Do you know what they are?"

"Heck, no I don't?" said Bertha somewhat indignantly with an impish look that said 'I am just a kid, what do you expect of me'.

"Alright, Roger, what do pages do?" asked Bertha.

"They assist the Congressman by delivering papers, copies of bills or amendments. They also work in the office of their Congressman, opening mail, writing letters, running errands and greeting visitors from the Congressman's home district. Actually pages stay very busy." Roger was well known in the cafeteria as before he became a doorman he was a page and knew many of the current pages.

"The Senate will be in session again after lunch," Roger informed the group. "The Assembly will not be in session so if you want to visit your man we can go look him up."

"Why do you always refer to men. Aren't there any lady Congressmen," asked Bertha indignantly.

"There are none at this point," was Roger's reply.

"Well, there should be some and I bet someday there will be a lady Senator or Assemblyman. President Lincoln will see to that," said Bertha with a haughty tone in her voice.

Roger led the way to the Assembly offices of the Capital. Edward knew their man was from Stevens Point. His name was Joseph Romanski. His office was located and the group entered. The aide behind the desk, looked up with a shocked expression on her face as the room filled up. Alice introduced the group and asked if Congressman Romanski was in. About then a large, heavyset man emerged from his personal office and introduced himself as Joe Romanski and offered his hand to all the group.

He was a jovial, apparently happy man that was in his second term. After greetings were exchanged, Joe invited the group into his office. Walter explained what had taken place at the hearing that morning.

"If you could push for the child care voucher program that would be a big help in your district and many others."

"I know why you guys are ringing a bell with me. One of my friends visited Antigo recently and someone told him that a Civil War soldier from Antigo and a nurse had been invited to visit President Lincoln. That was you, Walter and this young lady must be the nurse. Am I correct?"

"Yes, this is Florence Porter from Sparta. This is my brother Royce and we both spent two years with the 6th Wisconsin Iron Brigade. We were both injured at Gettysburg and we have both been discharged. Florence was at nurses training at the University in Madison and had gone to Hagerstown,

Maryland for a special training session with twenty-six other Wisconsin nurses.

"When the fighting began at Gettysburg, they immediately volunteered to go and help injured soldiers. I was seriously injured on the third day and was unconscious for three days. Florence took care of me and saved my life."

"Tell me more about the child care voucher plan. Let me get two of my aides in here to learn about it also." Shortly a young man and a young lady entered the room, both with writing pads. Royce explained the need for the program and he said he certainly agreed that the program could be a big help to getting more military goods as well as everyday goods at home.

"I doubt that anyone is working on this bill so I will try to get a bill put together if your group would help me rough it out," added the Congressman. "Two big questions. Who would qualify and where would the funding come from?"

"First of all," Florence said matter-of-factly, "the funds would go to mothers of young children that need to be cared for while the mother works outside the home."

"The job should be one that produces military goods," Royce added, "either directly or indirectly as well as goods and services needed on the home front, such as food, clothes, fuel and in some cases medicine."

"The funding could come from a temporary tax on alcohol and tobacco and reimbursement could be to the states and their county courthouses," said Walter.

"As you know," Erna offered, "Wisconsin voucher program for families has been very successful and it runs through the court houses.

"If this bill gets so far as debate on the house floor, Ann Freiburger from Antigo would be a wonderful spokesman in support of passage," stated Alice. "I must also tell you here, that Walter appeared with Ann at the Capital in Madison in support of the voucher program."

Assemblyman Romanski was hesitant on the funding issue. First of all, you don't like to hear about raising taxes in Congress and most will vote against any new tax. Increasing the tax on wealthy people won't work because President Lincoln will veto that. If we borrow money we would have to pay it back and interest these days is high.

"You folks have given us enough information to get started on. My aides and myself will investigate what kind of rates mothers might be expected to be reimbursed at and how much the program might cost. But my feelings are that this is such an important issue for the United States of America that we need to do something along this line and do it soon."

Assemblyman Romanski expressed gratitude for this fine group stopping in and assisting him and his staff for getting started on this child care voucher program. He assured them he would begin immediately working on drafting a bill and trying to win support for it.

The group thanked Assemblyman Romanski and his staff and said goodbye.

"How did the President react to the idea of a child care voucher program?" asked a female aide.

"He didn't seem to respond either way but his body language told me he was in favor of it," Florence responded.

"Having the Presidents support would be very important to this program," the aide said.

THE WASHINGTON MONUMENT

The group thanked the aides and followed Roger to the steps of the Capital.

"See that white tower over there. That is the Washington Monument. Construction has been halted for now but eventually it will be completed to be five-hundred-fifty feet tall and will be the tallest structure in the world at this time."

"Let's walk over to it," said Ernest.

"How tall is it now?" asked Bertha.

"I think it is about one-hundred-fifty-eight feet," Roger replied. The group walked as close as they could but the construction area was roped off. Dozens of huge white blocks were piled near the base of the monument. The group was impressed at the size of the base which tapered slightly as each new layer of blocks were added. Stairways were being built in the monument as each layer was added. Roger thought there would be an elevator operated by steam in the monument when completed.

"George Washington was called the Father of our County. He led the Revolutionary Army who defeated the British. He was elected to the office of President of the United States of America. The very first American President."

RICHARD'S PUB

The group held a meeting.

"What do we want to do tonight?" Edward asked. "I would like to suggest that tomorrow, since it is Friday we go to Philadelphia."

"Let's go someplace where they don't hold meetings," said a disgusted Bertha and her response drew a laugh from the group.

"I know of a pub downtown that serves food but also invites local music groups that play. I find the place enjoyable," said Roger enthusiastically.

The group made their way to Richards Pub. Roger was warmly greeted by Richard and they huddled for a brief time. And then Richard smiled at the group and told them to follow him. Tables were moved and presently all twelve were seated, six to a table but the tables were near each other. Maybe Alice arranged the seating but at one table, Walter, Florence, Ernest, Bertha, Erna and Roger were seated. The remaining were seated at the other table. Azalea and Royce ended up next to each other. Anyway, the group was in good spirits and when the small band started playing the group enthusiastically clapped and seemed to enjoy the music.

The meals were ordered and eaten. Mugs of beer had been ordered but not for Bertha and Ernest. Sarsaparilla was their drink. Finally the band played *When Johnny Comes Marching Home Again.* The entire pub crowd joined in. The crowd was so enthusiastic that the band played the song again. Several people got up and marched to the music and clapped their hands. When the song ended and the clapping and cheering stopped, Roger quickly stepped up to the area in front of the band.

"There are some Billy Yanks that came marching home and they are in the room now. There are two brothers who fought for the 6th Wisconsin, Iron Brigade, Army of the Potomac. Both were injured at Gettysburg and are now discharged. And they came marching home. Walter and Royce Rounds of Antigo, Wisconsin. . . please stand up." As soon as Walter and Royce stood up and acknowledged the crowd, the entire crowd cheered, clapped and rose to their feet. In a few minutes the din subsided and everyone sat down.

"Walter was severely injured and was unconscious for three days," Roger continued. "A lovely nurse in training at the University of Wisconsin had gone to Hagerstown for training. Those twenty-seven young nurses immediately volunteered to go to Gettysburg to treat the injured. When Walter finally regained consciousness, he looked at the beautiful, smiling face of Florence who had cared for Walter for three days.

"Walter recovered and was sent to Harrisburg and Florence went back to Hagerstown. Walter knew Florence would come to visit him or send a letter. Finally, Walter was healed enough to come home. Two months later he found out that Florence and two other nurses had been severely injured by a team of run away horses pulling a heavy wagon. Walter immediately went to Chambersburg, Pennsylvania, found Florence and for two months helped her regain her health. Florence, please stand up." Again the crowd rose, cheered and clapped.

When the crowd returned to a normal state, Roger continued. "Walter, Florence and Florence's mother and aunt attended the November 19th appearance of President Lincoln at Gettysburg to dedicate the war memorial and battlefield cemetery. Florence and Walter were able to meet the President and visit briefly. A short time ago Walter and Florence received a letter from the President requesting they come to Washington, D. C. as he had a task for them. They have met with the President and a special committee and they are about to leave Washington, D. C. All the folks sitting at their tables are family and friends that accompanied Walter and Florence to visit Gettysburg and Washington, D. C. to Philadelphia where the Rounds family lived until a few years ago. Thanks for the interruption."

Several people came to thank all three for their service. Several ladies approached Florence and thanked her for volunteering and tending to Walter and several others. Several asked if she was completely healed. All in all, the evening was fun and humbling for the entire group of twelve. Edward thanked Roger for being the instigator for calling attention to the accomplishments of Walter, Florence and Royce.

"Sir, it has been a high privilege to be included with your wonderful family for the past two days. I have been very attracted to Erna and with your and Mrs. Rounds permission, I would like to ask her to spend the night in my house. She would have her own room," said Roger hopefully. Edward smiled and put his hand on Roger's right shoulder.

"Roger, Erna is an adult lady and she can easily make up her own mind. Her mother and I would not think of advising her unless she asked. She is a wonderful, very capable young lady and if she is happy with your company, her mother and I are also."

It was nearly 10:00 p.m. and the group of twelve had enough to drink and had clapped and sung about all they could and it was suggested that the group head for the hotel.

"No, wait," said Ernest. "I had asked the violin player if I could use his instrument for one song. He said I could if Mother and Father approved. I would like to play, but Bertha has to perform the dance that goes along with the song." The group looked at each other with quizzical looks on their faces. Who knew that Ernest could play the fiddle.

Roger approached the band leader. He nodded and asked the violin player to come forward. Ernest and Bertha made their way to the band stand.

"What a surprise," announced Roger. "Young man Ernest will play the fiddle and his younger sister, Bertha will do a dance."

Ernest was nervous as was Bertha. Ernest took the fiddle, stroked the bow on the strings and began playing *Turkey in the Straw.* He enthusiastically swayed, tapped his foot and immediately engaged the audience. Bertha, daintily held up her skirt and began to jig to the music. Her nimble feet, quick hops and spins brought the crowd to their feet, clapping in time to the catchy tune. The song ended and the crowd went wild. "More . . More" was shouted from the crowd. Ernest and Bertha consulted briefly.

Ernest began She*'ll be Coming Around the Mountain.* His swaying, leaning and foot tapping style and Bertha's dance steps as she deftly held her skirt kept the crowd clapping and swaying with the music. Finally, the song ended and Ernest handed the violin back and the two performers rejoined the group to many accolades.

Roger was able to flag down the large coach and the group headed to the hotel. Roger had asked Erna to spend the night with him and they headed to his house. The remainder of the group entered the hotel and Edward approached the desk clerk and informed him that the rooms they were using would be vacated after tonight.

PHILADELPHIA

Friday morning found the group of eleven boarding a train to Philadelphia. Roger and Erna had joined the group for breakfast and Roger bade everyone farewell on the station platform. He promised he would visit Antigo when he could. Erna had tears in her eyes as the train pulled out of the station to clanging bells on the engine. The group felt a sadness about leaving Washington, D. C. It is such a fascinating place with plenty of excitement. The group felt great pride in being involved with the process with which the country operates.

Florence, Walter and Royce all had their own thoughts about their involvement with President Lincoln. Walter felt even greater admiration for this great man who had asked him and the others for advice concerning the war. Walter wondered if the suggestions made would be enacted or even parts of them. He felt the child care voucher showed some promise. At least the threesome's comments may start discussion that will lead to some meaningful changes.

Even though Florence and Walter had been together since they left Antigo, they have had no private time together. They sat together and held hands as the train rolled toward Philadelphia. Florence had watched Walter carefully during the past few days. She saw two times when Walter seemed to be struggling with the demons of the battlefield. She knew that when they got back to Wisconsin they needed to make wedding plans. She knew that Walter felt very strong about getting married soon and about the resulting child or children. She leaned her head on Walter's shoulder and wiped a tear of happiness.

Florence also left Washington, D. C. with mixed emotions. She felt that she and the Round's men had made important comments to President Lincoln and the committee. She felt proud that she and Walter had been invited to Washington, D.

C. and enjoyed the excitement of the nations Capital. She was so proud of Walter. This kind, friendly man is so willing to share himself and his ideas with anyone to help mankind.

RELATIVES

The train pulled into the station at Philadelphia. The cars were nearly full as there are several stops along the way, including Baltimore, Maryland and Willington, Delaware. The group stepped down off the train and were immediately met by two cousins of the Round's boys and girls. They were also named Rounds and were sons of Douglas Rounds, Edward's brother. These men were about Walter and Royce's age and warmly welcomed the travelers.

The boys had been friends and played together often when the Edward Round's family lived in Philadelphia. Cyrus was twenty-three years old and Earl was twenty-one. They looked very similar to Walter, Royce and Ernest as they were of moderate build and apparently quite athletic as they were quite lean and trim. They also had light colored hair. There was a daughter by the name of Lily and she was fifteen. She was not with the group which now included Douglas and Mary Rounds. Florence was amazed how much Douglas and Edward looked like each other. Both Douglas and Mary were very nice, polite people and Mary was a neat, well dressed lady with her hair pulled up with a stylish hat adorning her hair. Douglas wore a stovepipe hat and had a suit and tie on.

The five Round's men retrieved the luggage and a meeting was held on the railroad platform.

"Besides spending time with these fine relatives there are three things that need to be done in Philadelphia, Alice announced. "Florence, Olivia and I need to purchase a wedding dress for Florence. We need to visit the Liberty Bell Bank and Trust and we should try to visit Independence Hall."

Douglas and Mary invited the group to their home for the evening meal. It was decided that the three wedding dress seekers would visit two or three shops nearby. Jack and Azalea would visit Independence Hall. Alice told her five children to meet at the bank by 3:00 p.m. The five Round's young men took the luggage to a nearby hotel and secured rooms. On the way to the hotel, Erna and Bertha saw some dress shops that they would like to visit looking for some new clothes. Edward and Douglas had some property to look at.

Ever since Edward and Alice moved to Wisconsin, Douglas and Mary have been the overseers of the many properties that Alice inherited when her parents were killed in a train accident. They own one-hundred-seventeen row house apartments near downtown, a hotel with one-hundred-sixteen rooms and a Bank and Trust Company. They also own seventeen buildings downtown which are rented to various mercantile operations. They also own significant acreage on the edge of Philadelphia and some of that property is under pressure to be sold for development.

Douglas and the boys still operate the large nursery and landscaping business on the edge of the city. Their property is also desirable for development. Edward and Douglas spent the afternoon looking at the properties in question. After some discussion, the two brothers decided they wanted to explore the possibility of forming a company to develop these parcels. Edward's was fifty-five acres and Douglas had fifty acres which was now the nursery.

The possibility of forming their own construction and sales company entered the discussion. Douglas thought his sons, Cyrus and Earl, would like to do that with the nursery property. Both men thought that until the war is over, development of the property would be slow. Edward pointed out that to get the property surveyed, plats developed and approved by the county and the village of Drexel would take several months and many meetings.

Douglas said his inventory would have to be sold off, the property surveyed and platted also. The property is in Montgomery County and the village of Melrose Park. It may take several months to get approval and if we get started soon it may take several years before any building can start. Currently both boys, Cyrus and Earl are attending college. Cyrus at the University of Pennsylvania majoring in architecture. Earl is as Temple University majoring in engineering. Both are members of the Pennsylvania National Guard and were called into action at Gettysburg and fought on days two and three and neither were injured.

By the end of the afternoon, the two men thought they should keep the property separate and Douglas would oversee the development with the work being done by workers in the company. The two men would meet with Edward's three company lawyers on Saturday to get started drawing up company papers. After supper, the two men will discuss what they have talked about with Alice and Mary and seek their input.

The wedding dress shoppers found a beautiful dress for Florence to wear at her wedding. Erna and Bertha also found several items of clothing and shoes to purchase. They met up with Alice and their brothers at the Liberty Bell Bank and Trust.

THE BANK

The group went into the bank and were warmly welcomed by several of the workers. This impressed all of the Round's children. Why would these people even remember their mother since she had been gone for about eight years. Erna could see the surprise on her siblings faces and whispered behind her hand.

"It helps the memory when you are talking to the owner."

"You mean Mother and Father own this bank?" asked Ernest.

"That is correct," replied Erna emphatically.

Alice gathered the five Round's children around her.

"A few years before your grandfather and grandmother Miller were killed, they put ten-thousand dollars in savings accounts in each of your names. Your father and I have not told you until now for two reasons. First, your grandparents stipulated that the funds, plus interest, would not be available until you are twenty-one years old. They also wished that you would take a portion of these funds and do good for mankind. The second reason is that Erna and Royce have only recently turned twenty-one. Your father and I felt that you two really didn't need the money and besides we needed to come to Philadelphia to retrieve the funds. Walter just turned twenty-one in October. Ernest and Bertha have several years before the funds become available to them." The five Round's siblings were shocked.

"Ten-thousand dollars, that is a fortune," said Ernest enthusiastically.

"I don't even know how much money that is, but it must be a whole bunch!" said Bertha as she found a chair to sit on with her face in her hands. She got up from the chair and held her arms out, pretending to be holding a large object.

"Do you want to leave the funds here in this bank?" Alice asked the group once the back slapping and congratulations were completed. "If you do, you will have to come to

Philadelphia to retrieve the amount you are requesting, or you could draw the funds out and take that cash with you. I can tell you that both your father and I would strongly advise you not to do that. You maybe don't know this, but your father and I own a courier company that regularly delivers cash and other important documents to us or the bank in Antigo. There are many other companies that hire us to do this work for them also. I would recommend that you consider this option. These men are all bonded and insured and we have never had a loss in eight years.

"You could draw your funds, including interest and they would be put in the care of the couriers to be taken to the bank in Antigo, or any other bank."

"How about Bertha and I?" asked Ernest. "Can we transfer our funds too?"

"Yes, you can," Alice answered, "but you would not have access to the funds until you reach twenty-one."

"We totally understand that and we will happily wait," said Bertha, as she daintily raised her right hand and smiled sweetly.

"What should we do?" asked Royce.

"I want my funds in the bank at Antigo," said Erna emphatically.

"Me too," said Walter.

"Sounds good to me too," added Royce.

"Count me in," said Ernest.

"Well, I sure don't want to be the odd one out," said Bertha happily.

"We would not be able to arrange withdrawal of these funds until Monday, Mrs. Rounds," the bank manager told her. "Perhaps we could do the required paperwork today so Monday we could package the bills and entrust them to the couriers."

"That would be fine," replied Alice. The manager requested Alice's safe deposit box key and together they opened the box and Alice retrieved the paper documents for each of the

Round's siblings. They were signed and the proper bank documents were given to Alice. The courier company was in an office on the second floor of the bank. Alice asked Royce and Walter to accompany her to place the order to courier the funds to Antigo.

The manager gave Alice a warm welcome. Walter and Royce met the manager also and were impressed by the straight forward manner of this man. He called several of his couriers into the office to meet Alice and her sons. All were older, they were large, tough looking, imposing men. All wore a side arm that was holstered but was very visible.

"Antigo, you say," said Omar, the obvious boss of the crew. "I have been there at least six or seven times. It is out on the fringe of settlement but it is beautiful there. All those beautiful maples and friendly people at the bank. Have you built the railroad spur to your property?"

"The spur is in," Alice responded, "but that was just before it snowed and Edward has not been able to build any of the mill yet. Once this war ends he hopes to hire many men and get the mill running."

INDEPENDENCE HALL & THE LIBERTY BELL

The business at the bank was finished and Alice suggested, "All that wants to go, can come with me to visit Independence Hall."

Florence, Olivia and Azalea enthusiastically indicated they wanted to visit.

"If Florence wants to go," said Walter, "of course I will go . . . if it is alright with her." Florence gave Walter a playful slap on the shoulder.

"I would not visit there unless you do, silly." The few blocks were covered and before them stood one of the most famous buildings in American - Independence Hall. It was simple, but sturdy. It was easily recognized because it had been photographed often.

The group entered the main room, known as Assembly Hall, where the patriots that developed the Declaration of Independence and the Constitution held their meetings. One could imagine the men who labored here, the many debates that took place and finally reaching an agreement about both documents.

The group moved upstairs to 'The Governors Council Chambers'. This was the room where fugitive slave trials were held. Walter pointed out the instruments used by surveyors, Mason and Dixon when they established the Mason-Dixon line between Pennsylvania and Maryland.

Olivia, Azalea and Florence were very impressed to be in the same building where George Washington was appointed Commander and Chief of the Continental Army in 1775. Benjamin Franklin, John Adams and all the other signers who labored in the very room they stood in.

There was a plaque telling about the Liberty Bell which still hangs in the belfry of Independence Hall. In the 1840s the bell cracked after ninety years of service. It has not rung since then. There is talk of bringing the Liberty Bell down and displaying it. The famous inscription was shown. *Proclaim Liberty Throughout all the Land Unto all the Inhabitants Thereof.*

Olivia read the inscription and re-read it.

"What a powerful statement," she said thoughtfully. Alice told the group that the bell had heavy use. It was used to tell the early residents of Philadelphia when news was found and the bell summoned the people to hear the 'Town Crier' deliver the news. It also called citizens to meetings and other important events.

THE HOUSE

The afternoon had turned into early evening and Alice announced that it was time to go to Douglas and Mary's house. Alice led the way as the house of her childhood was only a few blocks away. There was snow on the ground but it did not hinder travel. Finally, the mansion came into view. Olivia, Florence and Azalea stopped and stared!

"It looks very much like the Antigo house," said Olivia. The large house had a sweeping roof with large overhangs. Large dormers looked out from parts of the roof. The house was dark in color with white trim around the windows and doors. The most striking feature was the large wrap around porch which appeared to be on three sides of this house. The house was on a large lot with many beautiful trees and shrubs. A large back yard looked like a nice place for kids to play. Picnics and parties could be held there or people could relax in the shade of the beautiful trees.

"This was my parents home which they built and I grew up here. Edward and I lived here before we moved to Antigo."

"Why would you and Edward leave this beautiful home to go to the frontier of Antigo?" asked Olivia.

"Edward felt closed in. We had inherited much property and Edward was managing it and doing a great job, but he was restless. He loved trees and shrubs. He and Douglas still had the nursery started by his father and we reached an agreement with Douglas and Mary to continue to oversee our property and they would live in this house as part of that agreement. Edward left the door open to return if the family really wanted to. Edward was immediately happy to leave Philadelphia, as I was too. It was a drastic change to move to Antigo but Edward loved it. The huge forests made him very happy. Building the house was a struggle, but we both knew eventually we would be very happy. The children loved our property at Antigo.

"I will say that our children missed their friends. Our Walter and Royce are the same age as Cyrus and Earl and they attended the same school. They were very good friends and they did many things together. They especially liked fishing together and hunting squirrels on the wooded hills near the city."

Inside the majestic house Olivia and Florence could see the arrangement was very similar to the Antigo house. The draperies and wallpaper were elegant! Beautiful pictures in elaborate frames adorned the walls. The floors were of maple and large oriental rugs covered the beautiful floors. The furniture was very sturdy and it looked expensive. Alice and Mary saw the visitors looking at the room and they could tell they thought the furniture, rugs and pictures were excessive.

"My father was a kind and generous person," Alice said, "he enjoyed elaborate surroundings. My mother was much less demonstrative. She never wore fancy clothes or put on airs. She did allow my father to build this elaborate house and decorate and furnish it as it is. My mother told me that she much preferred a less pretentious home and adornments but she came to appreciate these wonderful surroundings."

Everyone finally arrived, including Lily, the fifteen year old daughter of Douglas and Mary. She was in school and just returned home. She was fairly tall and slender. She wore her light brown hair down to her shoulders. She was a very pretty girl and she and Bertha were happy to see each other again. They had played together many times before Bertha and her family moved to Antigo.

As large and comfortable as this huge house was, the dining room table could not accommodate the seventeen people invited to dine. A second smaller table was set near the large table. Mary decided that the five Round's boys could eat at the smaller table. That was fine with the boys and the twelve other folks were seated around the large table.

Alice had sent a letter to Douglas and Mary regarding how

Walter was injured and how Florence nursed him to good health. She explained how they were separated and how Walter found the address for Azalea and knew Florence was there. He left immediately and went there and found a seriously injured Florence. That is as much as Douglas and Mary knew about Florence. They inquired as to her health. Florence told about Walter helping her to heal.

"Olivia, Azalea, Walter and I went to Gettysburg to listen to President Lincoln's address to dedicate the memorial and battlefield cemetery." She explained how they met the President and he later invited Walter and her to come to Washington, D. C. as he had a task for them.

"Edward and Alice had business here in Philadelphia. Walter wanted Royce to come to Washington, D. C. with us," related Florence. "Ernest and Bertha wanted to visit Gettysburg, as did Erna. We picked up Aunt Azalea on our way to Gettysburg. Jack is an old friend of my mother and we picked him up in Madison."

THE PRESIDENT BECKONS

"May I ask what the President wants you and Walter to do?" asked Douglas as he listened intently. Florence explained what the President asked them to do and briefly talked about both meetings.

"That is quite an honor to be invited to meet with President Lincoln. Were you impressed by the President?" inquired Mary.

"President Lincoln is a very impressive man," Florence smiled. "He is tall and thin and his eyes, well, they are piercing. He is very kind, friendly and honest. The tremendous weight of the many problems makes his life very stressful."

"How were you able to meet the President when he spoke at Gettysburg? The paper said about twelve thousand people were in attendance?" asked Douglas.

"My hero, Walter," Florence replied, "told me he wanted to meet the President so he took my hand and we made our way toward the speakers stand before the ceremony started, and there he was, stovepipe hat and all. Walter addressed the President, told him he had fought for the 6th Wisconsin Regiment and was severely injured a few feet from where they stood. He introduced me and told that I had saved his life. The President was very complimentary of the 6th Wisconsin and all Wisconsin Regiments. A few minutes later, one of his aides approached and asked for our names and addresses. Now you know the entire story of why we are filling your beautiful house with guests and eating this wonderful meal."

"Florence, you are indeed a very capable person and your mother must be very proud of you. I can tell that the Round's family of Antigo will be very proud and happy when you and Walter are married," said an impressed Mary.

The dinner and dessert was finished and all five Round's men offered to wash and dry the dishes. The two elder Round's men and their wives retreated to the den to discuss the two properties talked about earlier. Both ladies liked the idea of the land remaining in the family to be sold in small lots that the company would develop. The men planned to meet with the three lawyers that Edward retains to deal with the many issues encountered with the ownership of many properties. As the four discussed various aspects of the proposal, it appeared that indeed proper legal advice is needed.

Olivia, Florence, Azalea and Jack had retreated to the library. It turned out that Jack was quite the reader. He was very impressed by the hundreds of books on the shelves. Among them were *Moby Dick, Twelve Years a Slave, Last of the Mohicans,* and *Voyage of the Beagle,* were books that caught the eye of the group. Jack volunteered, "*Moby Dick* was based on a true story of a ship called the Essex, it was a whaler out of Nantucket that was attacked by a large whale that damaged the ship and it quickly sank. The crew got into the small whale boats used to row to the whale and harpoon it. Many sailors ended up dying but some made it to safety. Many months later, Herman Melville talked to survivors of the Essex and got the idea to write *Moby Dick.*

Finally, it was late and the eleven travelers needed to return to their hotel. Edward had made arrangements for a large coach and a team to arrive and take the group to the hotel. It was cold and a light snow was falling. The driver and footman provided blankets. Ernest and Bertha took seats by the driver. The team pulled the large coach through the quiet streets and shortly arrived at the hotel. The guests were helped down from the coach. Both addressed Edward as Mr. Rounds and seemed to be well acquainted with Edward. A gratuity was discreetly transferred and thanks were offered by the travelers.

Saturday morning found the Douglas Round's family joining the Edward Round's family in the hotel dining room. Douglas intentionally sought out Jack Sanders and sat by him at breakfast.

"Edward told me that you built a railroad spur from Antigo to his property. Was that a standard gauge?"

"Yes, it is, the same track that all regular trains run on. I think Edward may be thinking about establishing a 'narrow gauge' track to bring logs from deep in the forest to the mill. Those tracks are not as heavy and the rails are closer together. Many times these tracks are picked up and relocated after an area has had the desired logs removed. The engine and cars are smaller but are very useful moving logs to the mill."

SUZANNE AND PRICILLA

"I haven't seen any young ladies you two may have be-friended," Bertha asked Cyrus and Earl. "Is that going to change?" This brought laughter from everyone. Leave it to Bertha to speak what is on her mind.

"I have a lady friend," Cyrus smiled and answered, "and she will join us this afternoon. Her name is Suzanne and she is a student at the University of Pennsylvania. She is studying music. She plays violin in the Philadelphia Concert Orchestra as well as the University of Pennsylvania Concert Orchestra."

"I sure am looking forward to meeting Suzanne," Ernest announced. "I hope we can hear her play and I bet she is very talented."

"Suzanne is quite reserved but I hope she will perform a number or two," said Cyrus. "I will plead my case that my cousin Ernest is a young promising violinist and would very much enjoy listening to her play."

"Maybe Ernest can fiddle for her," Erna chimed in, "after all, he and Bertha stole the show at Richard's Pub in Washington, D. C. two nights ago." Ernest look embarrassed but pride of accomplishment shown in his eyes.

"Pricilla is my lady friend," said Earl, not wanting to be upstaged by his older brother, "and she is attending Drexel University and will soon transfer to Drexel College of Medicine. She is studying to become a doctor for children. I hope she can join us this afternoon also. You will like her and she is not reserved. Lily already knows this, but she will challenge you to a game of darts, card tricks and any other high-jinks she can dream up. She will enjoy you, Ernest and Bertha as you have 'spunk' that she really admires in young people."

Edward and Douglas left to meet with Edward's attorneys to discuss the steps necessary to develop both parcels of land on the edge of Philadelphia. The ladies all left to shop at the downtown shops. Before leaving, Edward reminded the ladies of the long train ride home and of the buggy rides, so keep that in mind when you make purchases.

Jack wanted to visit one of the companies that supplies switches to his railroad track company. He invited the five Round's boys but only Ernest accepted and on the condition that they get back to Douglas' home by afternoon as he did not want to miss meeting and possibly hearing Suzanne playing the violin. The other four Round's men opted for a pool hall. Mary had told everyone to be at her house for lunch by 1:00 p.m.

By mid-afternoon, lunch had been consumed but there was not a sign of Edward and Douglas. Pricilla was able to visit and she was an energetic pretty lady. Taller than most ladies, she had dark short hair and dark eyes. She was slender and seemed to have a permanent smile. After a few minutes she rounded up Lily, Bertha and Ernest and away they went to the dart board.

Pricilla was great at darts. Finally, she offered to toss her darts with her back to the dart board. She still won but there was much good natured ribbing by all three. Finally, she called her three opponents together in a huddle.

"I will tell you the secret to my success. Practice," she whispered.

Suzanne did indeed arrive by late afternoon. She did have her violin with her and Cyrus convinced her to play a number for the group that was gathered there. She tuned the instrument and began playing. Suzanne could really play the violin. Ernest was fascinated by the skill Suzanne exhibited. When she was finished Cyrus told Suzanne that Ernest had taught himself to fiddle and was looking forward to hearing you play."

"You mean Ernest plays jigging music?" With that she proceeded to play a fast moving, hand clapping tune that had everyone involved.

"Ernest, play us a tune or two," said Suzanne encouragingly.

"Naw, naw . . . I couldn't even come close to you."

"You let us decide, here is the fiddle." Ernest gingerly took the instrument.

"Bertha and I perform together," he told Suzanne. "I fiddle and she dances, is that alright?"

"Of course, it is alright and don't be surprised if a few of us join in."

Ernest looked at Bertha and saw she was ready to dance. He began to play and he dipped the fiddle, swaying back and forth and tapped his foot as *Turkey in the Straw* flowed from the instrument. Bertha had deftly held her skirt up and her feet flew as she danced to the music. All at once Suzanne jumped up and joined Bertha and a jiffy later Pricilla, Erna, Florence and Azalea joined in. All seemed nimble and all smiled as they jigged to Ernest's music.

Ernest played the song three times, one after the other. Finally he sensed the jiggers were beginning to tire. Ernest truly enjoyed playing for the group of lady jiggers. Suzanne had very high praise for Ernest.

"Where did you learn to play the violin?"

"We lived here in Philadelphia until I was seven years old. Mother had me take lessons from a Mr. Vitus Kohler." Suzanne had a shocked look on her face!

"Mr. Kohler was my teacher also. I loved that man. He was very patient but very strict with what he wanted me to learn. Mr. Kohler still has students and lives in the same house on Locust Street. In fact I sit by him during our concerts."

"I took lessons up until 1855 and it might be possible you were taking lessons then?" said Ernest.

"You know what? I had to wait until there was an opening and finally there was an opening in June of 1855, "replied Suzanne.

"My last lesson was in late May of 1855. When I left it may have made an opening for you," said Ernest.

311

Bertha asked Suzanne to play another tune.

"Want a fast one?" asked Suzanne.

"You bet," was Bertha's reply.

"This is a medley of Irish jigs and are popular here in Philadelphia because there are so many Irish people living here. In fact, there are several Union regiments from Philadelphia that are made up of all Irish. My brother fought for the 69th Pennsylvania and was killed at Antietam."

With that Suzanne made magical sounds with her violin. In seconds, the entire group found a place to jig. The Round's men were surprisingly good jiggers. Finally, the lilting music stopped and Suzanne played *When Johnny Comes Marching Home*. That signaled the end of the music. Suzanne told the group that the Philadelphia Concert Orchestra was performing this evening at the Academy of Music Auditorium on Broad Street near Locust Street.

"Starts at 7:00 p.m." said Suzanne with an inviting tone in her voice. "Besides I have a small solo tonight."

"Let's go," said Ernest.

"Let's see if there any other plans," cautioned Alice, "but it would be very nice to hear Suzanne and her orchestra."

There appeared to be much agreement within the group.

"We could have an early meal," said Mary, "and go to the concert. We better send one or two of the men to hold tickets for us. These mid-winter performances are well attended." Cyrus and Royce volunteered to go to the Academy office and reserve tickets. Pricilla indicated she would like to attend so the ticket count was seventeen. Away the men went hoping the group will be able to reserve enough tickets.

During the evening meal, Pricilla entertained the group with some of the classes she is taking at Drexel. She was a charming, engaging, young lady that had obvious communication skills. She and Erna had been classmates at primary school as well as high school

"You always were the brightest light in our classes. It certainly does not surprise me that you will be a doctor and my guess you will be a wonderful doctor. Your young patients will enjoy your great bedside manner," said Erna with an admiring tone in her voice.

THE CONCERT

Time to leave for the concert arrived. This large group made their way to the Concert Hall. Coats were checked.

"There is an after concert later in this lobby," Mary reminded the group. "The performers are here and people can visit with them or whoever they wish to."

"Ernest, maybe you could visit with Mr. Kohler," Alice encouraged her son.

The large group all had tickets, but could not sit together. Ushers found the proper seats for all and Florence and Walter were able to sit together a short distance from any others in the group. This was the first time since they left Antigo last Saturday that they had any private time alone.

"I have really missed you even though you have been near me," whispered Walter as he reached for Florence's hand. They snuggled close to each other. Florence reached over and with her other hand and put it on their clasped hands.

"I love you," Florence whispered and then gave Walter the same beautiful smile he first saw at Gettysburg.

The concert began but Florence and Walter were deep in their own thoughts and feelings. Walter had had several troubling incidents in the past week, none of which caused attention to be drawn to Walter. But he is more and more concerned that the battlefield memories are more often but not long lasting or severe. He is very worried that it may take him down. That thought is troubling to Walter as he is only twenty-one years old and he has some goals he is aiming at. The first is to marry Florence and to establish a home with her and the children born to them. Next is a little vague. He has seen some how the government makes decisions and makes laws. Perhaps he could get involved with local or state government. People seem to like what he says. He also is very interested in helping his father develop the flooring mill.

The concert continues and Suzanne is called to the front of the stage. A long concerto is played then Suzanne plays her solo and it is outstanding. When she finishes the audience gives her an ovation and the concerto continues. Florence is also deep in her thoughts as she holds Walter's hand. She also wants to marry Walter very soon. She looks forward to establishing a home for Walter and herself but also for anticipated children. Both she and Walter are looking forward to arrival of children and she knows Walter wants to have children soon as he is very concerned about the battlefield memories. He is worried of how they will affect their lives, if at all.

Florence and Walter are very much in love. Florence has made up her mind that she will stand by Walter forever. She hopes not, but the forever could be only a few years. She will do whatever she can to help him deal with the battlefield demons or to defeat them. She knows that her life could be chaotic but she absolutely will stand by Walter. Whenever she thinks about how he searched for her when she was injured and then he found her and helped her to regain her health, it brings a tear to her eye. She remembered how he was so happy to receive the plume back that he had given her as thanks for saving his life at Gettysburg.

Florence has given much thought to the plume. It was given to Walter by Lt. Col. Rufus Dawes as Walter lie unconscious from his wound at Gettysburg. Florence has wondered what may have gone on in Walter's mind as he lie unconscious. Maybe somehow he realized his commander had been there and presented the beautiful plume to Walter. Maybe he was processing the past two years of his life as a soldier. Maybe all those thoughts are dark as he recalled many of the horrors he has endured. Perhaps the plume was a bright and shining symbol about what was good about war. He probably knew his serious injury would prevent him from becoming a soldier again. Also it was given to him by his Commander, a man he greatly admired. He also felt he was doing his part to help President Lincoln to unite the Union and free slaves.

Florence knew Walter was a complex man, but yet very simple in his relationship with others. Everyone should be treated with dignity and respect, period. One issue that troubles him is that women are not allowed to vote. That is not right in Walter's eyes. Florence thought that issue would be worth fighting for in Walter's world. Not shooting at each other, but working within the Constitution that Walter loves and has studied.

As the concert wound to a conclusion, Florence squeezed Walter's hand and snuggled closer.

"I love you very much," she whispered to Walter. Walter looked at her smiling faces he smiled at her.

"I am the luckiest man in the world, Florence. I love you with all my heart," Walter whispered to Florence.

The concert finished, the guests and performers mingled in the auditorium lobby. Tea and cookies were offered and many people took advantage of this offer. Ernest and Bertha sought out Mr. Kohler, Ernest's violin teacher. Mr. Kohler saw Ernest and addressed him.

"Ernest Rounds, one of my best students. I thought you moved to Wisconsin."

"Mr. Kohler. it is very good to meet you again. This is my sister, Bertha." Bertha curtsied politely and offered her hand to Mr. Kohler as she greeted him.

"Ernest is a pretty good fiddler, thanks to you Mr. Kohler."

"I bet he is and I bet you can dance a mean jig, Bertha. Am I correct?"

"Bertha can really dance the jig," Ernest interjected, "and if she was around you for half hour you would want to pull all your hair out," said Ernest as he gently pushed against Berthas shoulder.

"Ernest, did you continue your violin studies in Wisconsin?"

"I would like to have, but where we live it is pretty much a frontier town and only a few years old. I just play for my own enjoyment and for Bertha to jig to," said Ernest wistfully. About then Alice and Edward joined the group. Alice greeted Mr. Kohler and introduced Edward

"I was very pleased to see Ernest again," Mr. Kohler smiled and told the parents, "and was very impressed to see the outstanding young man he is, of course, Bertha is pretty outstanding herself."

Edward excused himself from the group and walked to where Suzanne was standing. Eventually he was able to greet Suzanne, introduce himself and apologize for not being able to visit with her at Douglas's house. He told Suzanne how much he enjoyed the concert and especially her solo. He also expressed sympathy for the loss of her brother at Antietam.

"I went to school at the University of Pennsylvania and one of the students I knew was Benjamin Mason. Later, he also worked at organizing the regiment later identified as the 69th Pennsylvania. Many of my friends also joined the 69th. I fear that many of them are dead. I have wondered about my student friend."

"Did you say his name was Benjamin Mason?" Suzanne asked.

"Yes, that is his name," answered Edward.

"The letter to my parents telling of Paddy's death was signed by Col. Benjamin Mason. It was a sad letter," said Suzanne with a faraway look in her eyes.

The Round's families said good night to each other and went to their respective home or hotel. Olivia, Azalea and Jack decided to leave Saturday morning to return to Chambersburg for Azalea to go home. Whereas Olivia and Jack would continue on back to Madison.

The train schedule for departure was at 6:47 a.m. for Harrisburg. The plan was for all three to get off the train at Harrisburg and take the next train the Chambersburg. Azalea would be home then and Olivia and Jack would take the next train to Pittsburgh.

JACK'S GOODBYE

Jack invited the Edward Round's family, Florence, Azalea and Olivia to join him in the dining room of the hotel. He had checked earlier to see if it was permissible for women to consume alcohol beverages if they were twenty-one years old or older. It was permissible, so Jack asked the waiter to take drink orders, but Ernest and Bertha would have to have something else to drink. While the waiter was getting the drinks, Jack stood and asked if he could say a few words.

"We better take a vote first," Walter stood up and said.

"Yah. . .yah," said Royce with a wink at Jack.

"What are you guys talking about," demanded Bertha. "Jack is asking perfectly nice if he can say a few words and you two sound like you are not very kind to Jack, and I think he is a nice guy."

"It is time to vote," said Walter. "All in favor of Jack say aye." Everyone shouted aye and Jack laughed and went over to Bertha and gave her a hug.

"Thanks for the vote of confidence."

Jack finally got a chance to speak.

"A week ago you stopped at Madison and Royce pounded on my door and said, Olivia wants to know if you can go to Gettysburg and Washington, D. C.. In a jiffy, I grabbed some clothes and followed Royce and got on the train to Chicago. I had not met Royce, Ernest or Bertha. I was welcomed into this wonderful family like a long, lost son. The long train ride and meeting Azalea at Chambersburg was wonderful. The real experience was ahead of us yet. The visit to Gettysburg is a place every person in America should see. To see the place where fifty-thousand Americans were killed or wounded in three hard days of battle is a very sad sight to see and to contemplate what went on there. I think it is the saddest I have ever felt. What impressed me was that these two young he-

318

roes, Royce and Walter, took part of all three days of fighting and survived . . .Walter just barely. And to think that Florence caring for Walter is how this relationship started.

"The next stop was meeting with President Lincoln and seeing the effect of the terrible burden of the war and the terrible events that needed to be dealt with had on that man. It was a real privilege to be in his presence. To think that he invited Florence and Walter there to help him win the battle against Robert E. Lee was most impressive.

"Our time here in Philadelphia was wonderful. Meeting the Douglas Round's family, and Pricilla and Suzanne were a pleasure. Visiting Independence Hall was something I wanted to do since I was a kid in school. Edward, Alice and family. . . It has been a wonderful week. Thank you very much."

"Jack, you are almost like a member of the family," Alice rose and said. "And if a couple of marriages work out, you will be more like a member of the family. The room broke out in laughter and thanked Jack for his comments.

"See, I told you Jack was a great guy," said Bertha with an impish grin. Olivia and Azalea spoke and agreed with what Jack said. Both said they were very happy to be welcomed into the family and to participate in all the events of the trip.

"I have been to Gettysburg three times," Olivia said, "and each time it brings tears to my eyes and sadness to my heart."

VIOLIN

The next morning was Sunday and the group came down for breakfast in random fashion. Ernest and Walter came down the hall toward the dining room, when an older gentlemen rose from his seat on a bench and approached Ernest.

"Mr. Kohler," Ernest said excitedly. "How nice to meet you this morning." Ernest extended his hand in greeting as did Mr. Kohler. Ernest introduced Walter and they shook hands. Ernest told Walter that Mr. Kohler was his violin teacher here in Philadelphia.

Mr. Kohler told Ernest that if he could spare a few minutes, he would like to listen to him play the fiddle. He had brought a violin in a case and with a little hesitation Ernest agreed to play.

"Where will I play?" asked Ernest.

"How about right here," replied Mr. Kohler. Mr. Kohler handed Ernest the violin and a bow. Ernest tested the tuning and began to play, *The Turkey in the Straw*. Ernest bowed, swung his elbows, bobbed his head and tapped his foot. Occasionally he twisted his body but all the time producing beautiful music from the violin. After a few minutes, Mr. Kohler signaled - stop.

"Ernest, you did a masterful performance just now. I needed to hear you play to see if you still had a high level of skill I saw when you were a young boy. You were one of the very best students I have ever had and I was curious if you can still play at a high level. I would encourage you to continue to practice and learn other songs. I have some songs I would like to give you. If you practice diligently, paying close attention to the intervals, you will continue on to a path of being a concert violinist, if you wish. Ernest thanked Mr. Kohler and promised that he would play the music and would practice songs other than *The Turkey in the Straw*. Ernest invited Mr. Kohler to join them for breakfast and he happily accepted.

"That was certainly very nice of Mr. Kohler to come to the hotel and wait for you just to listen to you play. To give you songs to play is a very nice gift. It looks like you two certainly got along very well," said Walter admiringly. "I hope you will continue the violin even if the frontier of Antigo doesn't seem like a likely place to listen to a violin recital."

"Looks like this family has a young musician and soon to be a talented artist," said Edward as he sat down. "Maybe anyone that wants to could visit the Pennsylvania Academy of Fine Arts on Cherry Street today.

"The only thing planned for today," Alice told them, "is the evening meal at Douglas and Mary's home. Otherwise everyone is free to do as you wish. Walter and Florence headed to the Academy of Fine Arts on Cherry Street. The rest of the Round's children had friends they wanted to look up. Edward and Alice rented a horse and carriage to tour around Philadelphia.

FINE ARTS

Finally, Florence and Walter went along as they made their way to Cherry Street. They reached the Academy and checked their coats in the cloakroom. They held hands as they looked at the artwork hanging on the walls. Florence was very impressed by the skill of the artists and very much enjoyed the art work. Walter enjoyed the pictures also but he professed absolutely no skill when it came to artwork. The two love birds enjoyed being alone. There were very few other visitors and emotions of both were rising.

"Maybe we could go back to the hotel," suggested Walter. There was a pause.

"Since Azalea and mother left this morning, I am by myself in that room. We could go their and relax."

"Let's go!" said Walter. They quickly went to the cloakroom and retrieved their coats.

They hurried along headed to the hotel. Florence had a rosy glow on her cheeks from the cold weather. The two held hands and then Florence reached across with her other hand and held Walter's hand and arm with both of her hands. Both could feel their emotions rising as they approached the hotel. At the hotel, they proceeded to Florence's room. The door was closed and locked and Walter helped Florence with her coat and then he held her in his arms and they he sought out her soft beautiful lips.

The long kiss was finally interrupted as the two lovers began to remove their clothes. Walter insisted that they be careful and not start a family before they are married. The bed beckoned as both ducked under the covers. Some touching and feeling occurred and finally they could hold back no longer.

"I love you Florence, and I always will. I want to be with you always. I can not imagine my life without you by my side. I hope we can marry soon after we return to Antigo."

"My love, Walter, I feel exactly about you as you do about me. We will have a wonderful life together and yes we will marry soon after we return to Antigo." Walter was ecstatic!!

"That would be the best news I have ever heard." Walter held Florence in a powerful embrace and they kissed for several seconds. Walter could feel the emotions rising again as did Florence. Many minutes later they realized the day was turning into late afternoon. They decided they needed to get ready and make their way to Douglas and Mary's home for the evening meal.

THE DINNER

The Edward Round's and Florence made their way to the Douglas Round's home for a dinner of steaks and other wonderful entries. Wine was offered during the meal. Pricilla and Suzanne were seated at the smaller table with Cyrus, Earl and Royce. The mood was festive and everyone seemed happy. Alice and Mary wore beautiful gowns and had their hair nicely coifed and looked elegant. Edward and Douglas wore jackets with tails, ties and vests. Both men wore short beards and mustaches and looked every bit the masters of their domain. Both sets of elder Rounds exuded confidence in their station of the world they lived in.

The Edward Round's children were neatly dressed, but living out of valises for a week did not allow for very fancy dress clothes. Edward and Alice had made purchases on their travels that day as there had always been subtle competition between the brothers and their wives.

The Douglas Round's men wore ordinary clothes so as to not upstage the travelers. They were nicely dressed but not in tails and ties. Pricilla and Suzanne were dressed simply and both looked very attractive and easily fit into the conversation of the group.

After the meal, coffee was offered with a very rich cheesecake. Douglas asked if Walter, Florence or Royce had seen the daily Philadelphia newspaper. Walter confessed that he had not.

"Well, all three of you are quoted in an article in the newspaper. It told. . . no, let me get the paper and you can read it for yourselves. The paper was presented to Walter and he began reading it to himself.

"Hey, big brother, how about reading it to all of us," said Bertha a little perturbed.

Dateline - Washington.   By James Hosby.

After meeting with President Lincoln at his request, two Civil War soldiers and a nurse, all from Wisconsin, presented ideas to help the Union defeat Robert E. Lee and the Confederates. They appeared before a joint committee of the Armed Services Committee and the Department of the Army. Some suggestions were to sterilize all water used for cooking, washing utensils and washing hands. This would be done by boiling the water for three minutes to kill germs. Soldiers would wash their hands in sterilized water before eating, preparing food or cleaning up later. It was pointed out that for every Union soldier killed in battle, nearly three soldiers die from diphtheria, dysentery and other diseases along with bad food and severe weather. Soldiers should not prepare their own food and a well organized system to provide food and prepare it should be developed. Soldiers would be assigned duties for a period of time to help with preparing food, gathering firewood, sterilizing water and generally assisting the cooks. While on the march and during battle soldiers would have to rely on hardtack and other foods that were available. Also recommended were more blankets, raincoats and a folding stool, all to keep soldiers off the wet cold ground.

Shortages of nurses at Gettysburg showed that perhaps more nurses could travel with the troops and get training as part of their program. It was pointed out that the first two years of the Civil War, the 6th Wisconsin Regiment spent sixty-five percent of their time in camp, twenty-five percent on the move and ten percent of their time fighting.

A shortage of war materials and everyday materials on the home front could be improved if a child care voucher program could be adopted. This could allow mothers to join the work force while their children are being watched by a child care person or groups.

"Bravo, Bravo." Douglas said, "for your efforts with President Lincoln and the committee. Let's hope they will take actions that you have recommended."

"I was proud of the way my brothers and Florence presented the information to the large committee," reported Erna. "They did a first class job and I could tell the committee was impressed also."

The evening was spent in pleasant conversation. The Round's families said goodbye to each other but it was not an easy parting. In the few short days together, the families realized there were very strong ties between them. Pricilla and Suzanne certainly seemed like very nice people and would be a great addition to the Douglas Round's family. Lily and Bertha certainly got along fine and they were sad to be separated. Finally, the coach arrived and the final farewells were said. The Edward Round's family and Florence returned to the hotel. Alice passed the word that we need to be to the bank by 8:30 a.m. tomorrow. Edward announced that the train to Harrisburg departs at 10:37 a.m.

ROGER AND THE PRESIDENT

As the group entered the hotel, a familiar figure got up from a chair in the lobby. It was Roger, the Doorman! Erna quickly moved to him and they embraced. Roger was warmly welcomed by the group. He explained that he had the next two days off from work so he came looking for Erna. Besides, President Lincoln asked him to deliver a letter and here it is. He reached into his coat pocket and retrieved a letter addressed to Walter, Florence and Royce.

"I am not the President's personal messenger boy, but we talk and the President seems to value my judgment about people I allow into the White House. I mentioned I was going to find the group from Wisconsin up in Philadelphia. He said he wanted to send you a letter."

Florence read the letter to all. The letter said: *Florence, Walter and Royce. There has been movement on several recommendations you made. The child care voucher seems to have strong support in Congress. Your Wisconsin Representative Romanski is leading the charge and has great support. I have several large donations and hope for many more. Lt. Col. Schofield is moving rapidly to get provisions to sterilize water and get soap for all. High priority to upgrade the food system. Thought you might like to know this. Thanks from all Americans. A. Lincoln*

The group was very impressed that President Lincoln would go out of his way to communicate with the Wisconsin group. Roger said he would like to stay with Erna through Harrisburg and then he would work his way back to Washington, D. C.

"Anyone want to visit the pub down the street?" said Roger. All the Rounds siblings, including Florence, thought it was a good idea so off they went. A lively band was playing tunes that inspired many people to dance. Erna and Roger and Florence and Walter immediately began to dance.

Bertha kept after Ernest to dance and she finally succeeded and they began to dance. Ernest was very light footed and showed great footwork as they danced. Finally, Royce cut in on Ernest and Bertha beamed as she danced with her hero.

Finally, the pub closed and the group returned to the hotel. Roger had rented a room and he invited Erna to share it with him. She took some friendly ribbing from her siblings but she happily accepted Roger's offer.

Nothing was said for awhile but the message was clear. Walter wanted to share Florence's room. They also took some friendly ribbing.

"These two have earned this opportunity according to the great information in the letter from President Lincoln," said Royce. "I don't know what my reward is except a good nights sleep. Maybe I will find someone someday."

Walter went to Royce and put his arm around his shoulder.

"Brother if you can wait until you start class at Madison, I think there is a nurse there that you may find to your liking." Florence smiled and was pretty sure that Walter was referring to her friend, Beth McLaughlin. 'Yes, they would make a great pair, ' she thought.

HEADING FOR HOME

Monday morning arrived and an early breakfast was eaten. Luggage was packed along with clothes purchased in the many fine shops in Philadelphia. Shortly after 8:30 a.m. Alice, Edward and the five children were at the bank. The paperwork was taken care of and a message was sent to Omar, the boss of the couriers to come to the bank presidents office. The ten-thousand dollars plus interest was assembled for each of the children. All eligible siblings opted to take one-hundred dollars in cash and send the remainder to the bank in Antigo.

Omar presented sturdy courier bags and the bills were carefully put in two bags. The fifth amount was put in a third bag with funds and documents that Edward and Alice were sending to Antigo also. Alice cautioned her offspring not to tell anyone about the funds. Also, Omar assured the group that he and three other heavily armed couriers will be on the train with them toward Harrisburg.

"Your funds and documents are in good hands."

The hotel had taken the luggage and parcels to the railway station. Tickets to Harrisburg had been purchased. The group arrived at the train station and had some time before boarding.

Royce inquired to Roger about his status with the draft.

"As long as I work at the White House I am exempt. If I leave I will be subject to the draft from my county in Illinois. I am hoping the war will end in two years and the conscription order is lifted. I want to move to Madison and study under Professor O'Brien. I plan to visit Erna at Antigo with my next vacation time in June." Roger was a fun loving, happy man and appeared to be very intelligent and friendly. Alice had time to sit and observe Roger while they waited to board the train. She thought to herself, 'Erna , he is the one'.

The group boarded the train and in a few minutes the engine bell began to clang and they began to move. The engineer sounded the whistle at crossings and it took many minutes to get out of Philadelphia. The train picked up speed and the scenery became more rural. A couple of smaller towns were passed without stopping.

Within two hours, the conductor sang out, "Lancaster, ten minute delay." The train began to slow and in a few minutes the engine bell began to clang and the train station and depot came into sight to the passengers. Everyone stepped off the train to stretch their legs.

HARRISBURG

The bell clanged and the train began to move and in less than two hours the conductor announced "Harrisburg, end of the line." The group all stepped off and Edward went to the ticket agents window. The next train to Pittsburgh would depart at 3:12 p.m. Edward purchased eight tickets to Pittsburgh and one ticket to Lancaster and then joined the others in the lunchroom. The luggage and parcels had been retrieved and Edward told everyone the ticket agent suggested we get off at Breezewood and take a hotel room there.

Roger's train to Lancaster leaves at 3:10 p.m. so it is time for everyone to say goodbye to Roger. The entire family has very much liked Roger. Erna had tears in her eyes as she and the others said goodbye and boarded the train.

Bertha ran back to Roger before she was about to board. She hugged Roger, looked up at his face and said, "I hope you become my brother-in-law."

The rest of the group began to board the train toward Pittsburgh.

"Did you decide to stay in Pennsylvania?" a lady behind asked Walter as he was about to board. Walter turned and immediately recognized Margaret Poulette, the State Senator from District 8, in Pennsylvania.

"No, Mrs. Poulette, I am on my way back to Wisconsin."

"I bet you were called to Washington, D. C. by President Lincoln," chided the lady.

"Did you see an article in a newspaper?" asked Walter matter-of-factly.

"What you don't realize is that you are very well known in these parts," Margaret Poulette said with a wink. "You are correct, I read an article in a Philadelphia newspaper and I knew it was you and your beautiful nurse. I did not know about your brother, but if he is anything like you, he must be special."

Walter and Mrs. Poulette boarded and continued talking. The remainder of the group, except Florence, wondered what was going on. Walter introduced everyone and Mrs. Poulette remarked about what a supporting cast and how much she admired Walter and Florence.

"When Walter marched up to President Lincoln and introduced himself and Florence at Gettysburg, I was very impressed."

Walter realized that Mrs. Poulette was probably on her way home from Harrisburg, the State Capitol, where she works as a State Senator. The group settled into seats and Mrs. Poulette sat in front of Walter and Florence.

"Walter, I have some news. First, the State of Pennsylvania adopted a family voucher program and it is working just fine. The other thing, the child care voucher that you, Florence and Royce advocated for was an instant winner at the State House in Harrisburg. We got signatures from eighty-seven percent of the legislators to sign letters of support and to immediately seek development of legislation at the federal level. Also to seek a source of funds such as a tax on tobacco and alcohol. The child care voucher is certainly one of the most common sense things this country can do until this war is finished."

"I got that idea from an editorial in the Cleveland newspaper. We were happy to be in a position to bring it to the 'powers that be'," Walter confessed.

"You know something, Walter and Florence? President Lincoln saw an honest, sincere ally that he could trust in the short time you two were together at Gettysburg. You coming from Wisconsin, wherever in the heck that is, I know it is on the western frontier, but to come to Washington, D. C. at his request, signaled a strong desire to do what you could to help. When you showed up with this fine group in support, you definitely signaled that you two and your brother were going to give him information that he could trust."

"Three of my siblings and my mother and father wanted to see Gettysburg," Walter told her. "We all wanted to see Washington, D. C. Until 1855 our family lived in Philadelphia and my parents own property there that needed attention. We decided it was a good time to take a family trip. Also a visit to Independence Hall and the Liberty Bell were an attraction."

"Walter, you should be in the State Legislature of Wisconsin. I don't think you are eligible to be a National Congressman," said Mrs. Poulette matter-of-factly.

"Twenty-five years of age plus seven years of being citizen for Assembly and thirty years of age for Senate plus nine years a citizen," confessed Walter.

"Sounds like you know the constitution," said Mrs. Poulette, with a hint of jealousy in her voice.

"Mr. McBeth was my high school history teacher in Wisconsin. He made us all copy the U. S. Constitution but we debated many issues and especially the free speech amendment. That was a hot issue but it really is at the heart of freedom in America. Many days I was disgusted with Mr. McBeth, but he made us all realize that we all have rights and responsibilities, but so do our neighbors."

"Sounds like Mr. McBeth was a very good teacher and he made you question many parts of the Constitution."

"Houstontown, Houstontown, next stop," sang out the conductor.

"That is my stop so I must say goodbye," said Mrs., Poulette, as she got up and shook hands with everyone in the group.

"We all knew Walter was a real smarty britches," said Bertha as she could not resist, "but he must have bamboozled you too. Thanks for being his friend, he needs all he can get," as she hugged Mrs. Poulette. This kind lady took Bertha's head in her hands and said, "Your brother is very special, take care of him." When she came to Walter and Florence, they both hugged her. Florence had tears in her eyes as Mrs. Poulette stepped off the train.

The train continued toward Breezewood. It was late afternoon and getting dark as the train rolled through the Pennsylvania mountains. Finally, the conductor announced, "Breezewood, Breezewood, ten minute delay." The Round's group stepped off, as did Omar and his couriers. Rooms were secured at the hotel. The Round's made no sign that they knew anything about the mysterious, tough looking men with leather pouches over their shoulder. The group had supper in the hotel dining room as did two of the couriers. When those two finished eating, they left and the other two couriers came in and ate. Royce had inquired about the time of the next train to Pittsburgh and found it was 8:11 a.m.

Breakfast was eaten and all were at the train station by 8:00 a.m. The couriers were there prior to the Round's group. The train was boarded and the engine bell began to clang as the train started to move. Today would be a long day on the train. The goal was to pass through Pittsburgh and on to Cleveland to spend the night there.

WEDDING TALK

Walter thought this was a good time to talk to Florence about their wedding plans.

"Yes, your mother, my mother and myself have pretty much planned most of it but a lot still remains to be done after we get back to Antigo. The ceremony will be at your parents home. The wedding will be at 1:00 p.m. on a Saturday and we will ask a minister from Antigo that your mother is familiar with. We thought my matron of honor will be Erna and Bertha will be a bridesmaid. You could ask anyone to be your best man. Do you have someone in mind," asked Florence.

"I guess I thought it would be Royce," answered Walter sounding mystified. "Then Ernest would be a groomsman, if that is alright with you. I just want to get married and if it alright with you , it is alright with me."

"We felt there should be a reception afterward, but because there is little extra room for guests to spend the night, we felt the reception should be finished early enough so guests could get back to Antigo before dark."

"What will the reception be like?" asked Walter.

"Your mother thought there should be a meal by mid-after-noon. The food could be displayed in the dining room and the guests could serve themselves. They could find places to sit and eat. There may be places for the wedding party to sit at the dining room table," Florence eagerly said.

"Who would make the wedding cake?" inquired Walter.

"Your mother volunteered that Erna could bake it, but we would have to ask her."

"Who will provide the meal for the reception?"

"Our mothers thought they could take care of that and planned to ask Mr. Peroutka for suggestions about a menu."

"Perhaps we should ask Mr. Peroutka if he could provide a meal and, of course, we will pay for it," said Walter.

"You know, that is a good idea, if Mr. Peroutka can do it. He did tell my mother to keep him in mind for the wedding. Maybe he could see to baking a wedding cake, if Erna is uncomfortable attempting a cake like that. She may not have the necessary utensils and pans, either," said Florence.

"Are we going to have music and beer at the reception?" asked Walter.

"What are your thoughts on that?" asked Florence.

"Did our mothers discuss that at all?" Walter wanted to know.

"They seem to avoid discussing that. Neither of them are teetotalers but they clearly don't want a drunken brawl. About music they thought that was a good idea if there was room for a small band but where would people dance, if they wanted to. Your parents house is large, but it has its limits."

"There is a musical family that lives on the east side of Antigo. There are three middle-aged men and I have heard them a couple of times. They play the fiddle, accordion, banjo and they also play the harmonica and washboard and they do sing. They play fast moving, foot-kicking music but also some slow ones. They definitely get people involved with their songs. I would like to have that band play at our reception," Walter offered enthusiastically.

"Who would we invite to the wedding and is there going to be a shower?" inquired Walter.

"Both mothers thought we should keep the number of wedding guests to not over thirty, besides your family. Because of the small size of the guest list and the short notice the guests will have, the mothers thought there would not be a shower. They do expect guests will bring a wedding gift," answered Florence.

"Will any guests plan to sleep over that night?"

"The nurses that I invite will very likely sleepover but they will have to sleep on the floor in the living room."

"Ted, my one armed friend from Merrill, and his wife, will have to spend the night if he can attend," said Walter.

"It looks like the first thing we need to do is set a date that the minister can attend. If we plan to have a band they need to be available on that date, too. Perhaps Mr. Peroutka will have to be available. Of course, our parents, brothers and sisters will have to be available too, especially Royce, Ernest, Erna and Bertha," replied Florence.

The train approached Pittsburgh in early afternoon. "Pittsburgh, Pittsburgh, end of the line." The group got off the train as did the couriers. Both groups went to the railroad stations lunch room. The Round's siblings retrieved the luggage and parcels and brought them to the lunchroom. Edward and Omar sought out the ticket agent and found the train to Cleveland left at 2:41 p.m. on Track six.

The two groups boarded the train at the prescribed time. The bell on the engine signaled the start of movement and the train slowly began to move. Once the outskirts of Cleveland were left behind, the train picked up speed. At times the tracks ran beside the Ohio River and barges could be seen loaded with coal headed to Pittsburgh. Mules pulled both loaded and unloaded barges. In a few miles the tracks left the Ohio River and continued on toward Cleveland.

Bertha sat by herself and asked Walter to move up and sit with her for a few minutes.

"Why did Mrs. Poulette know so much about you if she lives in Pennsylvania?" Bertha asked inquiringly.

"She is a State Senator in District Eight in Pennsylvania. That means she works at Harrisburg in the Pennsylvania State Capital. Do you know where the State Capital of Wisconsin is?"

"Silly, it is Madison," replied Bertha sounding a little exasperated. "If you were a State Senator in Wisconsin you would work at Madison when the Senate is in session."

"Our State Senator is Robert Haynes and he lives at Wausau," Walter offered. "He and Mrs. Poulette have about the same job. They both debate about the merits of new laws that are being developed and later voted on. There are committees made up of Senators and some committees deal with education, agriculture, railroads, waterways, banking and many others. The committee deals with problems and decides if legislation is needed," explained Walter.

"Do you think you would want to be a State Senator?" asked Bertha. Walter was silent for a time.

"I think I would be interested," he replied after some thought, "because I could help people." Walter looked away and seemed to focus on a faraway point. Bertha was alarmed by Walters reaction. She looked at her brother with a look that said, 'what is wrong'?

Florence also noticed Walter's condition. She immediately reached for Walter and held him. She continued to hold Walter and finally he hugged Florence and seemed to return from wherever he had been. He looked at Bertha and saw tears in her eyes.

"Bertha, I am sorry I scared you. It scared me also," Walter said softly.

The train pulled into Cleveland and the conductor announced, "Cleveland, Cleveland, end of the line." It was dark as luggage and parcels were retrieved and the group headed to a hotel nearby. Royce checked with the ticket agent and was told the train to Chicago left at 8:07 a.m. A meal was eaten at the hotel dining room and everyone turned in early. Florence, Erna and Bertha shared a room. Walter shared with his brothers.

The next morning was cold. The group boarded the train to Chicago, as did the couriers. The railroad car had a small heater but it was cold for the travelers. As the train rolled toward Toledo the day warmed up some. Walter wondered how his old friend, Charles Sullivan was. He and Charles developed a strong bond during the time of helping Florence with her rehabilitation. By late morning, Toledo was reached and an ten minute delay was announced. Walter hoped Charles would be able to visit this fathers flooring mill once it was running. By late afternoon, the train slowed as it went through the steel mill district of Gary, Indiana. By the time the train reached the train station it was nearly dark. "Chicago, end of the line," said the conductor dutifully. Hotel rooms were secured and an evening meal eaten.

The train to Madison departs at 8:20 a.m. on Track number five.

The next morning was still cold as the group boarded the train to Madison. The engine bell began to clang and the train slowly pulled away from the station.

"We are going to be in Antigo today," said Bertha happily.

"We have had a wonderful time on this trip," said Alice, "but it will be good to be home." The train rolled out of Chicago and into northern Illinois. More snow covered fields were seen and by mid-morning the train crossed into Wisconsin. Stops were made at Beloit and Janesville. Many more snow covered fields were seen as this was prime fields for corn, hay, wheat and other crops.

"Madison, end of the line," announced the conductor. The train slowed as it approached the station. The station platform came into view and Bertha announced, "There are Olivia and Jack!" Sure enough there they were. The group stepped off the train and everyone greeted Olivia and Jack who had arrived at Madison the day before.

The train to Wausau departs in one hour. Florence and Alice approached Olivia and asked if they could address some issues about the upcoming wedding. The group decided to gather around a table in the dining room. Walter was invited also. The first thing would be to set a date and go from there.

Alice had a calendar and they studied the dates. Finally Saturday, January 21st was selected. Florence and Walter would contact Rev. Inar Raccola. Florence will ask Erna to be maid of honor and Bertha to be a bridesmaid. Walter will ask Royce to be his best man and Ernest to be a groomsman

Both mothers liked the idea of asking Mr. Peroutka to prepare a simple meal. Florence wanted to ask Erna if she would want to make the wedding cake. Walter brought up the band and made it apparent that he wanted the Three Brothers Band. And that was alright as long as the size of the band was established. Olivia asked about beer.

"Most wedding receptions around Antigo seem to have beer," offered Alice.

"Let's have beer," said Florence. Walter said that he would contact the Three Brothers Band about their music.

The guest list was finally addressed. All agreed that it should be kept to around thirty, plus the Round's family plus Olivia and Jack. The time of 1:00 p.m. seemed fine for the wedding, with the reception to follow. The dancing and socializing would follow the meal. Some local folks will have to get home before dark.

Florence said she wanted to invite at least ten of her nursing friends with the idea that they may have to sleep on the floor. It was agreed that both sides need to make guest lists as soon as possible. All four thought for awhile to see if anything else needs to be addressed.

"What about invitations?" asked Alice.

"Whoa, that one completely went over my head," said Florence at little sheepishly.

"I know Florence and I need to get a marriage license," said Walter somewhat proudly.

"Walter and I can do that at the Court House the same day we talk to the minister, Mr. Peroutka and the Three Brothers Band. Maybe we should stop at the print shop, if the date and time is approved, and order invitations," added Florence enthusiastically.

The hour was nearly up so goodbyes were said to Olivia and Jack and the travelers boarded the train for the next to last train leg toward Antigo. It was cold but this railway car was warmer and everyone appreciated that. The train moved out of Madison and headed north. In a little over an hour Portage was reached along with a ten minute layover. The train continued north and by mid-afternoon the city of Stevens Point was approached. After a ten minute delay, the train continued north, now running beside the Wisconsin River. By late afternoon the conductor announced Wausau, end of the line. The travelers stepped off the train as did the couriers. Luggage and parcels were retrieved and Edward consulted the ticket agent and found the train to Antigo would leave in eighteen minutes. Tickets were purchased by both groups and loading the car began a few minutes later. Royce estimated that the group would reach Antigo while it was still light.

All the travelers were happy they were on the last leg of their long trip. There was about two feet of snow on the ground, but it did not hinder the train as it moved northeast from Wausau.

"Antigo, end of the line," announced the conductor. This man lived in Antigo and smiled.

"Welcome back home folks. It sounds like Walter, Royce and this wonderful nurse had important information to tell the President and the committee. There was a nice article in the paper yesterday. Thanks for helping win the war,"

"We don't know if we did any good while in Washington, D. C.," relayed Walter. "We answered President Lincoln's request to come and talk to him and he seemed to appreciate it."

The train slowed and the engine bell clanged as a snowy rail station came into view. Bertha was looking out of the window.

"There are lots of people on the platform," Bertha announced excitedly. "They seem to be waiting for something to happen." The train finally came to a stop and many people saw the travelers through the windows and began waving and shouting.

"What the heck is this all about?" Ernest asked.

"Lets get off the train and find out," Erna said. The travelers began to move toward the exit.

"Walter, Royce and Florence, you step off first. These folks are here to welcome you back home," said Alice as she smiled and gently guided them to the exit.

Alice was right. Somehow the word was passed from Madison that this group was headed for home. More than likely the telegraph was used and, if the paper carried an article about their trip to Washington, D. C. this combination brought these people to the railroad station. When the embarrassed travelers stepped off the train, the crowd cheered and clapped.

Ann Freiburger stepped to the front of the crowd. "Florence, Walter and Royce, our little town is proud you were invited to Washington, D. C. at the invitation of President Lincoln. Your meeting with the committee must have been a success and we thank you and welcome you back home." The rest of the travelers were welcomed with back slaps, hand shakes and words of welcome. The couriers also stepped off the train and headed for the bank. Not once, on this long trip, did either group acknowledge the other.

Ernest and Edward retrieved the luggage and parcels. As they took them off the baggage car, two men from the livery offered to carry the items to their two sleighs waiting a short distance away. Edward was very happy and he quickly settled with the livery owner, a nice gratuity was also included. Finally, the crowd disbursed, the passengers, the luggage and parcels were loaded. Royce drove the larger sleigh and Walter manned the smaller sleigh. As they drove down Fifth Avenue, several people waved and shouted words of thanks and appreciation. The entire group felt proud of the reception received. It was a complete surprise.

The sun had set and twilight had set it. The group knew the last third of the trip would be in the dark.

"Oh no, it won't," announced Ernest. "Tonight is full moon and in a few minutes we will see a beautiful moon rise in the northeast. This cold weather brought a nice clear sky."

"Mr. Smarty Britches," chided Bertha.

"Miss Doubting Thomas, look toward the northeast?"

"Nothing, Mr. Sm…. . Oh, I do see a light area. I suppose the next thing I see is the full moon."

"Ernest, we are all impressed with your power of observation," interjected Alice. About then the very top of the full moon appeared above the horizon, several tall pine trees appeared on the face of the moon. A few minutes later the entire moon was above the horizon providing light and long shadows, but the road toward home was easily visible.

"If you look to your left," said Bertha, "you will see a bright star-like object. It is the planet Venus and right now it is an evening star. In a few weeks it will be a morning star."

"Mother," said Edward, "it looks like we have a couple good observers with us tonight. I am impressed, Ernest and Bertha."

The group was in high spirits. All at once, Erna's beautiful voice was heard singing *When Johnny Comes Marching Home.* She was joined by the entire group. Many songs followed as the moon rose higher. At last the large home of the Round's family could be seen in the grove of oak trees. As they approached the house, the travelers noticed lights in the windows.

"Someone must be in the house," observed Ernest. As they got closer, smoke could be seen coming from both chimneys.

"Our neighbor must have found out we were coming home and readied the house for us," said Edward. "That Amos is a very good neighbor."

The travelers were indeed happy to be home. Luggage and parcels were unloaded and brought into a warm, well lighted home. Walter, Royce and Ernest took care of the horses and sleighs. Erna immediately noticed that the cook stove was warm.

"We can open a jar of canned elk, fry some eggs and at least have something to eat," said Erna. Luggage was unpacked and parcels were put away.

"There must be soiled clothes," said Alice. "Put them in the kitchen and they will get washed and ironed eventually."

Erna prepared a nice meal. The entire family, including Florence, sat down together.

"Alice and I were very proud of our family on this extended trip," stated Edward. "It was wonderful to see the respect we were all afforded. I feel confident that Florence, Walter and Royce's advice will bear fruit. The child care voucher seems to be well received. Thanks to all of you for helping America to grow."

"Father and Mother," Royce offered, "thanks for covering all the expenses of this trip. We also are very proud of our mother and father. You have shown us the way."

WEDDING ARRANGEMENTS

Friday morning dawned and it found Walter driving the large sleigh with Florence seated beside him, wrapped up in heavy blankets. Ernest and Bertha huddled under heavy blankets also. They were anxious to see their school mates even though someone would need to pick them up and bring them home that night. Walter stopped the sleigh close to school and the two students got off and ran into the school, very excited to be back with their friends and teachers.

The very first stop was at the home of Rev. Inar Raccola. Walter and Florence were welcomed into the ministers home. They explained that they wanted a minister to perform their marriage ceremony in the parents home at 1:00 p.m. on January 21st. The minister consulted his calendar and found the date and time would be fine. He would be happy and proud to perform the marriage ceremony for two such wonderful people. He reminded the couple to get a marriage license. Other than that there was no other requirements. Walter and Florence liked the minister and can see why Alice had recommended him.

Next stop was the Court House to obtain a marriage license. The county clerk was excited to meet Walter and Florence. She thanked Walter for working with Ann Freiburger in getting the family voucher program established.

"It is working very well. The proposed child care voucher is an excellent idea and I hope Washington, D. C. will adopt it," she said. Walter thanked the clerk and introduced Florence.

"You saved Walters life at Gettysburg and he helped you recover from some very serious injuries. Oh, yes, you two are very well known around here and very much admired."

Florence and Walter accepted the praise and then asked to purchase a marriage license. The clerk was ecstatic.

"You two are going to marry? Now that is exciting." The license was completed and the small fee paid. By the time Florence and Walter were ready to leave, the clerk's office had several other courthouse workers that had found a reason to visit the clerks office. Walter and Florence smiled and acknowledged the admiring and curious workers.

The next stop was to see if the Three Brothers Band could play at the reception.

"All the attention is somewhat embarrassing," Walter said on the way.

"Let's enjoy it now as it may not last long," Florence replied. The Three Brothers Band was home and after introductions and compliments about their music, Walter inquired if the band would be available the afternoon of January 21st. A quick check of their calendar showed that indeed they could play for their reception. Florence was impressed by these three fun loving musicians that could barely speak without cracking a joke of some kind.

The next stop was the print shop. Florence had written out what she and Walter wanted on the invitation. The printer showed samples of the paper stock he would use for invitations and envelopes. Finally, a sample was selected and next was the style and size of type used to print everything. Florence had a good eye for this selection and in a few minutes the size and style of type was selected. The printer looked at the information for the invitation and made two small suggestions. The printer would have them done in one week, which was fine.

Peroutka's Meat Market was next. After greetings, Florence inquired if Mr. Peroutka, or his business, could provide a dinner at the reception on January 21st.

"No, I don't do that sort of thing, but my daughter does," said Mr. Peroutka with a large smile. "She is working in the back so I will call her." Sharon came from the back wearing a long apron and wiping her hands.

"Ah, the love birds my father told me about," said Sharon with a large smile on her face. Sharon and her husband Ralph could indeed put on a meal the afternoon of January 21st.

Florence and Sharon discussed the menu and the use of the kitchen stove, if needed. Sharon told Florence that she could furnish several small folding tables with chairs. Walter offered to pick up the tables and chairs on Friday, January 20th and return them on Monday, January 23rd. The menu of a small steak and other fixings were agreed on. Mr. Peroutka gave Florence a small sack of slices of beef sausages, 'to snack on as you head for home'.

One last stop was the General Store. Alice and Erna had a long list of supplies needed to restock the Round's kitchen. As soon as Walter and Florence stepped into the General Store, people began welcoming them and thanking them for helping America. The clerk took the list and in a few minutes the order was filled. The boxes of groceries and other things were stowed on the sleigh. Walter headed the sleigh for the school, as it was time to pick up Ernest and Bertha.

Here they came and there was a man with a coat and tie on with them. 'Oh, no,' thought Walter, 'that looks like Mr. Bugni, the principal'.

"This doesn't look good," said Walter to Florence.

The threesome arrived at the sleigh. Walter had jumped down from the seat as they approached. Walter could see that Bertha was definitely happy.

"Walter, this is Mr. Bugni, the school principal," Ernest said. Mr. Bugni offered his hand and introduced himself. Walter introduced Florence and she stepped out of the sleigh.

"Walter and Florence, there is much excitement about you two being invited to Washington, D. C. by President Lincoln. The students of the school would really like to have a Civil War veteran of Gettysburg, and the nurse that saved his life, come and talk to them and tell them about Mr. Lincoln. Many of the classes are studying Mr. Lincoln's Gettysburg Address. Bertha told me that you and Florence met President Lincoln before he made his two minute speech. Bertha also told me the President was so impressed by you and Florence that he invited you two to come to Washington, D. C. and help him win the war against Robert E. Lee."

"Bertha is mostly correct and our family, Florence and her mother visited Gettysburg. Ernest should tell about what he saw there. We went on to Washington, D. C. and met with President Lincoln and he arranged a meeting with an important committee. Ernest and Bertha were at both meetings. They could do a good job of telling about President Lincoln and what went on in the committee meeting."

"Ernest told me that you may be able to spend some time at the school Monday morning when you bring these two bright lights to school," Mr. Bugni explained.

"What do you think, Florence?" Walter asked as she looked at her.

"Walter, we could not possibly turn down Mr. Bugni. Perhaps Ernest and Bertha could help out. They went to Independence Hall and learned about the Liberty Bell in Philadelphia besides meeting and speaking to President Lincoln."

"How about that, Ernest and Bertha?" asked Walter with a 'you better say yes' tone in his voice. Bertha was quick to say she would but Ernest was a bit more shy however he straightened up and said, "I will be happy to help." Mr. Bugni was very pleased and told the foursome that he would call for an all school program after roll call on Monday."

On the way home, Bertha was a regular chatterbox. Ernest also spoke several times. It seems like their classmates were anxious to hear about Gettysburg, Washington, D. C. and Philadelphia. Florence and Walter were going to ask Royce to come with them on Monday morning. They also thought this might be a good time to tell these two what the wedding plans were. Both Bertha and Ernest were excited about the wedding plans.

"One more thing," said Walter. "Ernest, I would like to ask you to be a groomsman when Florence and I get married."

"What do I have to do?"

"You would stand next to Royce, if he accepts being best man. Your man job is to catch me if I faint, or if Royce faints," said Walter with a happy smile. "You would have to wear a suit and tie and polish your shoes. What do you think? Can we count on you?" Ernest was silent for a time.

"Can I kiss the bride?" he finally asked.

"Well, I do that first, but after me, it is alright with me but the one who really gives permission for that is Florence."

"Ernest, you may kiss me after Walter does," said Florence with a nice friendly smile. Ernest seemed quite pleased with the prospect of kissing Florence. He had already thought that if Walter did not marry Florence, he would be interested!

"Bertha, I am asking you to be a maid of honor at our wedding," Florence said as she looked at Bertha.

"I accept," said Bertha excitedly. "I was hoping you would ask me and I would be very proud to stand by you and Walter."

"Both of you, please mark you calendar for 1:00 p.m. January 21st," said Walter as he went on to explain what the plans for the wedding were. "If either one of you want to invite a friend to the wedding, we will give you an invitation when they are ready. Keep in mind that the sleeping arrangements will have to be worked out, or a ride back to Antigo before dark.

As the ride home continued, Bertha and Ernest had happy faces. They both admired Walter and Florence and thought they would be a perfect couple. They both felt proud that they had been asked to take part in the ceremony.

Upon arrival home, Florence and Walter approached Erna and Florence asked her if she would accept being matron of honor at their wedding. Erna was excited and went to Florence and gave her a hug.

"Of course I will. I would be very happy to be part of you and Walter getting married."

"January 21st, 1:00 p.m. here in the house. The wedding plans were explained and Erna was asked if she would like to bake the wedding cake.

"I need to talk to Mother to see what utensils and pans we have - also I need to know what kind of cake you want."

"One more thing, if there is someone you would like to invite to the wedding, we will give you an invitation when we get them in a week. It is a long way from Washington, D.C. but one never knows how things work out unless one tries." Erna gave Walter a smug smile and went to Walter and gave him a hug and then a playful punch in the gut.

Later in the evening, Walter and Florence approached Royce.

"Are you going to be around at 1:00 p.m. on January 21st?"

"Why, what is going on? Are we going fishing or something?" Royce asked light heartedly.

"Really, Florence and I are getting married here in this house and I want you to be my best man. Do you think that will work for you?"

"Wow! Congratulations. I knew you had talked about it and there was some questions about when and where. Of course, I would be honored to be your best man."

Walter explained what was planned and until the minister was secured today, we could not be sure of the day. Ernest will stand by you and you don't have to have any special clothes. Just a suit and tie will be fine. If you have someone you would like to invite, feel free to do so and we will have invitations in a week. Walter told Royce about Mr. Bugni inviting the three of them to speak to the students Monday morning. Ernest and Bertha will help out about Independence Hall and the Liberty bell and their reaction to Gettysburg and President Lincoln.

"Count on me," Royce replied.

SCHOOL

Monday morning found Florence, Walter, Royce, Ernest and Bertha on the way to school in Antigo to meet with Mr. Bugni and talk to the students. Upon arrival, the group found Mr. Bugni was true to his word. After roll call was taken all the students grades five to twelve were called to the assembly room. This serves as a hall to study when not in class.

Mr. Bugni introduced the group and turned it over to them. Walter asked if anyone had any questions.

"Why did you and your family take the trip?" a high school girl asked. Walter told about going to hear President Lincoln's speech at Gettysburg.

"We heard you were injured at Gettysburg. Was that the same time the President was there?" Walter explained the difference in dates.

"Why were you there in November if you were hurt in July?" Florence offered to answer that. Florence explained how she nursed him back to health and then he was sent to a hospital in Harrisburg. Florence and two friends were on their way to visit Walter and got run over by a run away team and wagon. After two months, Walter found me in the hospital in a town near Gettysburg. He stayed with me for two more months and helped me heal. November 19th President Lincoln was coming to Gettysburg to dedicate the memorial and the battlefield cemetery. Walter wanted to meet the President and he introduced me to President Lincoln."

"Do you remember the speech?" asked a young boy.

"Yes, I do, every word of it and with that Florence recited the entire Gettysburg address by President Lincoln.

When Florence finished, the entire body of students and teachers cheered and clapped and gave Florence a standing ovation.

"After four months I was finally able to return to Wisconsin and there was a letter from President Lincoln asking Wal-

351

ter and me to come to Washington, D. C. as he had a task for us. We left for Washington, D. C. the next day. Our route took us through Gettysburg and all of the Round's family wanted to see the place where Walter and Royce were injured.

"The Round's family lived in Philadelphia until 1855 and owned property there. The family had business in Philadelphia and we all got to visit Independence Hall and learn about the Liberty Bell."

"Gettysburg is a site of a three day battle," Royce took over and said. "About fifty thousand soldiers were killed or wounded and this counts the Confederate soldiers. It is a very sad place and I know our brother Ernest was deeply affected by what he saw."

"What I saw was the saddest thing I had ever seen," said Ernest as he stepped forward. "Thousands of markers with dead soldiers names on them. Long row after long row. Think of who they were, young men like my brothers here. They will not be going home to their families or to their sweethearts. Besides, the dead soldiers, there are many thousands with serious injuries, like missing arms and legs. Many will survive the battles but the battles in their minds are never finished."

Ernest stepped back. The room was very quiet. After a few seconds a student began clapping. The entire room clapped and then stood and gave Ernest a standing ovation.

"We left Gettysburg," Royce continued, "and went to Washington, D. C. Walter produced the letter from the President to allow us into the White House. Florence and Walter went in to meet the President and Walter asked if his family and Florence's mother and friend could come in to the office also. President Lincoln said absolutely, if they came all the way from Wisconsin to be with you they are very welcome." Royce asked Bertha for her reaction to the President.

"President Lincoln welcomed our entire group of eleven," Bertha began cautiously. "He shook hands with everyone but me. I stepped up and hugged Mr. Lincoln and told him to keep on with his plan. . . President Lincoln is a very distinguished man. His eyes are distinctive and seem to see everything. He treated all of us with dignity and respect. I admire him."

Walter asked if anyone else had any questions.

"What about the 6ᵗʰ Wisconsin Regiment? My dad says they are very good soldiers. Is that true?" asked a high school boy.

"Royce and I joined the 6ᵗʰ Wisconsin when it was organized at Camp Randall on the west side of Madison. Our Commander was Lt. Col. Rufus Dawes and he is an outstanding leader. In two years we fought at Bull Run, Fredericksburg, Antietam, Chancellorsville and Gettysburg. At Gettysburg, the 6ᵗʰ Wisconsin and other regiments of the Iron Brigade charged into a large group of Confederates from Mississippi and captured a few hundred, including their General. In three days at Gettysburg we lost about half of our regiment of over four hundred troops. Royce and I were injured on the third day and Florence saved my life."

"Why did President Lincoln invite you to Washington, D. C.?" asked a high school girl.

"The President apparently thought Florence and I might be able to offer some ideas on how to win the war against Robert E. Lee. We offered several suggestions of ways to provide sterilized water and soap since for every Union soldier killed in action almost three die of diphtheria, dysentery, bad food and weather."

"Where is Gettysburg?" a young boy asked.

"From Antigo, take the train to Madison in southern Wisconsin, next go to Chicago, then east to Toledo and Cleveland, Ohio. From there, continue east to Pittsburgh, Pennsylvania then southeast for about one day on the train to Gettysburg which is a small town like Antigo. The battle was south of the town along a battle line of about four miles. Over three-hundred thousand troops fought for three days in the tremendous heat of July 1ˢᵗ , 2ⁿᵈ and 3ʳᵈ of 1863."

"I heard my parents talking about child care vouchers," said a high school student. "I think they said you had something to do with that."

"We suggested that to the President and the committee," chuckled Walter. "We also told that I had seen that in an editorial in the Cleveland newspaper. Apparently we spoke of that to the right people and at the right time. It would let mothers join the workforce at a time when our country desperately needs war materials and goods and services needed on the home front. The voucher would pay for someone to look after children while the mother worked."

Things were winding down when Bertha asked if she could speak.

"We visited Independence Hall in Philadelphia. My brothers and I lived in Philadelphia until 1855. It still gave me a thrill to visit that famous building. Where four-score and seven years ago the Declaration of Independence of the United States and the Constitution were written inside. The Liberty Bell still hangs in the belfry but it is cracked and has not been rung for some time."

Time was up and the students clapped and cheered. Several came up and spoke or asked questions. Two or three just wanted to shake hands with Civil War soldiers. Mr. Bugni and several teachers thanked the group.

"Looks like the Rounds boys are making history for the United States," said Mr. McBeth, Walter and Royce's teacher. "Thanks for your great contribution in being a Union soldier."

"Mr. McBeth I still have my copy of the U. S. Constitution," said Walter. "Thanks."

"I think both of you have much more to offer," said Mr. McBeth. "Good luck."

Walter, Florence and Royce returned home. A sleigh and team from livery was in the yard. Walter put the sleigh and team away and joined the others in the house. Mr. Cutler and two of his engineers were in the house and sat at the dining room table with several large sheets of drawings. Edward and Alice had been studying and listening intently. Royce and Walter were invited to join the group. Mr. Cutler was from Milwaukee and his company helps lumber and flooring mills utilize the space needed to develop a mill to be able to access all the necessary buildings and area. A large sketch of miniature buildings and tracks showed the entire view of the finished operation.

Walter and Royce studied that sketch and noted the scale. They looked at each other and finally Royce said, "This is going to be huge, bigger than I had envisioned."

"What are these little houses on the far west side?" Walter asked.

"Those are houses for the workers and their families," Mr. Cutler explained.

"I count sixty houses," observed Walter.

"There is room for more to the northwest of the others," added an engineer, "your father and mother are considering a central water and sewage system for the sixty homes. Heat will be provided by steam from the fire hole steam system. If our company were hired, we would bring a steam shovel here on our rail car and dig footings, water, sewage and heating lines, pointed out Mr. Cutler.

"How is the big band saw working?" asked Walter. Mr. Cutler referred the question to one of the engineers.

"The single cut saw is working fine. We still have things to work out on the double cut saw. We will definitely be able to have the large band saw, single edged cut in this state of the art mill."

Walter excused himself and went looking for Florence. She was in Walters bedroom which is where they decided to hang out and sleep. Florence took one look at Walter and saw that he was in trouble. She went to him and held him. She could see that he had that far away look in his eyes. She guided Walter to the bed so he could lie down. She took another blanket and covered him and then snuggled up behind him and under the blanket. In a few minutes, Walter was sleeping. Florence took his pulse and it was faster than usual. He didn't have a fever but in a few minutes he began to shake, then he began to hold his hands over his head, like he was fending off something. Walter finally was sleeping without shaking and Florence continued to hold him.

Sometime later, Walter woke up and wondered why he was in bed.

"You had an episode but now you seem to be alright. I would suggest that when Royce goes to Madison to register for the second semester, we get an appointment with a doctor I know at the Medical School that may be able to help you," said Florence. Walter was completely in favor of that. Royce had received information from the University that registration was the week of January 9-13.

THE CHRISTMAS TREE SEARCH

Christmas was near. Alice and Erna got out Christmas decorations and everyone helped decorate the house. Ernest knew of a place to cut a balsam fir for a Christmas tree. He led the way as Walter and Royce followed on their horses. They traveled three or four miles on a logging trail until Ernest veered off the trail and in a short time a small grove of balsam fir appeared in front of them. There was about a foot of snow on the ground and immediately tracks of a herd of elk were seen. These fresh tracks led into the grove of firs. The three men studied the tracks in the grove ahead of them.

All at once, a commotion was heard on the far side of the grove. A pack of timber wolves had sneaked up on the herd of elk and were trying to pull down an elk cow. The herd was on the run . . .right toward the three riders. Royce had a rifle in his saddle boot and immediately began to load it. As the elk got near, the horses began to get jittery. The elk saw the men and horses and veered to the south. The pack of wolves had spread out and a large grey one was trying to stalk the right side of the herd as it ran west. The wolf was fixated on the elk cow and had not seen the three men on horses. All at once, it ran right among the horses, which immediately spooked and then turned back the way they came from.

Ernest was loading his rifle which meant he had to pour gun powder down the barrel, put a lead ball in the barrel and push it down with the ramrod. He had gotten that far but still needed to add the cap to the hammer when his horse spun rapidly and dumped Ernest in the snow. He held on to the rifle but when he regained himself he saw the big wolf only a few feet away. The wolf was not trying to attack Ernest or any of the three riders. Being in the midst of the three horses, the wolf was temporarily confused. Walter and Royce were able to stay on their horses but they began to run away to the west.

Ernest had time to only use his rifle to push at the wolf to keep it away from him. The wolf all at once realized where it was and immediately stopped and turned around and fled into the grove of firs.

Ernest was not hurt but he had been scared big time. The elk disappeared as did the wolves. Walter and Royce were able to get the horses under control and return to the snow covered Ernest. He was a little dazed as he did a flip and ended up landing on his head. His rifle was covered with snow. Walter and Royce dismounted and rushed to Ernest. He handed the rifle to Royce, put his hands on his knees with his head down.

"Man, that happened fast," said Ernest with a lopsided smile on his face as he tried to straightened up.

In a few minutes, Ernest seemed alright. Walter had ridden after Ernest's horse, caught it and returned with it. Finally, things settled down and Ernest felt like continuing on. They led the horses into the grove of firs. In a few minutes a nice tree was selected and cut. Royce tied the tree to his saddle and the mighty loggers headed for home.

"These woods are filled with excitement and thrills," Ernest said smugly, over his right shoulder.

The brothers returned with the beautiful tree, they thought. Alice, Erna, Florence and Bertha studied the tree from all angles. The three loggers sat on their horses fully expecting the inspecting judges would reject it and they would need to try again.

"Looks a little straggly on this side," said Erna with a hint of sarcasm.

"The top looks a little crooked, the star we put there will lean a little," followed Alice.

"There should be more branches on the bottom. It is too sparse there," said Florence getting her two cents worth in. Bertha looked and looked. By now the three loggers could smell a rat.

"Come on Bertha, can you find anything good to say about this tree. After all, a timber wolf nearly bit me (wink-wink). We really are afraid of going back into the wolves den. What do you think?" pleaded Ernest.

"I really respect my elders and all of them had nothing good to say about the tree. I really think it is . . . the most beautiful tree I have ever seen," said Bertha. The other three judges pooh-poohed Bertha's remark and waved their hands in a 'I don't believe it wave'.

"Ladies, we have been outvoted," Alice commented. The three went to Bertha and hugged her. All in all the tree was beautiful and the three loggers got another lesson of life in the forest.

Christmas was a wonderful family event. On Christmas Eve, a wonderful meal of roast goose from Peroutka's Meat Market and several other dishes provided a meal fit for a king. The men washed and dried the dishes as Alice oversaw covering the leftover food and putting foods in the ice box that required cooling. The next thing was singing several Christmas songs and hymns. This family could sing! Erna played the piano and finally Ernest went and got his fiddle. "Play *Little Town of Bethlehem* please," he requested of Erna. The two played the old Christmas song and it was beautiful. Ernest had obviously practiced some of the music that Mr. Kohler had given him. The next time through, the family and Florence sang along, many with tears in their eyes.

RETURN TO MADISON

Royce, Florence and Walter prepared to go to Madison on Monday, January 9th. They would take Ernest and Bertha to Antigo for school, would leave the horse and sleigh at the livery and board the train to Madison. Little did Royce know that a meeting with Beth McLaughlin may be in his future. Royce had been told that Walter was planning to see a doctor at the University Medical School. The three of them would stay at Jack Sander's house on Mifflin Street. Olivia and Jack had assured Florence that it would be fine. Olivia had warned Florence about trying to match Royce with Beth.

"I know you are shooting at Beth and Royce but you may miss him and hit Walter instead. Just be careful." Florence knew her mother had a sixth sense about these sort of things and she briefly thought about pulling back from introducing Beth to Royce.

The next day Royce headed to the Forestry Department at the University. Florence and Walter went to the University Hospital and sought out Dr. Curran. The receptionist was happy to see Florence, but the doctor was out of town today. The earliest appointment is 1:00 p.m. tomorrow. Walter planned to visit some of the buildings at the University. Florence was off to visit her nurse friends.

Walter left the hospital and headed toward the Science Hall. Halfway there he felt strange. He fixed his gaze on a student walking toward him. Walter had stopped and waited for this student who was alarmed by the distant look in Walter's eyes. The male student stopped by Walter.

"Sir, are you alright? Can I help you?" Walter continued looking toward the student with a faraway look.

All at once, Florence and Beatrice came running toward Walter and the student.

"Walter, Walter, I am here." Florence reached Walter and held him and consoled him. Florence thanked the student and told him that he has these episodes from time to time.

"Is he a Civil War veteran?" asked the student with an understanding tone in his voice.

"Yes, two years and five battles and the last one was Gettysburg." By now, Walter had snapped out of his episode.

"My brother fought for the 7th Wisconsin Regiment and was wounded at Gettysburg. He is haunted by his memories of the battles and many times I have seen him like this veteran was a few minutes ago."

"We are here to have Walter meet with Dr. Curran tomorrow. I hope he can help."

"So far, nothing has helped my brother. He has been fired from two jobs and is sad all the time."

"Does your brother live in Madison?" asked Walter.

"No, he lives at LaCrosse with my parents. They are very worried about my brother. I need to get to class. Thank you for your service, Sir." The student reached for Walter's hand and looked into Walter's intent eyes.

"I am alright now," Walter told Florence. "I can make it by myself."

"No, my sweetheart, I will go with you wherever you want to go," Florence told him. Beatrice went back to her duties and Walter and Florence walked arm in arm to the Administration Building.

Shortly after the two of them entered the building, an older man with a handful of papers crossed the lobby in front of them.

"Are you a new student, Sir?"

"No, no. My brother is enrolling in the Forestry program at this time. I am just looking around. This is my fiancé, Florence Porter who is in the Nursing program."

"You mean the Florence Porter who saved many soldiers at Gettysburg? Then she and two of our other students were run over by a team of horses and a wagon?"

361

"Florence, I am John Bascom, President of the University of Wisconsin."

"Mr. Bascom, I want you to meet Walter Rounds, one of the soldiers I helped save at Gettysburg," said Florence respectively.

"Walter Rounds, 6th Wisconsin Regiment, Iron Brigade, political activist that helped get the family voucher program going. Bigger yet, both of you and your brother have given President Lincoln advice on how to prevent disease from germs of diphtheria, and others. Florence gave credit to the University for some leading edge work on germs. Equally important is your suggestion of the child care voucher. Walter and Florence, you and Royce are real giants among us. I have the greatest respect for your accomplishments during these terrible war years."

Walter and Florence bade the University President goodbye and left the Administration Building. They went to the Science Building wondering if they would find Royce there. Walter asked a student if she knew where the Forestry Department was.

"Straight up the stairs and the three classrooms on the right are forestry rooms. The office is just past the third classroom," answered the student as she hurried on her way.

Florence and Walter went upstairs toward the office. In the third classroom they saw Royce meeting with an elderly man in a plaid shirt with suspenders holding up his trousers. This man appeared to be interviewing Royce. There were about a dozen other people in the classroom. Most seemed to be dealing with paperwork. Two of the students were ladies. Walter and Florence stepped into the office and were greeted.

"Good Morning, are you here to register for classes?" asked the lady, apparently the person in charge of office activities in the forestry department.

"No, my brother is meeting in the next room. I would like to leave him a message. Do you have any idea how long he may be meeting with the gentleman?"

"They will take a lunch break, but then continue into mid-afternoon," replied the pleasant lady. She had already left her desk and stood behind the counter in the office.

"I am going to take a guess. Your brother is Royce Rounds," said the lady with a pleasant smile.

"Yes, Royce is my 'brudder'," said Walter with a hint of brotherly love.

The lady produced a piece of paper and pencil. The note said for Royce to come to Jack Sander's house on Mifflin Street when he finished his business with the Forestry Department. Walter thanked the lady for giving the note to Royce. He and Florence left the office and walked to the hospital. Walter waited in the reception area as Florence sought out two or three of her nurse friends.

In a few minutes Florence returned and she and Walter left the hospital and headed to Jack's house. By now it was early afternoon and Walter wanted to visit the Capital to see if the Senate or Assembly were in session. Florence did not want Walter to go by himself, so after lunch the two of them headed for the Capital. The State Senate was in session. Walter and Florence found seats in the balcony overlooking the Senate chamber. Serious debate was underway on a bill that would allow other state colleges to be established. Several cities were mentioned. Finally, the bill was voted on to send it back to committee and return when the cities mentioned could produce a bid for that program. The cities should tell what they would offer and what are the support plans from the city. The cities mentioned seem to be in eastern and southern Wisconsin.

By this time it was late afternoon and Florence and Walter walked to Jack's house. Royce had just arrived and seemed quite excited about the classes he would take and the Forestry program in general.

"On our way to the Forestry office, we saw you meeting with a man with a plaid shirt. Was he one of the instructors?" asked Walter with a curious tone in his voice.

"Yes, he teaches 'cruising' which is to determine the amount of board feet or cords in a certain amount of land, such as forty acres. He is also the Dean of the Forestry School and seems like an alright guy. The classes I will take this semester sound very interesting and I hope they are."

Part of the plan was to have Olivia, Jack, Florence, Walter and Royce all go to *Smokey's* for an evening meal. Several of the nurses will be there also, including Beth. Before the meal, the group intermingled around the bar. Before long, the maneuvering put Royce next to Beth. Florence looked at Walter and winked. Walter read that to mean 'poor Royce, doesn't stand a chance'.

The next event was to sit around the tables arranged for the group. Beth and Royce ended up sitting together and really seemed to enjoy each others company. Walter seemed to have put his feelings toward Beth behind him. He did admire how she carried herself as it accentuated her curvy figure. She was very outgoing and engaging, with her pretty face and flirty eyes. Walter wondered how Royce was getting along as he had about as much experience with women as he did before he met Florence. He really wondered if he had any better understanding of women like Florence now. He just knew he loved her very much.

The meal was finished. The nurses decided it was time to call it a night and the group left. Royce and Beth decided to hang around for awhile. Walter wondered how Royce was getting along. He really loved his brother. He did not want this to turn out bad. He realized that Royce is a grown man, and is a very intelligent person with very good thinking skills. Walter finally decided that it was really none of his business.

Walter and Florence sat up late and finally went to bed. The next morning Royce came down to breakfast with the rest of the people. Walter did not hear Royce come in but was happy to see him. He seemed happy and ready to face the day. Small talk dominated breakfast. Apparently, everyone was waiting for Royce to tell all the details of last night. More small talk. 'come on Royce, what happened last night' was on everyone minds.

Finally, breakfast was finished and Royce excused himself. In a few minutes he announced he was going to the University and would see everyone later. After Royce left, Olivia looked at Florence and Walter.

"That is a tight lipped man," Olivia remarked.

"What do you think, Walter?" Florence inquired.

"I have never seen him like this before," answered Walter. "He certainly seems to have a poker face. He is probably laughing his head off thinking he really fooled us, or . . . he is in a state of shock."

"Beth could do that to Royce or maybe other men," Olivia said as she glanced over at Walter. Walter caught the entire message and felt his face get warm.

Walter quickly rose and took Florence by the hand and took her upstairs. Barely at the top of the stairs Walter turned to Florence, pulled her to him and held her tightly. They engaged in a long emotional kiss. Walter gently led Florence to the bedroom.

"The first baby can come any time, can't it?"

Florence and Walter arrived before the appointed time to meet with Dr. Curran. Some paperwork was completed and they were ushered in to a small consultation room with a table in it. Dr. Curran entered and gave Florence a hug and welcomed her back to the world of 'well people'. This was the first time the two had seen each other since Florence had been hurt in Pennsylvania.

"What is the reason you are here today?" the Doctor began. Walter explained about the injuries at Gettysburg.

"Let's take a look." Walter peeled off his shirt and sat at the end of the table. The Doctor looked at him and had Walter lie down.

"Looks like a rifle bullet did this. Were you in the hospital a long time?"

"I treated Walter when he was brought to the hospital tent I was assigned to," Florence offered. "He was unconscious and an army surgeon removed the bullet. He was unconscious for the first three days. A Doctor and I treated him for the next week. He was then transferred to a hospital in Harrisburg where he remained for about seven weeks."

"I see." exclaimed the doctor. "Walter, were there complications?"

"Yes. There was an infection and a surgeon had to reopen the wound and treat it. Finally the doctor said the infection was gone and I was going to be discharged."

"Have you been able to regain your strength and endurance."

"No, I have not. I tire easily but there is another issue. I have had many episodes of 'battlefield memories'. They now occur more often. Most are minor, but lately some have been longer. I don't threaten anyone and Florence holds me and I return to normal."

"Florence, can you add anything about his episodes?"

"He seems to have a far away look on his face and in a few minutes he seems to return to normal. On a few occasions he has spoken out or made whimpering sounds."

"Walter, I want you to step up and down on this footstool for a short time." The Doctor took his pulse and listened to his breathing before stepping up and down on the stool. After six or seven minutes Walter was noticeably tired and the Doctor told him to stop. He immediately took his pulse and listened to his breathing.

"Walter, sit down." The Doctor pulled his chair near Walter. Florence got up and stood by Walter with her right hand on his bare shoulder.

"The Confederate bullet did considerable damage very close to your heart. The subsequent infection apparently did very serious damage to your heart and the surrounding lung tissue. Your heart and lung performance is only about forty percent or less than it was prior to the injury. The episodes occurring more often signal that you give . . . " Walter had a faraway look on his face, stood up and grabbed the Doctor and pulled him off his chair.

"Stay down, they are coming." He turned toward Florence and was about to grab her, when just as quickly as it has started, Walter snapped out of his trance like episode.

Florence pulled Walter to her and held him.

"What happened?" asked Walter innocently. Florence held Walter with her right hand behind his head.

"You were having a battlefield memory," she said as she looked into his eyes.

Dr. Curran had picked himself up off the floor and put the chair upright and he too, went to Walter and put his left hand on his bare shoulder. He looked carefully into Walter's eyes and then reached for an instrument with a lens in it and looked in both eyes. He paused and seemed in deep thought and then looked in Walters eyes again. The Doctor pulled his chair to within a couple feet of Walter. Florence stood by Walters side. Walter reached up and took Florence's hand. He knew he was about to get bad news.

"Walter and Florence, I know all about what a great soldier you were, as was Royce. All of the hospital knows about your trip to Washington, D. C. at President Lincoln's invitation. You both have a lot to offer each other and the world. Walter, unfortunately, your injury and infection has caused abnormal growth to develop in the area of the old injuries. This growth will very likely continue and it has already restricted blood flow to your body but especially to your brain. That is one reason for the increase and frequency of your episodes."

Walter sat with a forlorn look on his face. He turned and looked at Florence and she pulled him toward her. Florence had tears in her eyes and deep sadness in her heart. For a short time there was no conversation. Dr. Curran looked at this young man that he knew would very likely not recover from his injury at Gettysburg.

"Doctor," Walter finally asked, "any idea how long before my story comes to an end?"

"It could be as short as a year or less, but maybe five years or more. We can hope that a procedure would be developed that would stop the spread of this abnormal growth. I have a colleague at the University of Chicago that I would be happy to schedule an appointment with so he could examine you."

"We will have to think about it, but Florence has great respect for you and your work. I trust your diagnosis. Thank you for your service training young doctors and nurses."

Walter offered his hand to the Doctor and Dr. Curran congratulated them on their upcoming wedding and told them to enjoy it.

FINAL DETAILS

The next morning Walter, Florence and Royce boarded the train in Madison and headed to Antigo. The three had plenty of time to visit and Royce offered that he and Beth seemed to be getting along just fine. Beth knew of a vacancy at a rooming house near her apartment. Florence and Walter could detect a definite attraction to Beth. Royce was impressed by the people he met in the Forestry Department and was looking forward to starting classes next Monday.

Walter told Royce what the Doctor had told them. It brought tears to Royce's eyes. He suspected the Gettysburg injury was worse than originally thought, but he thought Walter is young and will overcome these episodes. Royce was immediately sad. Walter could see that Royce was down. He moved to the empty seat beside him and looked into his eyes.

"That bullet could have been one inch closer to my heart, big brother. I have been given extra time on this earth. I am going to love Florence and new baby, hopefully. We have a wedding next week and Florence and I will continue down the highway of life and we will do what we can to enjoy the trip and make this world a little bit better for being in it."

"Little brother," Royce said, "count on me to stand with you. Let's hope a procedure can be developed that can reverse this thing that is causing all the trouble."

On the way north, the three made some final decisions about the guests invited to the wedding. The ten nurses Florence invited will attend. They all received a day off to ride the train to Antigo. The plans now are for the ten nurses and others like Roger, the doorman, will spend the night in the hotel near the railroad station. Florence, Walter, Royce, Erna, plus Ted Liskau and Matilda would all spend the night in the hotel after a night of socializing and a meal in the dining room. Ernest has invited a friend, Pollyanna and could pick her up

369

on Saturday morning. Bertha invited a friend, Rosemary and both girls live in Antigo so Ernest could pick them up and the extra chairs and tables from Peroutka's Meat Market.

"Be sure to ask Mother and Father if they want to spend the night also," Royce said. "Maybe Ernest and Bertha would enjoy staying at the hotel also." Florence was thoughtful for awhile. "Maybe we should see if we could rent the dining room and have a party among our guests and family."

"We could try to get another band to play some kicking music," Walter quickly said. "Ernest mentioned a band that asked him to join their band. Maybe he could talk to them about that when we get home. First thing, though, we need to determine how many hotel rooms we need and get them reserved. Next talk to the owner, Jack Dawson, about renting the dining room."

"Maybe Jack would not allow a band as there may be other hotel guests," Royce offered.

"Maybe we could rent all the hotel rooms if Edward and Alice are willing," chimed in Florence.

The train pulled in to Antigo and the sun was about forty-five minutes above the horizon. The travelers headed straight to the hotel and found Jack looking after things. Walter asked if the Rounds family could reserve twelve rooms for next week Friday and at least ten rooms for Saturday. Jack consulted his ledger and that would be fine he said with a smile.

"If possible," Florence said, "we would need meals for Friday night, breakfast Saturday, and Sunday morning early. The number of meals would be twenty-three at this time. These arrangements are for guests and family members attending Walter and my wedding on Saturday, January 21st. Many of these people will be arriving on the Friday evening train and leaving on the early Sunday morning train."

"One more thing, after the Friday meal, would it be possible to rent the dining room for a little party?" asked Walter hopefully.

"Well," said Jack thoughtfully, "there are sixteen rooms in the hotel and if someone rents the other rooms they would have to agree to the party, or you could invite them to the party."

"I will rent the other four rooms!" said Royce, all of a sudden. "If someone is planning on staying in your hotel, I will offer to take their luggage to the Northern Hotel just up the street." Jack agreed to the proposal and everyone had smiles on their faces. The trio quickly walked to the livery, hitched up the team and sleigh, paid the bill and headed north toward home.

THE WEDDING

Friday afternoon, Edward, Alice, Erna, Royce, Florence and Walter took their valises and headed to the hotel. Ernest and Bertha would walk from school. Ernest was told to bring his fiddle. Edward dug his concertina out of the closet and the plan was that Edward and Ernest would play a few tunes that people could dance to.

The train pulled into Antigo and the folks on the platform gave the arrivals a warm welcome. Royce and Beth were very happy to see each other and they embraced. However, that was overshadowed by the embraces and kisses that Erna and Roger gave each other. Beatrice was carrying a banjo which made Edward and Ernest smile. 'Maybe she can play a song and we can limp along' seemed like a reasonable guess as to their thoughts. When the remainder of the luggage was retrieved, an even bigger surprise awaited. There was a trombone case! Who would claim that? It was Roger! Now Edward and Ernest really felt good. Maybe this will turn out alright. Edward, Ernest and Bertha took the team and sleigh and went to pick up Pollyanna and Rosemary as they had been invited to attend the doings at the hotel and spend the night in Berthas room. Edward assured both parents that their daughters would be safe and attended to.

The hotel bar was busy. The entire group seemed to be in a party mood. Roger had met the nurses in Madison and he had entertained them with his wit and good humor. Ted and Matilda Liskau got on the train at Wausau. One of the nurses, Marilyn, recognized Ted as one of the soldiers she treated at Gettysburg. She was very happy to meet him again and they spent the time on the train in friendly discussion. Matilda and Marilyn had gone to country school together near Merrill and they had much to talk about. Ted seemed to really appreciate meeting the nurse that cared for him shortly after the rest of his shattered arm had been amputated.

Jack and his staff prepared a very nice meal which was presented family style to the guests. Everyone was in good spirits and much laughter was heard. Finally, the meal was finished, the dishes cleared, and the tables arranged for seating, leaving space for dancing. For Edward and Ernest the moment of truth had arrived. Beatrice tuned her banjo, Roger got his trombone out of the case and tuned it. Roger let out a loud blaring short tune that brought applause and cheering.

It became clear that Roger could really play the trombone. The other three looked to him to lead the little band. He knew several polkas that got nearly everyone out on the dance floor. Edward and Ernest picked up these tunes as did Beatrice. Actually, this pickup band was pretty good. Roger, the showman, announced the 'fabulous four' would play a schottische, next, get ready to do 'an elbow swing'. He started slow as the threesomes swung their legs to the right and then to the left. After a few stanza's, the pace picked up and the dancers elbow swing between them. There was plenty of action on the dance floor. Suddenly the pace of music drops to a slow pace and kick to the right and then kick to the left and then the groups do more elbow swings. Ernest ducked out from the band to invite Pollyanna and Rosemary to dance this dance with him. Walter and Royce danced with these girls after the next set.

The music and dancing continued. Absolutely everyone was having a wonderful time. Roger, the showman, called for a halt in the action.

"There is a young musician who has been 'hiding his light under a bushel', but we are going to hear him play now. Ernest, get out here where we can see you. Bertha, get warmed up and ready to jig. Whenever you two are ready."

Ernest began *Turkey in the Straw*. He bobbed and weaved as Bertha deftly lifted her skirt and began to jig in a lively manner. Ernest turned around and around at the appropriate time kicked his right foot high in the air. The crowd was clapping and Bertha beckoned everyone to come out and join her, and they did. After three times through, Ernest finished by jumping up and clicking his heels as he played the last note.

Finally the evening was winding down. Roger announced, "We are having a wonderful time tonight, but somewhere young men, maybe some from Antigo, are in camps or fighting somewhere, trying to end this terrible war. Let's finish with *When Johnny Comes Marching Home.* This song is dedicated to the three brave soldiers in this room who were able to come marching home."

The little band began and everyone joined in. By the time the song was finished there were no dry eyes in the crowd.

Alice and Florence had seen to making room assignments. Bertha was like a little mother hen being sure Pollyanna and Rosemary were welcome and made to feel comfortable. Alice saw that the three of them were satisfied with their room and sleeping arrangement. The hotel bar was closed and the guests had all turned in for the night.

The next morning a leisurely breakfast was served and afterward several sleighs were brought around. Those sleighs were loaded and began the trip to the Round's house. Edward had another livery team and a covered freight sleigh as he went to Peroutka's Meat Market and picked up folding tables an chairs so they were protected from the snow.

The minister, Inar Racolla and his wife were picked up by the livery sleigh as was Ann Freiburger and her husband and brought to the Round's house. The preparations for the wedding were completed. Just before 1:00 p.m., Erna and Bertha took their places as did Walter, Royce and Ernest. The ministers wife played the wedding march. Olivia and Florence made an entrance from the kitchen. The minister indicated that the guests should rise. Florence looked radiant with a wide smile on her face as she approached Walter and the others.

The minister began the ceremony. The vows were exchanged as were the rings. The minister declared them man and wife and to Walter said, "You may now kiss the bride." Walter and Florence embraced and kissed to the applause of the guests. The minister announced, "I now present Mr. and Mrs. Walter Rounds." He indicated the guests could rise as Mrs. Racolla played the recession.

Due to the arrangements and the guests, Walter and Florence along with the remainder of the wedding party immediately returned from the kitchen and formed a moving reception line. They proceeded to greet all the guests, as did the wedding party. Ernest took his turn with congratulations and he kissed the bride. Mrs. Racolla continued with appropriate music. Guests were invited to step into the living room and partake of some champagne.

Ernest and Royce got busy and set up the small tables and arranged the chairs that Edward brought from Antigo. The dining room table was repositioned with seating for the wedding party on the side of the table opposite the display of food. Sharon, and her husband Ralph, began to carry food, dishes and side dishes out to the dining room table.

A photographer was hired to take pictures of the wedding party, parents and guests. The Three Brothers Band arrived and were promptly told that they should go through the food line right after the wedding party. The minister said a prayer and the feast began. As ordered, there were those nice juicy Peroutka aged steaks done to perfection. A nice Antigo baked potato from Stanley Diercks field went nicely with the steak. Olives and pickles were among the side dishes which included wild rice. Compliments flowed aplenty as the guests consumed the sumptuous meal.

The meal was finished and dishes picked up and taken to the kitchen. Next the wedding cake, baked by Erna, and jointly decorated by her and her mother, was presented. Florence and Walter cut the three layered wedding cake and it was served to the guests on small plates by Bertha, Pollyanna and Rosemary. All at once, someone began tapping a glass with a fork. That was a signal for the bride and groom to rise and kiss. If those two are a little slow to rise, there is a much louder clanking of glasses.

After toasting by the best man and maid of honor, Walter rose and produced the plume from inside his jacket pocket.

"Florence saved my life at Gettysburg. This plume will be a symbol of our long and lasting life together."

Guests were invited to the living room where a small bar was set up. Edward served what was requested. With his beard, mustache and colorful vest, he looked like a very skillful bartender. The Three Brothers Band continued to set up as the small tables and chairs were taken away.

The gifts had been placed on a table to the right of the entrance door. Walter and Florence were opening them and making comments about the wonderful gifts and thanking their guests for them. Suddenly, Florence picked up an envelope. It was from President Lincoln! Apparently Roger, the doorman, had brought it with him. The card inside wished them well and a long and happy marriage. On the bottom of the card was a note stating that there has been significant action on some of your suggestions. Signed, Your Friend, Abraham Lincoln.

The band leader called for the bride and groom. Florence and Walter stepped on to the dance floor and proceeded to show good aptitude toward dancing the polka. The guests cheered and clapped and then Walter motioned everyone to join them. The dance floor was filled with enthusiastic dancers. The vocal sounds by the Three Brothers added to the enthusiasm. A bit later, a favorite by the band was played, *The Chicken Dance*. Immediately the dance floor was filled by dancers flapping their wings and acting like chickens.

Ernest and Pollyanna were indeed good dancers. Both were very light on their feet and seemed to float around the floor. Bertha and Rosemary were having a wonderful time dancing, even if they were a little inexperienced. Another couple that was noticeable was Ted and Matilda Liskau. For a big person with one arm, Ted was a skilled dancer and Matilda was very light on her feet.

If voting had been done, the winning couple might have been Erna and Roger, whose real name was Roger Hammer. Both of these slender, attractive lovers were especially skilled at spinning Erna under Roger's outstretched hand. Both showed great body control and charm besides being very light on their feet.

The Three Brothers announced, "No wall flowers allowed and no dancing with your partner." Immediately the men sought out the ten nurses. James Diercks and Ernest had their sights on the same nurse, but Ernest stepped aside. The men present easily asked the nurses to dance. Walter was the odd man out so he asked his mother for a dance. One of the Three Brothers put his banjo down and danced with the ministers wife.

After one dance, the two brothers in the band announced "Gentlemen, move one partner to the right." With new partners the two man band proceeded to play a fast moving polka with plenty of vocal sound effects. When the song was finished, the band announced the next song would be a schottische. "Men, grab two ladies." The music started and the legs began to swing from right to left. The tempo changed and the elbow swinging began. Abruptly the tempo changed and the dance continued. The band was definitely very good and people loved their music and the commentary that the Three Brothers Band contributed.

Some guests left before it was dark to enable them to have light to get to Antigo. The livery had rigged their sleighs with lanterns so the revelers going to the hotel could stay well after dark. Finally the energy of the dancers ran low and everyone made preparation to leave and go to the hotel. The Three Brothers Band loaded their instruments and left also. Everyone but Edward returned to the hotel to spend the night. Florence and Walter were exhausted and Walter was dragging. When they finally were alone, Walter was so tired all he could think about was going to sleep. Florence crawled in bed and snuggled next to him.

"I am so happy my darling. Just sleep and get your strength back." Walter had already begun to snore and Florence thought 'this is not how I thought we would spend our wedding night and I know Walter had other plans too. Oh, well, tomorrow is another day'.

Breakfast was eaten and the guests going to Madison on the train went to the station. Olivia and Jack were staying a couple more days. Royce had to begin classes the next day, so he joined Beth on the train. Roger also had a difficult time leaving Erna who had briefly toyed with the idea of going to Washington, D. C. with Roger. In the end, she realized that she had responsibilities, but her friendship with Roger was very strong.

Ernest and Bertha had returned Pollyanna and Rosemary to their homes. Both girls said they had a wonderful time as did Ernest and Bertha. On the way home Bertha could see Ernest was love-struck and she encouraged Ernest to continue to being friends with Pollyanna. Bertha thought she was a very nice, friendly girl and had enjoyed being with her the past two days.

Walter did regain his strength overnight. He and Florence woke up and remembered that they were married. Florence was very pleased when she realized Walter seemed fine. They were a little late for breakfast but they were happy.

Later that day the house had been straightened up, the gifts and those who gave them were recorded and the family relaxed around the dining room table. Walter and Florence had only told Royce what Dr. Curran had told Walter. Florence held Walters hand and began telling the family.

"Walter has met with Dr. Curran, a doctor at the University Hospital who is very well regarded," said Florence. "After questions about Walter's symptoms, doing an exam and doing an exercise stepping up and down on a foot stool, the Doctor declared that Walter's heart is functioning only at about forty percent. The damage caused by the bullet very near his heart and the subsequent infection has created an abnormal growth in the heart and lung region, that will apparently continue to grow. This growth affects the flow of blood and especially the flow to the brain. This causes the battlefield memories to increase in frequency. Walter had an episode in Dr. Curran's office when he pulled the Doctor off his chair and onto the floor and told the Doctor to 'stay down, they are coming'. In a few seconds Walter returned to normal but he could not re-member what had happened.

"Walter asked Dr. Curran if he had any idea of when his story may come to an end. The Doctors reply was a year or less and maybe five years or more. The Doctor did not know of any procedure that could reverse or stop the growth. We are hopeful, but Dr. Curran did not sound very optimistic."

Bertha had begun to cry. She got up from her chair and came to Walter and hugged him as he sat in his chair with tears in his own eyes.

"It is not fair," sobbed Bertha. Erna and Alice also came to Walter, who stood up and all three hugged Walter as the tears flowed. Florence hugged the entire group.

"I have been given some extra time," Walter continued af-ter several minutes. "I could easily have died at Gettysburg. So far I have met the love of my life, Florence, who saved my life. We are now married and hope to have children. Florence and I need to try to plan for our future, whatever that is. Flor-ence has promised to stand by me, but that is not fair to her

379

and her goal of being a nurse or an artist. We have to decide where we will live and what we will do to earn a living. Much has happened in our lives in the past few days. If it is alright, Mother and Father, we need to live here for a time to try to get an idea of where our lives will go."

Edward had been quiet as had Ernest.

"Walter and Florence, you can live here for as long as you wish," said Edward as he headed over and put his hand on Walters forearm. Ernest got up from his chair, came over to Walter, shook his hand and left the room. In a few seconds, his sobs could be heard in the distance.

WHAT NOW?

By late March, the days are longer and the sun is higher. The snow is melting and there is a hint that spring is around the corner. Late one morning, a team of horses and a sleigh drove into the yard. It was Ann Freiburger and a man that Walter recognized as Robert Haynes, the State Senator from Wausau. Walter and Florence welcomed them and Ann introduced Mr. Haynes to Florence.

"Due to my health and other factors, Robert Haynes told Walter, "I will not be a candidate for the Wisconsin State Senate District that we both live in. Ann has told me about you and your contact with President Lincoln. She thinks you would be a wonderful State Senator and that is what I am here for. I want to encourage you to run for the job."

Mr. Haynes explained what the job entailed and that the election would be in November. He told of some of the people he needed to convince and in what towns they live in. You will be asked to attend many events by election day.

"You need to file your candidate papers by April 15th and I have a copy of that form," said Mr. Haynes.

Walter looked at the forms. He saw that he had to declare a political party and he immediately saw a conflict. He really felt he was an independent thinker and did not want to be told how to vote by one party or another. If elected he planned to vote for whatever is best for the people in his Senate District. He knows that it is quite unrealistic but that is the way he felt. And if he didn't get elected then that is the way it is. Walter told that to both Ann and Mr. Haynes.

"Walter, I will support you no matter what party you align with and I really feel that people that know you will not care either. Your promise to do what is best for them may be unrealistic but they want to hear that," Mr. Haynes added.

"You will find that in order to get support for your constituents you will have to support other Senator's bills. From what Ann tells me, your honesty is beyond reproach and that is a good reputation to have."

"You two are very close and support each other," commented Ann. "If you decide to file for the job you will find out that you, Florence, will have to share Walter more that you may be comfortable with."

"I just found out that the wound suffered at Gettysburg may limit my life to just a few years."

"That is very bad news," said Ann sadly.

"From what I know about you," Mr. Haynes stated, "the people of this District will benefit from your leadership no matter how long you serve."

Alice prepared a light lunch and invited the guests to join the Rounds. Edward and Erna came in from outdoors and were introduced. Mr. Haynes had many questions about the flooring mill which was about to be built. He was very impressed by the scope of the project. He and Ann bid goodbye and left.

Edward inquired as to the reason for the visit from the State Senator. Walter explained and immediately sensed that his parents and sister were in favor of Walter applying for the job.

"The next few years will be critical for this frontier country," Edward commented. "Development of the railroad and good roads and bridges will be very important. Health care, law enforcement, education and development of our resources are a few of the problems that need to be addressed."

"Walter, you would be a wonderful Senator," interjected Alice. "You and Florence need to decide how it would affect your personal lives, which may include children. The other big issue is how will this job affect your health and how will your health affect your job." Erna was silent but supportive of the idea of her little brother being a Senator at Madison. She would offer to help but Walter already knew that that was a given. As she sat looking at her empty soup bowl 'Senator Walter Rounds, sounds right'.

Later that afternoon, Walter and Florence spent time with Walter's mother. She made several good points, both pro and con. She did not try to convince them one way or the other. She definitely realized the predicament they were in. Walter definitely would stand by Florence on whatever she wanted to do with her life. Florence will definitely stand by Walter on whatever decision he would make.

Walter feels a strong encouragement from others to help serve mankind. He also feels a strong urge to help people. He has always felt that everyone should be treated with dignity and respect. His mother, whom he loves dearly, once told him as they watched an obviously handicapped boy struggle to walk, "There but by the Grace of God goes I". It took awhile to understand what she meant as he was only six or seven years old at the time. Since then he has looked on anyone who is struggling in the light 'that could be me'. His mother told him once before he and Royce joined the army.

"You have a wonderful gift of wanting to help others. People have looked on you as a very kind hearted person who will come to someone's aid, if needed."

Walter needed to really realize that his life was going to be over in a few years. It was like he could not make plans because of the uncertain time schedule plus the uncertainty of how his health will affect his life. All in all, it was very confusing.

Walter and Florence continued to discuss all of these issues.

"With all the issues we are dealing with, here is another. We are going to have a baby!" Walter pulled Florence to him and they locked in an emotional kiss. Walter looked away as tears began to flow. He turned back to Florence as she wiped his eyes. "This is the happiest moment of my life. It also makes me feel sad that I will not be here to help raise this child. I feel that you will have a burden to bear, because I wanted an ancestor and a child I could hold and love. The baby is part of you and it is wonderful that this little baby is part of both of us. You will have something of me to see and hold. I can't explain it, but it just seems wonderful that this little baby is carrying both of us. That seems very special. I hope we can raise it together for many years."

The news of a new baby in the family was greeted with excitement. For Alice and Edward, it was their first grandchild. For the brothers and sisters, it will be the first niece or nephew. Florence wrote letters to her mother and to her Aunt Azalea about the wonderful news.

THE DECISION

Florence and Walter were bogged down in decisions that were waiting to be made. Another one is where will they live? The lake house would be a wonderful home and perhaps Olivia and Jack could live with them from spring to fall. A deal to live there must be worked out with Edward and Alice. Maybe they have other plans for the house. After all, it is their house. Walter and Florence decided to approach his parents about the use of the lake house. Ideally it would be great if a suitable road could be constructed between the two homes.

Another decision to be made is where will the baby be born? Who will be the doctor or should they use a midwife. Walter said definitely no to the midwife. They both concluded that the best medical facilities were at Florence's old hospital, the University Hospital in Madison. That would mean getting accepted with a doctor in Madison, or nearby, that practices at University Hospital. It would mean regular checkups in Madison and finally moving in with Jack and Olivia, if that is alright with them. The baby should be born about the end of October. A discussion with Edward and Alice about the use of the lake house went very smoothly. Olivia and Jack were also welcome to use the lake house. A suitable road could be built between the two houses. Maybe Jack and his crew could build this road.

The last day of March found Florence and Walter on the train to Madison. The first stop would be at the University Hospital to find out which family doctors use the hospital for baby deliveries. They found two family doctors that deliver babies there. Florence contacted one of her nurse friends who worked in the obstetrics part of the hospital. She showed her the two names and with no hesitation she pointed at Stanislaus Wojek.

The Doctors practice was not far from the hospital and Florence and Walter went there to make an appointment. They found the earliest was the next day at 2:30 p.m. The next stop was Jack and Olivia's house. Olivia was not home as she was a student at the University again. She was studying to finish her degree so she could get a job teaching history.

Jack was happy to see Florence and Walter. "Your mother is ecstatic about the baby and so am I," said Jack excitedly. "Your mother will be home in a few minutes. She enjoys the classes and spends a great amount of time reading and taking notes. About then Olivia came in the door. Greetings were exchanged and Jack was right . . . Olivia was excited about the baby. She told about her classes and needed to leave again as she had a 1:20 p.m. class. Lunch was eaten and while still at the table Florence told about their plans to live at the lake house and Olivia and Jack would be welcome to live there too.

Olivia was excited about living back in the beautiful lake home.

"I don't know, I hope to graduate in June and will be looking for a job teaching history. Jack will be spending a fair amount of time at your parents home putting railroad tracks in for the new flooring mill."

"Maybe the Antigo school will be looking for a history teacher. Mr. McBeth has been there for many years and may be ready to retire," Walter offered.

Olivia returned to the University for her class and she needed to do some research in the library. Jack was doing some remodeling in the kitchen so Walter and Florence decided to go to the Capital just to observe what was going on there. They decided to visit Senator Haynes office to meet the staff and see how the office is set up. Senator Haynes was not in but his staff was very happy to meet Walter and Florence. The two young ladies, Lisa and Joanne appeared to be in their twenties and both were form Wausau. Both seemed to know about Walter. They thanked him for his work on the family vouchers. Joanne had plenty of praise for both of them for what they had accomplished in Washington, D. C.

"Do you have information about events in Washington, D. C.?" asked Walter.

"Yes, messages come into this building on the telegraph. Copies are written out and carried to each office that pays the fee. Senator Haynes and others get information this way," described Lisa.

"Do you have recent news from Washington, D. C.?" asked Walter.

"Just this morning, this message came in," replied Lisa as she handed the paper to Walter. He shared the paper with Florence. *Congress today passed the child care voucher program. Mothers can join the work force as this voucher will pay for someone to care for her children. This program is expected to increase production of war materials and materials needed on the home front. Men off to war have seriously depleted the work force. The program will be run through city halls and county court houses.*

"You and Florence were very much instrumental in getting this much needed program," stated Joanne.

The girls explained what their duties were and how they helped Senator Haynes with research on bills. They served as a sounding board for comments received from the Senators constituents. They answered all correspondence by taking notes on what the Senator wants to say, presents the letter for him to sign and then mail it.

"There is much work to do in this office, " said Lisa.

By now it was late afternoon and Florence and Walter were leaving the Capital when suddenly Walter reached out and grabbed Florence's arm.

"That man is Lt. Col. Rufus Dawes," declared Walter enthusiastically.

"Commander Dawes" shouted Walter as he began running toward the Commander who had stopped and recognized Walter. The two men ran to each other and gave the other a

387

powerful hug. Greetings were exchanged and Florence was reintroduced to Commander Dawes.

"Florence, I certainly remember you. I could tell that you were giving Walter special care."

"We are married now and our little baby is due in October. We are here to meet with a Doctor tomorrow," said Walter proudly.

"Congratulations on both accounts. I learned you were very seriously hurt. Walter found you and your mother and he helped you heal for two of the four months. Both of you have been huge news makers, both in Wisconsin and in Washington, D. C. Just a few minutes ago I learned that the child care voucher program is approved. Congratulations to both of you."

"Are you still Commanding the 6th Wisconsin?"

"No, I finally had to step aside. A couple old injuries and exhaustion made it impossible to continue. Florence, do you or Walter have the plume?"

"That is Walter's most prized possession other than his life," laughed Florence.

"Commander, I have heard from Senator Haynes, your old childhood pal, that you are very interested in politics in Wisconsin. Is that why you are at the Capital?"

"Well, yes it is. I just filed my papers to run for a Senate seat from Madison. It looks like I will have opposition also."

"Walter has been approached by Senator Haynes and Ann Freiburger to consider being a candidate for his seat," offered Florence.

"Walter, that would be great. If we win, we could work together again," said the Commander as he put his arm around his shoulder.

"I have still not decided whether to run or not. I have more and more battle field memories so Florence got me to visit Dr. Curran. He determined that my heart and lungs are only working at forty percent and it will get worse. He gave me a few years. I know running for office will involve travel and

388

meetings. With Florence being pregnant it will be a challenge for both of us."

"Walter, that is very bad news. I know Dr. Curran and there is no doubt that he is a top doctor. I am sad for both of you. Knowing that you two act as one and from what I know about you Walter, you feel guilty about the possibility of leaving the raising of your child in Florence's hands." After a pause, "What is Royce doing now?"

"He is attending the University and just started classes in January. He is going to be trained as a Forester so he can manage our parents forests. My parents are in the process of developing a large flooring mill north of Antigo and I was going to help with that. I may still try to do what I can."

That evening, Florence and Walter visited Royce at his apartment. He had books spread on the kitchen table and he welcomed Florence and Walter to his place. After exchanging pleasantries, Walter told him about the baby and he was excited for them.

"That would make me an uncle."

The three sat and mulled the pro's and con's about Walter running for the State Senate seat. In the end Royce was noncommittal but Walter did not feel any negative feeling from him.

There was a knock on the door and when Royce opened it there stood Beth. She was happy to see them and she told them how much she enjoyed the wedding weekend. When told about the baby, Beth was very excited and she also agreed Dr. Wojek was a very well respected baby and mother doctor. Beth and Royce certainly seemed very compatible.

The next day, Florence visited Dr. Wojek's office. The Doctor was a jovial man with a semi-bald head and 'owl like' expression but very friendly. Florence and Walter immediately liked the doctor who promptly put them at ease with his bedside manner. He asked many questions of both of them. He especially asked about the overall health of members of

Florence's family. The questions were asked of Walter's family. The doctor gave Florence an exam, took her weight and gave her a paper that suggested meals that she should consider eating to provide nutrients the baby needed and that will keep Florence's weight in the proper range. She is to have no alcohol and get plenty of exercise like walking.

Finally he listened to the baby's heart beat. He had the nurse give a stethoscope to Florence so she could listen to the heartbeat. When she heard the first heartbeats it brought a wide smile to her face. She handed the stethoscope to Walter and he also had a wide smile on his face. The doctor assured them that everything looks good and he expected Florence to come in for a visit every month. The doctor was thanked and goodbyes said. The next appointment was made for the end of April. Walter and Florence went to Jack's house to spend the night and would head to Antigo tomorrow.

The next day on the train heading north, Walter and Florence realized that they needed to make a decision about running, or not running, for the Senate seat. Florence remained completely noncommittal on a decision. Walter sensed that she had reservations but she remained quiet about recommending one way or the other. They got to Wausau and were waiting to board the train to Antigo.

"If I did become a candidate," Walter asked, "do you think I could beat someone else?"

"Silly, that would depend on who was running, wouldn't it?"

"That certainly is correct. Let's say I won. Do you think I could do the job?" asked Walter pensively.

"Walter, I think you would be a wonderful Senator that would look out for the people in our district," said Florence as she put her hand on Walters forearm.

"Would you hate me if I decided to be a candidate?"

"No, Walter, I would not hate you. Go ahead and file the papers. I will stand by you and do whatever I can to help you." A huge kiss sealed the deal.

"Do you remember that you need fifty qualified voters from your district to sign supporting your nomination and that is to be sent in with the application?"

The next few days in April were spent getting the fifty names required to accompany the application for the Senate seat. Walter felt that he should get a few signers from Wausau, Merrill, Wittenberg and Marathon. Walter and Florence spent the day going to Wausau, rented a team and buggy, and visited Marathon, west of Wausau. Even people in Marathon had heard of Walter and were happy to sign. Wausau was also friendly toward Walter. By the time they had to catch the train to Antigo they had sixty-one signatures for the day. Both were encouraged by Walters acceptance by the people they met that day. Between the Antigo names and the sixty-one names that day the total was two-hundred-eighty one names.

Not wanting to take a chance in being lost, Florence and Walter took the train to Madison and delivered his application and signatures to the proper authority at the Capital. This friendly man looked at the application, looking to see if it was complete.

"Independent party, eh?"

"Is there anything wrong with that?" asked Walter a little perturbed.

"No, no, it is just that your Independent application is only the third one I have seen in ten years," answered the official. He was very impressed by the two-hundred-eighty-one names Walter turned in.

"That is an impressive list of names. You must be some sort of folk hero in your district." The gentlemen shook hands and wished Walter good luck.

In late April Florence and Walter moved to the lake house. Olivia and Jack lived there when they could, but Olivia had classes at the University through May. Jack spent time overseeing the railroad track at the new flooring mill. A steam shovel arrived on the railroad and was busy digging trenches for water pipes and steam pipes.

Olivia had inquired about any openings for a history teacher in Antigo. She was told an opening was anticipated and she should write a letter of application. In late April, Olivia wrote a letter to the principal and she said she would send a copy of a transcript of her grades when the semester ended.

In July, Olivia was offered a teaching job in the Antigo high school. She would be replacing Mr. McBeth who had retired. She was very happy to be offered the job and looked forward to classes beginning in the fall. She and Jack would continue living at the lake house but Jack would still retain the house in Madison.

THE CAMPAIGN

The summer and early fall were filled with a monthly visit to Dr. Wojek to check on the progress of the mother and baby. All is going just fine. Florence followed the recommended diet and she and Walter spent many hours walking. The Doctor was pleased with the progress of both Florence and the baby. Many hours were spent visiting with the people in the district. Advertisements also were developed and they appeared in the newspapers in the district. His main theme was very simple.

"I will treat everyone with dignity and respect. I will have the best interest of this district's people at heart." On the bottom of the ad was this simple statement, "6th Wisconsin Regiment, Iron Brigade."

Walter and Florence attended as many community events as they could. They scheduled meetings when they could meet anyone who had interest in meeting him and asking questions. He wanted people to know that he would only vote for bills that benefited the people of the district. He told the people that he was well aware of the political atmosphere in Madison. On occasion he may have to vote for some other Senator's bill in order to get that Senator to support one of his bills.

Some things that needed attention would be the protection of the many beautiful lakes, rivers and streams. Pollution of these waters must be regulated. Building roads would be a high priority as would be developing railroad lines. There seemed to be no end to things that needed attention and some regulations. The one issue that Walter definitely wanted to accomplish was that women would be able to vote in Wisconsin.

By late September, Florence and Walter moved to Madison and lived at Jack's house. The Doctor said the baby should be born about October 21, 1864. Florence felt tired but excited as the days clicked off toward October 21st. Walter thought

Florence looked beautiful during her pregnancy. He loved to rub her belly, put his ear up to her belly and put his hand on the bulge to feel the baby kicking and moving.

The morning of October 20th, Florence's water broke. Walter grabbed the valise she had packed and they headed for the hospital a few blocks away. Everything was normal and after several hours of labor and Dr. Wojek's assistance, a baby girl came into the world. Florence was exhausted but eagerly held the baby. What a beautiful feeling, being a mother, thought Florence. Walter was allowed into the room and beamed when he saw that Florence appeared to be alright as she held the baby girl. The baby had a small amount of light colored hair. She weighed seven pounds four ounces and was twenty inches long.

Finally, Walter held his daughter. This produced a feeling that Walter had never felt before. He was thrilled as he looked at the newly born baby making faces and opening and closing her hands. She was so soft and delicate. She was making suckling motions with her mouth.

"Time to give you back to your mother."

Florence had moved to an arm chair and Walter gently handed this beautiful little girl to her. She opened her robe and the hungry little girl knew what to do. Florence and Walter had spent time discussing possible names. Now the time had come to decide. Walter had already come up with a name recently but had not talked to Florence about it.

"Your mother is Olivia, my mother is Alice. How about Alicia or Alivia," said Walter hopefully. Florence was thoughtful for a few minutes.

"I like Alivia," said Florence emphatically.

"How would Alivia Florence Rounds sound?" asked Walter hopefully. Florence was silent as she looked at the nursing newborn.

"I think that name is beautiful, just like this wonderful little girl," said Florence proudly.

Several days later, Florence and Walter took Alivia Florence to Jack's house where a nursery had been established in the bedroom. This room was adjacent to Walter and Florence's bedroom. Since Walter was unopposed for the election to the State Senate, they had decided that at least for a couple months Walter, Florence and Alivia would live at Jack's house.

Edward, Alice and Erna took the train to Madison and came to see the new granddaughter and niece. Royce visited in the hospital and he and Beth had visited in Jack's home on two occasions. The new baby girl charmed everyone that came to see her. Everyone took turns holding and talking to Alivia. Olivia and Jack came from Antigo the next weekend. Olivia loved her job and Alivia impressed both her and Jack.

The November election took place and Walter easily won as he was unopposed. Walter checked the Court House in Antigo the next day and he found he had indeed won. The first day on the job would be the next Monday. Walter headed back to Madison to Florence and Alivia.

He could hardly wait to hold Alivia. He really loved that little girl just under one month old. He arrived at Jack's house and Alivia was sleeping. Florence was concerned about Walter. She went to him and they embraced. Walter felt his emotions rising and at that moment Alivia woke up and announced that she needed attention. Walter changed her diaper, picked her up and held her. It gave Walter a powerful feeling of love for this tiny girl.

He planned to go to the Capital to size up the situation, find out as much as he could about his budget, staff, postage and other office expenses. Also he needed to find out about his own pay for serving as a Senator and what per diem expense may be allowed. Travel expenses back and forth in this district should be covered, he thought. He didn't expect any great amount of money, but he hoped it would be enough to cover expenses.

Senator Haynes was in his office, and enthusiastically welcomed Walter and congratulated him. He encouraged Walter to retain Lisa and Joanne as they were very capable and did a wonderful job of taking care of the office, responding to any correspondence and visitors to the office. They are also very knowledgeable about how the legislative process works and are very good at drawing up new bills.

"The first meeting next Monday will be an organizational meeting. Committee assignments will be handed out. Votes will be taken to determine the President of the Senate and other jobs. You are the only Independent elected to the Senate. Have you decided which party you will caucus with? There is one more Republican than Democrat. If you caucus with the Democrats there is no majority. For the purpose of determining a majority, you must determine one party or the other. You will need to decide by Monday morning."

Walter decided to see if he could find out if Rufus Dawes was elected. He checked with Lisa in the office. He found out that indeed he had been successful and was assigned an office to which Lisa gave Walter directions to.

"Counting you," Lisa told Walter, "there are seven new Senator's, three Republicans, three Democrats and you."

"Any advice you could give me about Monday morning? Not to scare you, but if it turns out to be lousy advice, I will fire you." Walter waited a few seconds before saying, "Don't worry, I would never fire you, but it did give you a start, didn't it?" Walter looked at her with a big grin.

"Mr. Rounds, Monday could be a very long day. Talk among my peers is there is no clear front runner for President. However, the Senate rules of order require voting to continue until a President is chosen. That is all I can tell you," said Lisa.

Walter went to Rufus Dawes office and his old Commander was there. They exchanged pleasantries and talked about their upcoming Senate terms. Rufus sounded much more knowledgeable about what went on in the Senate. He really didn't know what to expect Monday morning when it comes to choosing a President of the Senate. They talked about committees that all Senators are appointed to.

"I would hope you and I would be appointed to the Veterans committee. We may have a period of time after election of our President to list preferences on up to three committees as I understand it," said Rufus Dawes enthusiastically.

Walter left the Capital and headed to Jack's house. The thought of being with Florence and Alivia made him smile. He began to walk faster but in a few minutes, he began to feel weak. He stopped and rested for a few minutes and then began to slowly walk toward home.

When Walter stepped in the house, Florence could immediately see that he was tired. She went to him and embraced him.

"Lie down on the bed and I will bring Alivia to you." Walter lay on the bed and Florence put his baby girl on his chest. Alivia was happy and made gentle baby sounds. Walter loved this beautiful baby. He talked to her and kissed the top of her head. Florence lay down beside Walter and Alivia. Walter lay on his side with the baby between them. She waved her arms and kicked her feet. Both parents were unbelievably happy with this precious little girl.

"What will her life be like?" asked Florence happily.

"Whatever is in store for her, I hope she can have good health. I hope she can live a happy life and be a good citizen," said Walter lovingly.

MONDAY AT THE SENATE

Monday morning found Florence looking after Walter as he put his suit and tie on. She and Walter embraced and then he kissed Alivia on the head and took a long look at her. Florence wished him well and he was off on a venture he was excited about but very unsure of the outcome.

The Senators assembled in their chamber. The Parliamentarian held a vote to select a moderator of the election for President. A Senator from Beloit was selected. The process for the election began. A Senator from Green Bay was nominated. Ballots were passed out and voting took place. Ballots were collected and counted by the Parliamentarian. Walter didn't have any feeling for how the vote would go. The candidate was a Republican and Walter was caucusing with the Democrats. Results of the vote came in and it was a tie.

A Democratic Senator form LaCrosse was nominated and had the same results . . . a tie vote. The next three votes also ended in a tie. Finally, Rufus Dawes nominated Walter.

"This man is a registered Independent and caucuses with the Democrats. Walter served with me and I can assure you that I have never known a more honest and fair man. He will be an outstanding President of the Senate." The vote was taken and Walter won by five votes. Walter about fell out of his seat! His fellow Senators gave Walter a round of applause, with a stunned look on his face.

"We have all been elected by the people in our districts to do good things for them and all the people of Wisconsin. Treat everyone with dignity and respect," Walter told them.

The remaining elections were held. Walter asked each Senator to list three committees they would be most effective being a member of and leave it with the Parliamentarian before you leave today. The executive committee will establish committee assignments and we will reconvene at 6:30 p.m."

Walter called the body to order at 6:30 p.m. and committee assignments were handed out. Some discussion about possible goals for this Senate session were discussed and Walter gaveled the meeting adjourned at 8:30 p.m.

The walk home to Florence and Alivia was dark except for lamps lit on certain street corners. Walter was exhausted and had to rest twice before he finally reached home. Florence took one look at him and helped him to sit in a soft chair and rest. Alivia was sleeping but after a few minutes, Walter got up and went to look at his precious baby girl. Oh, how he loved her.

He returned to the chair and Florence pulled another chair closer and after sitting down, she reached out to take Walter's hand. She was very interested in Walter's day and when he told her what went on she listened intently. Walter told her the Senate elected him President. She put both hands up to her mouth and inhaled. Walter asked her if that was a sign of pity or happiness. They both laughed and Florence got up and embraced him as he sat in the chair.

"Honestly, I don't know if I am up to this task," declared Walter with a hint of uncertainty in his voice. Florence was silent for a moment.

"The people of your district and the other Senators have expressed confidence in your leadership. I know you will be very fair and will treat everyone with dignity and respect. You will not fail, there may be some tense moments but your skill at reading people will win the day."

Florence took Walters hand and led him to the bedroom.

"Let's talk about a playmate for Alivia." Walter was tired, but not that tired. After all, they were just going to talk, weren't they?

The Senate schedule was set by law. They would convene from that Monday in November until the end of the week before Christmas. They would reconvene from mid-January until the end of May. They would not meet again until the following November unless the Governor called them into session. Walter spent the remainder of the week in his office and attending committee meetings he was assigned to. He also spent many hours talking to Lisa and Joanne, who he found to be very knowledgeable about what went on in the Capital and especially in the Senate.

Walter took each day as it came. He didn't continue getting weaker but he was tired at the end of the day. Florence had made an appointment for Walter to see Dr. Curran when the Senate adjourned for Christmas. The Doctor examined Walter and gave him the same test of stepping on the footstool many times.

"Walter, you already know that your heart and lungs are functioning at less that forty percent. I wrote a letter to the Doctor in Chicago to see what he would recommend. He basically said that he knows of no treatment that would help. He also said that he knows of three cases similar to yours that chose to attempt to correct it with surgery. All died on the operating table. Your heart and lungs have such reduced capacity that the surgery alone overtaxes them more than you can handle. I am sure both of you have considered the possibility that in your case it would be successful. To increase your chances it should be done now. The longer you wait the weaker you will become. As your Doctor I am advising you to enjoy Florence and your baby girl and get all you can out as many days as you can."

The Christmas break found Florence, Walter and a well bundled-up Alivia on the train to Antigo. Christmas was held at Edward and Alice's home. Royce and Beth spent several days at home. After Christmas, Roger was there to visit Erna. Ernest and Bertha were home for the vacation. Olivia and Jack came over daily and everyone was overjoyed to see, hold and enjoy Alivia.

This fun loving group spent many happy hours together.

There was an ice fishing trip to the lake by the lake house. Edward, Ernest and Roger played a few tunes that got the group clapping and tapping their feet. The hit of the gathering was the story telling event. The only rule was that the story could not take more than fifteen minutes to tell. Edward was the time keeper. There were some beauties! Bertha and Roger were the most energetic and animated. Laughter and clapping were all the story tellers received as a reward. It was greatly enjoyed by all and this ability to tell a story in front of family and friends astonished the others.

Walter went to the Capital to attend to his duties there. In the Human Services committee, Walter worked to get approval of a bill that would allow women in Wisconsin who were twenty-one years of age or older and a citizen of the United States to vote. Even though the election laws of the United States don't allow it, maybe if Wisconsin indicates it is in favor of it, the law may change.

"It is not right that my mother and my sister are not allowed to vote," said Walter emphatically After much discussion, this bill was passed out of committee.

The Senate was reconvened and there were several bills that were approved to be on the agenda. The woman's voting bill was debated with strong feelings on both sides of the discussion. Finally Walter called for a roll call vote. The final tally was close but the bill was defeated by one vote. Newspapers from throughout the state were in attendance and all the bills presented were covered but the woman's right to vote was clearly most popular with the newspaper. Walter read several accounts of the discussion before the vote. Four papers had editorials supporting women voting, no other paper had editorialized which might mean the paper was against it. Generally there was a positive reaction to the bill even though it was defeated. In the next month Walter's office was swamped by letters running eighty-five percent for the bill. There were also some nasty letters against the bill.

THE WAR ENDS

On April 9, 1865, the long and bitter war ended. General Grant met General Lee at Appomattox Court House and the surrender was completed. The Confederates must surrender their rifles, but officers could keep their side arms. Those men with horses could take them with them. And all men, except parolees, were free to return home. The season for spring plowing was here and the men of both armies were needed at home.

The Senate was in session on the Monday after the signing. There had been great celebrating on Sunday everywhere. When Walter convened the Senate he called on Commander Dawes to come forward with another Senator that fought with the 7th Wisconsin Regiment. The three men stood in front of the Chamber to thunderous applause and cheering. Walter asked Commander Dawes to speak.

"It is over. Now is the time to heal and grow. To the seventy-thousand Wisconsin men that trained at Camp Randall, we are proud of your performance on the battlefield. Walter and the Senator from the 7th Wisconsin spoke briefly and then it was on to the business at hand.

END OF SESSION

The end of May signaled the end of the 1864-1865 Senate session. Several bills were passed, three failed and two were postponed to the next session in November. All in all, the Senators worked together and were able to compromise bills the Assembly passed so they could be sent to the Governor for his signature and adoption.

Walter was definitely getting weaker. He went home to Florence and Alivia as quickly as he could. For the past three weeks it was an effort for him to walk and after two blocks he had to stop and rest. His skin had begun to take on a darker shade. Walter knew that he was near the end. One day he closed the door to his office.

Dated May 27, 1865, Dear Alivia, You will very likely not remember me. I am your father, Walter Miller Rounds. Your mother and I conceived you because of our deep love for each other. With a love that strong, we knew we wanted a child and what a child we got! Our love for you is difficult to describe. We both want to hold you as much as we can. We know you will outgrow letting us hold you and we will have to be content to watch you grow into a fine young lady.

I will not be able to watch you grow, but your mother will give you enough love for both of us. You are reading this letter at an age your mother knows you will understand what I am writing.

As you grow into a fine young lady, I would like to tell you something I would have told you if I had been there with you. Treat everyone with dignity and respect. Be a good student and select a career you will be happy doing. Continue your education all of your life. If you have the ability to help others, use it. My mother, your grandmother, Alice Rounds, told me as we watched a young person struggling to understand his environment, 'There but by the Grace of God goes I or you'.

My big battle was slavery. You will have big battles in your life. Sorry I had to leave. Your loving father, Walter Miller Rounds.

Walter folded the letter, put it in an envelope and addressed it, *Alivia Florence Rounds - to be opened when her mothers thinks it should be.* Walter then sealed the envelope.

Walter got a second piece of paper and an envelope.

May 27, 1865. Dearest Florence, When I opened my eyes and saw your beautiful, smiling face, I knew at that instant that you and I were meant for each other. I thought that you also believed that about me. Your wonderful care to save my life, told me it was true.

Florence, our lives together have been wonderful. Our support for each other show how much we love each other. My love for you and your love for me is difficult to explain. I would do anything for you and I know you would do anything for me, which you have done since I first saw you at Gettysburg.

I am very sad that I can not be with you the remainder of your life. I am very sorry that I will have left you the task of raising Alivia without me helping you. I know you have enough love to do a wonderful job of raising her.

My life has been very full, thanks to you and others. Florence, I am sorry to leave you and Alivia but I will save a space in Heaven for both of you. Your loving husband, Walter Miller Rounds.

P. S. Life is for the living. Mourning is a good place to go, just don't stay there very long.

Walter folded the letter and put it in an envelope and addressed it to *Florence Olivia Rounds. Open this letter shortly after the funeral.* Walter put them in his suit coat pocket and headed home.

Walter could only walk a block at a time without resting. Finally, he reached home. Florence could immediately see that Walter was in trouble. She cradled Alivia in her arm and hurried to Walter. He looked into her eyes as he stood unsteadily.

"I think my time has come, Florence, please help me to the big chair and let me hold Alivia."

Florence guided him to the chair and when he settled in she handed Alivia to him. Walter smiled and cuddled her in his right arm. Alivia made baby sounds and for the first time she reached up and gently touched Walters lips and smiled. She squirmed around and with Walters help she put her hands around his head and her lips on his forehead. She leaned back and looked into his eyes for a very long time.

Walter had tears in his eyes and he returned her to the crook of his arm. He motioned Florence to take the baby, and when she did he stood up with great difficulty and embraced her and Alivia.

"Florence, I love you will all my heart," he said softly as he looked into her eyes. "I am sorry." He stumbled back to the soft chair and collapsed into it. Florence was horrified. She put Alivia in her crib and returned to Walter. She could tell Walter was gone. He looked peaceful but she recognized the signs she had seen too often at Gettysburg. She burst into sobs and knelt in front of Walter and cried in his lap. Her sobs were powerful and told the world 'my best friend and loving husband is gone.' How will I carry on.?

THE FUNERAL PLANS

Florence could not leave Alivia, but the next door neighbor, a pleasant lady had offered to watch the baby if Florence needed her. Now was that time. She took the baby and knocked on the door and told her of Walter's passing. The lady and her husband were horrified!

"Yes, yes, I will come and watch the baby."

"She is about ready to go to sleep," said Florence in a calm clear voice.

Florence explained that her brother-in-law Royce lived in an apartment near the University and she would contact him to help her with plans. Florence got the neighbor lady settled in with Alivia. Florence hurried to Royce's apartment and when she told him about Walter, he cried.

"What should I do?" asked Florence sadly.

"Did Walter ever say anything about where he wanted to be buried?" Royce asked.

"The only thing was on two occasions when we went past the Antigo Cemetery and he remarked that is a beautiful place," said Florence, with a helpful tone in her voice. "I will take him home to Antigo and to the family. Then I can make arrangements."

"Beth and I will go with you and Alivia. I think Commander Rufus Dawes would want to know. If it is alright with you," Royce said, "I will go to his house tonight and tell him. He may want to attend the funeral."

"Please do so. Meanwhile, how do we get Walter's body to the train station?" Florence asked. "I just can't deal with Walter's passing now."

"When I am going to Commander Dawes house, I will pass close to a mortuary and I will see about a casket and other arrangements, if that is alright."

"By all means make arrangements and I will pay for it. I need to get back to Alivia. I don't know how I will sleep tonight," said Florence sadly.

Florence returned home, thanked the neighbor and settled in, wondering what would happen next. There was a knock on the door and it was Royce.

"The mortuary people will be here soon. They will put Walter in a casket and take him to the train station in the morning. They will take Walter to the mortuary for the night." Royce and Florence looked at Walter peacefully sitting in the chair. His right hand was under his suit coat.

"Isn't that strange," said Royce. "Do you suppose he felt pain or maybe he was reaching for something."

Florence went to Walter and opened his jacket. Immediately she saw the ends of the two envelopes in the suit jacket inside pocket. She retrieved the two envelopes and read the address and the information on them. Florence immediately burst into tears and cried on Royce's shoulder.

"That is just like Walter, thinking of others instead of himself," she sobbed.

In a few minutes there was a knock on the door. It was Commander Dawes. He immediately gave Florence a huge hug. They both had tears when they separated.

"I loved Walter and Royce like sons. Florence, your husband was a wonderful, kind hearted hero, as was Royce."

"Florence, this is difficult but you need to give some thought as to the funeral arrangements," said Royce. "I know my parents would be pleased to hold the wake and the funeral at their home. I am sure that they would be grateful to do everything they could to honor their son and your husband and in a way that is fitting for this special man.

"I will be in Antigo," said Commander Dawes, "and I feel certain that other Senators would want to attend also."

"Maybe we could ask the mortuary if they have a caisson that you could rent. That could carry Walter from my parents home to the cemetery in Antigo," Royce commented.

407

There was a knock on the door and it was two well dressed men from the mortuary. Florence welcomed them into the house. Royce inquired about a caisson.

"Yes, our firm has a very nice caisson that we would be happy to accommodate you with during this very difficult time. We could provide just the caisson or because we have a special railroad car, we could bring a team of black horses to pull the caisson. If you wish, we could provide an appropriately dressed driver to drive the caisson to this veterans final resting place."

"Can you provide the rider-less horse?" Commander Dawes asked.

"Absolutely, the railroad car is designed to allow for that in the event it is requested. What about embalming the veteran?" requested the owner of the mortuary.

"I have not thought about that, but could you remove Walter and by that time we can make some tentative plans for the wake and the funeral," requested Florence.

The three retreated through the kitchen to do some planning.

"Today is Friday," Royce began. "You, Alivia and Walter can take the train to Antigo tomorrow, which is Saturday. Walter could be dressed for preparations made on Sunday. The wake and funeral could be held Monday or if it was Tuesday, it would allow additional time for guests to arrive."

"My guess," Commander Dawes offered, "is that there will be a large number of Iron Brigade soldiers in attendance and they will definitely want to march with Walter and the family on the way to the cemetery."

The men completed the task of removing Walter to the waiting hearse. Florence told of the tentative plans, which included getting embalmed for the wake and funeral on Tuesday.

"How will Walter get from the train station in Antigo to his parents home," asked the mortuary owner.

"It certainly would not be very appropriate to load him on a freight wagon," Royce answered, "I have never seen a hearse wagon at the Antigo livery."

"Since the funeral is Tuesday, we could load our hearse and black horses on our special railroad car and take Walter to Antigo tomorrow. We could return to Madison with the hearse on Sunday and return on Monday with the caisson and rider-less horse," said the owner enthusiastically.

"Do you have many American flags on a staff that the soldiers could carry?" Commander Dawes inquired.

"Oh yes, we have at least fifty American flags and about twenty regimental flags for the 2nd , 6th and 7th Wisconsin."

"I will cover this expense," said Commander Dawes with his 'this is what we will do' expression on his face. "Is it possible to get another thirty American flags? There will be a great turnout of Iron Brigade soldiers," said Commander Dawes emphatically.

"We will bring them with the caisson. We may have to rent a team and wagon to transport the flags to the funeral site." The owner assured Florence that their firm would do their part to make this funeral a fitting tribute to a Civil War hero and a State Senate President. "We are very proud to be of service to such a distinguished man and his family. Our condolences to you, Mrs. Rounds and to your daughter."

Florence was finally alone with Alivia who was sound asleep in her crib. What to pack and what will she wear? She began to lay out her clothes and then began getting Alivia's clothes and toys ready. How she wished her mother was with her now. She and Jack won't know any sooner than the Round's family. She wished she could tell Walter's family that he was gone. She felt a great sadness and finally collapsed on the bed and sobbed, loud, heart wrenching sobs. How she missed her Walter. A half hour later she sat up on the edge of the bed.

"Walter, my love, I don't know if I am strong enough to live without you. I know you are by my side now as you were before. I know we can survive and with your help I will be strong just like you were. I love you Walter, Good night." Florence said out loud with a forlorn tone but also sounding determined.

Saturday morning Florence had the packing for her and Alivia done and she wondered how she would get all of it to the train station and still carry the baby. A knock on the door solved that problem. It was Royce and Beth. Greetings were exchanged and Beth offered her sincere condolences. They had left their luggage at the railroad station before coming to help Florence. Between them all, they were able to get everything to the train station. The hearse with the black horses was being loaded on a special mortuary railroad car. Florence watched and tears came to her eyes as she pictured Walter all alone in this casket. It was a very sad thought and Beth quickly put her arm around her and tried to comfort her.

The boarding of the cars began. Royce had purchased three copies of a Madison paper. The front page story was of Walter's passing. Apparently Commander Dawes had informed the newspaper and provided some of the information. There was a picture of Walter presiding over the Senate. It was a very good story and praised Walter as a great American. One of our finest.

Finally, Wausau was reached and there was a thirty minute layover. The special car with the hearse had to be switched out of the Madison train and added to the Antigo train. Florence watched the proceedings and whispered, 'getting close to home, my love'. Many people on the train had realized there was a special traveler on the train that day. Many men tipped their hat or cap to Florence and Royce.

The last leg of the train ride began. Florence had to feed Alivia. This little seven-month old must have sensed something different was going on as she was very good and did not fuss at all. Florence hugged her and whispered to her as she nursed. Florence was thankful that Walter wanted to marry as soon as possible. He apparently was afraid his days were short. Here was their special little angel that they both loved but Walter could not hold her enough.

Deep in her thoughts, Florence was reminded of the fact that she may be pregnant. That thought brought a smile to her face and then she realized that it would be difficult to care for two little ones at the same time. Then she thought 'Walter, we will just do it.'

Royce had thought they would have to rent a buggy and a team from the livery in order to get the three of them, plus Alivia and the luggage home. As the train pulled into Antigo and near the station, they could see a large crowd that over-flowed the platform.

"What is going on?" asked Florence as she looked at Royce.

"Somehow the word must have reached Antigo. I am sure these people are here to welcome you and Walter home," Royce said as he helped Florence to her feet.

Royce helped Florence and Alivia to the door of the railway car. The conductor helped her down and then she saw Olivia and Jack and behind them was the Round's family. There was no sound, just people wanting to show their respect and condolences by their presence. Florence, Royce and Beth were amazed by the turnout. Tearful greetings were exchanged with Bertha, Erna, Ernest, Alice, Edward and Olivia.

The crowd watched the unloading of the hearse and the team of black horses. The hearse had glass sides and Walter's casket was draped with an American flag. Finally the proces-sion was organized.

Walter would be taken to his parents home where Royce, Ernest, Edward and the mortician would take Walter into the house. Florence and Alivia would spend the night with Olivia and Jack. When the family and hearse got home there were six blue-coated Union soldiers ready to help.

"Sir, we would be proud and honored to carry our brother into the house, but we will step away if your family would rather have that honor," said a tall, strong Sergeant.

"If you soldiers could carry Walter to the front door," Edward said after careful thought, "that would be fine, then Sergeant, if you would select three of your soldiers to help us carry him into our home."

"Sir, that would be a high honor for us. We served with Walter and there was none better."

The six soldiers moved Walter to the doorway where the undertaker had placed a stand to put the casket on so the transfer could take place. As the three Round's men and three soldiers lifted Walter, the tears flowed from Ernest, Royce and Edward. The undertaker moved the platform into the house and Walters casket was placed on it. All six soldiers came near the casket, removed their Iron Brigade black hats and reached out and put their hand on top of the casket for a few seconds. They stepped back, put their hats back on and each one snapped a salute to Walter.

The undertaker would take care of changing Walter from his suit to his 6th Wisconsin uniform. He requested that Royce and Ernest help with the change of clothes. The task took thirty minutes but when finished Walter looked like the top notch soldier he was. The hole made by the Confederate bullet was visible and no attempt was made to cover it. His wallet and watch would be given to Florence. The undertaker took the hearse to Antigo and loaded it on the special car. The two black horses were boarded at the livery.

Florence and her mother spent the evening talking about events so far and what the agenda was for the wake and funeral. Having her mother with her at this time reinforced Florence's resolve to be strong through the next days and beyond. This was not the time to worry about the future.

Sunday morning found Florence, Alivia, Olivia and Jack at the Round's house. Royce asked if they wanted to see Walter. They agreed that they did, so Royce opened the lid of the casket and held it. Florence looked at Walter with his blue uniform on and reached out to her mother.

"He looks so strong. He looks just like the man that found me and cared for me in Pennsylvania. He was so kind and loving and we were deeply in love. I am so thankful he wanted to get married as soon as possible. He loved our little Alivia so much and so do I. He felt sorry for leaving me with the task of raising her by myself," said Florence as she wiped her eyes. Her mother put her arm around her and Florence put her head on her mothers shoulder.

Edward and Alice had talked about what to serve after the service. Finally, Edward mounted a horse and rode to Antigo to find Sharon and Ralph, Mr. Peroutka's daughter, to see if she could put on a lunch for up to three hundred people. When Sharon heard that number she gasped, but regained her composer.

"We can do it if a picnic is alright."

"Anything you want to put on will be fine."

"Oh, boy, Ralph, you and I and my dad need to get to work."

Next stop was the railroad depot to visit with the ticket agent/telegraph operator. First he thanked him for sending his son to our home to tell us about Walter.

"I would like to rent three railroad cars to take guests to the funeral at our home."

"Let me check." He stepped to the telegraph machine and tapped out a message to Madison. In a short time an answer tapped back.

"Need an engine?"

"No, we will use ours."

"Will be on the Monday train," was the answer a few taps later.

Next stop is at the ministers house, Inar Racccola and his wife. Edward told them what he wanted for a service. He

413

asked Mrs. Raccola if she could play hymns that most people could sing along without a hymnal.

"How about *The Old Rugged Cross?*"

"That would be fine and play two verses only. Can you play *When Johnny Comes Marching Home?*"

"Yes, I can."

"Inar, please don't have a long service. It is all about Walter and he was a believer but not overly so," said Edward.

While Edward was away, the family and Florence decided on a position of the casket and where Florence and the family would stand to greet visitors. Visitation will be from 11:00 a.m. to 1:00 p.m. Because of the anticipated large crowd it was decided that lunch would be served before and after the service. The subject of pallbearers was brought up.

"See those six Union soldiers camping out there," Royce said, "they want to be Walter's pallbearers."

"Would that upset anyone if they were the pallbearers?" asked Florence. The group looked around at each other and no one seemed to object.

"How about you, Ernest? Would you object to not being Walter's pallbearer?" asked Florence in a quiet, sympathetic voice.

"Not if I can help lower Walter into the grave," answered Ernest with a 'I gave a little, but I won't give on this' tone in his voice. Florence went to Ernest as he sat in a chair.

"This is very hard. We all want you and all of us to grieve for Walter in our own way." Ernest got up and moved away from his chair and turned to Florence and hugged her.

"Walter was the best brother anyone could have and I loved him. It will be hard to realize he is not coming back to us. I am thankful that I had him for sixteen years."

Bertha had been wiping tears. She got up and came to Florence and hugged her and put her head on her shoulder. "I want to speak tomorrow at the service. I don't know if I am strong enough but for Walter I must be strong. I must be strong for this family. I am so proud of all of you. This wonderful family was Walters rock. The love in this family naturally led Walter to help others and I want to tell that tomorrow."

"You may be the baby of the family," Alice said as she came to her baby, Bertha, and pulled her close to her, "but you are a giant and Walter knew that. He told me twice that Bertha will out shine all of us. For Walter, use your great speaking skills to tell about your brother."

Edward arrived home and reported on securing the food service and he agreed that serving lunch before and after the funeral would be about the only way to serve all the anticipated visitors. The three railroad cars made everyone smile. Edward would speak to the engineer that worked for him. He told about securing the minister and his wife and the two songs she would play.

"Who is going to help me lower Walter into his final resting place?" asked Ernest.

"I will," answered Royce.

"I will," said Edward.

"I will," said Erna.

"So will I," said Bertha.

"So will I," said Alice. This loving family looked at each other. 'Yes, that is fitting,' thought Alice.

"Walter would like that."

"Are we going to shovel the dirt in also?" asked Ernest, "because I want to."

"Let's all do it," said Bertha.

Florence asked if Walters hat with the beautiful plume could be placed on the casket after the flag as been placed there.

"Of course," said Alice, "and I think it should be taken off the casket and given to you Florence, before it is lowered."

"Maybe it could be by his left shoulder during the visitation," said Florence.

"I know Commander Dawes will be here tomorrow," said Royce, "and he will want to speak at the service. He also has arranged for up to one-hundred American and Iron Brigade Regiment flags on staffs. He and I discussed the anticipation of many veterans to attend. His thought was that these soldiers would walk on either side of the hearse and the family carriage. The soldiers would be arranged so that half would walk beside the hearse and the remainder would be split walking in front of the hearse and walking behind the carriage. He also arranged for a bugler to play *Taps*. Also a squad of five riflemen will give a fifteen-gun salute to Walter. Several drummers will accompany the flag bearers."

"I want to speak at the service also," said Erna. "I will make it short but Walter would want me to, and for Walter I will speak."

Just then the ticket agent/telegraph operators son knocked on the door. Edward went to the door and accepted a slip of paper. The paper was addressed to Erna and it was from Roger. The note said he was coming to the funeral.

By now it was nearly dark. Edward had gone out to visit with the six Union soldiers that would be the pallbearers on Tuesday. They were very comfortable and did not need anything.

"Sir, we are very sad for losing Walter but we are very proud to have served with him. You and Mrs. Rounds must be very proud of Walter."

"We would like to stand guard for Walter when the visitation starts," another Sergeant addressed Edward. "With the families approval, two of us will stand on either side of the steps leading up to the porch, two more will stand on either side of the entrance door and two more will stand behind the casket with Walter."

"If you are wanting to perform that service for Walter," Edward said, "I am sure our family will be very happy. Thank you very much."

416

Monday was a quiet day. The plans seemed to have been made and everything seemed to be in readiness. Royce asked Ernest and Erna if they wanted to take a carriage with him to Antigo to see if there are any guests that arrived on the Madison train. They hitched up and headed to Antigo. They arrived a few minutes before the train did. They watched the passengers step off the cars. Commander Dawes was with a large delegation of Union soldiers. Several drums were unloaded from the baggage car. Five long rifles in cases were also seen. Royce went to Commander Dawes and introduced Erna and Ernest.

"Ernest, I am so happy the war ended before you had to be drafted. Your family has paid enough already."

Royce noticed several men that he guessed were Senators and other governmental people. Commander Dawes had Royce, Ernest and Erna meet a man he introduced as the Governor of Wisconsin.

"I traveled to Antigo to honor Walter," he said, "and there is no need to make a fuss about me. I have admired Walter ever since he and Ann twisted the arms of the Senators and got a family voucher passed. Your brother had a very bright future ahead of him."

All at once, Erna saw Roger and ran to him and gave him an embrace and kiss. Erna was very excited as was Roger. The sadness of the loss of Walter temporarily could not hold back the emotions of those two.

Royce noticed an older lady looking around and thought she was familiar. He went to her and then he knew.

"You are the State Senator from Pennsylvania"

"Yes, I am Margaret Poullette. I can tell you are Walters brother. I was so sorry to read about Walter, I said goodbye to my husband and made my way to Antigo."

"Please come with us to my parents home and you can sleep in my room. This bunch looks like they want to stay up late into the night. My father has a bottle or two if you would like a little nip," said Royce convincingly.

"Is Roger coming with us?"

"Of course, I am, Margaret. After all this beauty is my special friend," said Roger. Royce had told Commander Dawes about the three railroad cars that will bring visitors that come to the house.

"I don't know when the cars will leave, maybe if they get full, they will leave and come back," said Royce.

Royce, Ernest, Erna, Roger and Margaret loaded up in the carriage and headed for the house. Edward and Alice warmly welcomed Roger and Margaret. A light meal was eaten and the discussion around the big table was brisk and didn't seem to reflect the somber attitude of the earlier two days. Maybe some of the grieving has been completed.

Florence had been nursing Alivia and came in to the dining room and immediately embraced Roger and thanked him for coming from Washington D. C. He expressed his condolences. He asked to be allowed a few minutes in the service the next day.

"This country lost one of its brightest stars," Margaret told Florence. "Walter was an exceptional person as are you and Royce. I can see where Walter got his 'star shine' from. I think Ernest and Bertha are waiting to follow Walter's pathway. Royce and Erna are already on that pathway. Edward and Alice, what a family you have. And now Roger is making plans with Erna to join the family. Roger, get ready for a ride into the stars. And now there is a baby girl. With her pedigree she will do great things also."

True to Royce's hint, Edward brought out a couple bottles and glasses. This was a rarity in this house, but so was a funeral of a young son.

THE FUNERAL

Tuesday morning. The food arrived and provisions to feed guests were set up. The six pallbearers assumed their position as Walters guardians. Before 11:00 a.m. mourners began to arrive as the first round of railroad passengers arrived. Once empty, the engineer returned to Antigo for more passengers. Florence and the Round's family, plus Roger were scattered in various parts of the living room and dining room. Florence stood by Walter and began the task of greeting people.

As dozens of people passed Walters casket, Florence saw two young men in Confederate uniforms. They approached her and removed their caps.

"Madam, we are very sorry for your loss. You may not remember us, but you cared for us just like your troops at Gettysburg. We knew we would be welcomed and wanted to thank you and honor Walter." Florence thanked the young soldiers and gave each an embrace.

A few minutes later, Ann Freiburger came through the line and she was with Ted Liskau. After condolences, Ted told Florence, "I want to be appointed to complete Walter's term in the Senate. I definitely would run for that position in the next election cycle." Florence thanked Ann for all she has done.

"Walter admired you and had great respect for you."

Olivia and Jack were caring for Alivia. It was a beautiful day, sunny and warm, just a wonderful day, just not nice for Walter, thought Florence.

As the 1:00 p.m. hour neared, the living room was arranged to hold the service. Windows were opened so people on the porch and outside could hear what was said inside the house. The minister did a good job of making it a simple service. Mrs. Raccola played *The Old Rugged Cross* and the people really sang along. The minister asked if anyone wanted to speak.

Bertha spoke and told how much she loved Walter and how much he loved her and all of the family. His love for Florence was so strong that he went to Pennsylvania and found her. She was injured and he helped her heal, just as she did when he was injured at Gettysburg. Our family loves each other very much and we will miss Walter but maybe we will try to carry on with his kind hearted spirit.

"I served with Walter," said a man with one arm, dressed in Union blue, "and was injured at Gettysburg. I rode on the train with Walter on two occasions. The last time I had just gotten out of the hospital in Madison because of an infection in my stump. Walter could see I was in a bad way since I hadn't worked for two months. This kind hearted man dug in his pocket and gave me forty dollars. I told him I would pay him back. And Walter said, No, Ted, when things are better for you lend it to someone that is up against it."

Next was Erna and Roger.

"Walter was always a special person," Erna began. "He would always help another kid that was having a hard time fitting in. He sought out kids that did not seem to come from the right side of the tracks. One day I asked him why. He said that our mother and he watched a little boy that seemed to have a hard time comprehending. Mother told Walter 'There but by the Grace of God go I, or you.' In Walters young life he lived by that simple phrase. I loved him and will miss him."

"My name is Roger, the door man. I guard the door at the White House. The President had invited Florence, Walter and Royce to come to the White House. The President had met Walter and Florence when he gave the Gettysburg address. This entire family, and a few others were attempting to smuggle into the White House on their invitation, but I stopped them dead in their tracks." Roger paused and looked around for effect. "I would not open the door unless I could get a date with this lovely girl here." With that the crowd broke into laughter. I worked with the President and we are all very sad about his recent death. On more than one occasion the President told me how much he admired Florence, Walter and Royce. Their help was a great assistance in ending the war. President Lincoln was a great leader and he told me once that Walter was one of the finest young men he had ever met.

Commander Rufus Dawes spoke next.

"I commanded the 6th Wisconsin for over two years. Walter and Royce were with me through Gettysburg when Walter was seriously hurt and Royce was injured also. Florence nursed Walter back to health. I visited Walter in the hospital tent when he was still unconscious. I traded my plume and this is it, with Walters shot up plume and this is it, as he held up both plumes.

"A bullet hit his plume on the first day at Gettysburg. I wore Walter's plume in honor of one of the greatest soldiers I ever commanded. In a few minutes we will form a procession to take Walter to his final resting place. The soldiers carrying the flags have the greatest respect for Walter. I agree with President Lincoln, we have lost one of Americas finest men. His desire to serve mankind got him elected to the State Senate. He, Florence, and Royce were instrumental for the start up for family vouchers and family child care vouchers."

Mrs. Raccola began with *When Johnny Comes Marching Home*. The crowd joined in and really rocked the place. The minister announced lunch would be served for the next hour and then procession to the cemetery would begin. The train will make trips as needed.

When the hour was up, the lunch was eaten. The caisson had been pulled up near the porch. The six pallbearers carried the casket with the American flag draped on it. Walters cap with the plume rested on top of the flag. The casket was loaded and secured to the caisson and the rider-less horse was hitched to it.

The carriages for the family were loaded behind the caisson. The flag bearers and drummers were positioned on the road to Antigo. At last, the signal to begin was given. The drummers immediately began a steady beat. When the caisson reached the place where a flag man waited, the soldiers marched to the drum beat and the entire procession began the sixteen mile trip to the Antigo cemetery. It was impressive to see one-hundred flag bearers escorting the beautiful caisson with the black horses and the rider-less horse. It was also very sad. A gentle warm breeze made the flags wave beautifully. Twenty-five or more horses and carriages brought up the rear of the procession. After one mile there were several wagons waiting to pick up the flag bearers as it had been determined the sixteen mile hike would take too much time. Once the soldiers had been picked up, the procession moved along at a more rapid pace.

At the cemetery, the soldiers with flags formed a corridor to guide the caisson near the dug grave. As the drummers beat out a solemn rhythm the pallbearers placed the casket on two wooden rods that were laid across the grave. Three ropes were laid across the grave also. The minister said a prayer, the fifteen-gun salute was given and *Taps* was played.

"Anyone that wants to come up and place your hand on the casket can do so at this time," the minister said. Nearly everyone in attendance did, including the nearly one-hundred soldiers, who all saluted after touching the casket.

Walter's hat was removed and given to Florence. Next the American flag was carefully folded and given to her. This solemn ceremony brought tears to nearly everyone's eyes. The Round's family members went to the casket and held their hands on it for a few seconds. The men and Erna were on the end ropes where as Alice and Bertha held the middle rope. On the signal, the group lifted the casket and the pallbearers removed the wooden bars. On Edwards signal, the family slowly lowered Walter into the grave. Finally the casket settled at the bottom. Six shovels were brought up and the family began to shovel the dirt into the grave. Tears were flowing from all the family and from Florence, Alivia and Olivia as they stood nearby. Finally the grave was filled. The family, Florence, Alivia and Olivia loosely held each other and all said their final goodbye to Walter.

In a short time, other mourners moved in slowly and began placing their outstretched hands on the shoulders of the Round's family, Florence and Olivia. The Iron Brigade flag bearers began to encircle the group. As other mourners moved up and placed their hands on those in front of them, the flag bearers moved up and also put their hands on the those in front of them. The drummers began a solemn beat.

All at once, Erna's beautiful clear voice was heard, slowly singing *When Johnny Comes Marching Home.* The entire crowd joined in and then the song was finished. In a few minutes, the flag bearers backed up and began to lower their flags. They marched to the beat of the drums and left the area of Walter's grave. The ceremony was complete. Walter had been shown great respect and honored for the impact he made on the people of America.

EPILOG

By mid-summer a white marble cross was placed at the head of Walter's grave. The horizontal arm had *WALTER M. ROUNDS* engraved on it. The vertical staff reads *6TH WISC. IRON BRIGADE.* On the back of the horizontal arm was engraved, *TREAT EVERYONE WITH DIGNITY AND RESPECT.*

A simple white marble flat stone was placed at the foot of his grave. Engraved on it was, *THERE BUT BY THE GRACE OF GOD GO I.* Below that were the numbers 1843 - 1865. There was also an Iron Brigade hat and plume engraved below the inscription.

Ted Liskau, the one-armed soldier from Merrill was appointed to complete Walter's term in the Senate. He was elected to three more terms as State Senator.

Walter was correct that his mother would come up for the best name for his families lumber enterprise. It was named Edward's Lumber. It was a very large operation that grew and employed over two hundred men and women. The reputation was that it was a very good place to work.

Erna and Roger were married. Erna joined Roger attending the University of Wisconsin at Madison. Both graduated with degrees in Business and were part of the family ownership of Edward's Lumber. They looked after the overall management of that vast enterprise, plus the families holdings in Philadelphia.

Royce graduated from the University of Wisconsin with a Forestry degree. He and Beth McLaughlin married and had a daughter and a son. Beth worked as a nurse in Antigo. Royce oversaw all management of the forest which included harvesting and replanting of the beautiful family forest. He became very well known in the forestry field. The management of Edward's Lumber timberlands was viewed with awe and admiration.

Florence was pregnant when Walter died. A son was born and named Miller Walter Rounds. Alivia was indeed a special young lady. Florence gave her Walters letter when she was ten years old. Alivia read the letter several times and then held it to her heart. The next trip to Antigo she asked to be allowed to visit her father by herself. For an hour she visited with Walter. Finally she told him, "Your big battle was slavery, mine will be women's vote. Bertha and I will see that come true." Alivia knew her father had great love for her.

Florence never finished her nursing program. She and Ernest were married a few years later. They had a son and a daughter born to them. Ernest and Florence, along with the four children, lived at the lake house. Ernest began his involvement in Edward's Lumber by being the woods boss in charge of all the woods crews, which cut the trees selected under Royce's careful watch. Ernest also oversaw transporting logs to the mill via a vast narrow gauge railroad system. As Edward began to slow down, Ernest moved into the overall operation of the mill. Ernest did continue the violin and became a skillful violinist.

Florence became a very well known artist and her work was very much sought after. She put on workshops for aspiring painters. Florence visited Walter on many occasions. They talked and she planted flowers on either side of the cross and either side of the stone at the foot of the grave. Alivia and Miller were the joy of Florence's life. She just knew Walter was watching their two lovely children and he was very proud of them.

Florence and Ernest's son and daughter were welcomed into this loving relationship. The four children were happy companions and grew up in a wonderful environment at the lake house.

Charles Sullivan of Toledo, showed up at the mill one day and introduced himself to Edward. He told of Walters friendship and was very sad to hear of his passing. He and Edward spent many hours talking lumber talk. Edward and Alice invited him to stay and he did for a little more than two weeks.

Florence and the Round's family received many, many letters and notes. Two weeks after the funeral, a letter came from Sparta to Florence. It was from the class of students that Florence and Walter had visited.

Dear Florence, We are very, very sad to hear that our hero Walter has died. We feel very, very sorry for you. All of the students in our class want to be like you and Walter. It will be very hard to do because both of you are so nice and friendly. Love from all of us, The letter was signed by all twenty-six 6th graders.

Olivia and Jack did not marry but remained good friends and they both lived in the lake house in the summer. Olivia taught history in Antigo and because of the distance from the lake house they purchased a home in Antigo and lived there during the school year. Olivia was a wonderful grandmother.

Edward got the Edward's Lumber operation going at full speed. Maple and oak flooring was shipped to many markets. It was a standard for the industry. The two hundred or more employees took great pride in the operation of the mill and producing very high quality flooring products. To utilize all sizes of wood scraps, Edward's Lumber began a manufacturing operation and made furniture and other products.

Alice remained the matriarch of the family and was loved and respected for her unassuming life style. Even though she had been raised wanting very little, she was a very good money manager. Her role in the Edward's Lumber operation was to oversee the entire monetary picture at all times. She was a loving grandmother also.

Bertha attended the University of Wisconsin at Madison majoring in Political Science. She was an activist and was elected to the Student Senate. After graduation, she tried to get involved with Edward's Lumber but it did not fit. She returned to school at the University of Chicago and obtained a PhD in Political Science. She became a Professor at University of Wisconsin, Madison. First came terms on the Madison

City Council. Three terms on Dane County Board of Supervisors was next.

A failed try as United States Assemblyman and finally a successful campaign which led to four terms in Washington, D. C. She returned to Madison and taught at the University for eighteen years, and then was elected to the United States Senate at age sixty-five. The drums were beating to allow women the right to vote. The Round's family renegade got into the fight with both fists punching. She remembered Walter and his spirit.

She teamed up with Alivia and fought for women's suffrage. In 1920, the 22nd amendment was passed which both women had battled for on the front line. They made a special trip to the Antigo cemetery and visited Walter and told him the good news. Finally, Walter knew 'women voters will be treated with dignity and respect'.